Emigration vs. Assimilation

ALSO BY KWANDO M. KINSHASA
AND FROM MCFARLAND

*Black Resistance to the Ku Klux Klan in the
Wake of Civil War* (2006; paperback 2009)

*The Man from Scottsboro: Clarence Norris and
the Infamous 1931 Alabama Rape Trial,
in His Own Words* (1997; paperback 2003)

Emigration vs. Assimilation
The Debate in the African American Press, 1827–1861

KWANDO M. KINSHASA

McFarland & Company, Inc., Publishers
Jefferson, North Carolina, and London

The present work is a reprint of the library bound edition of Emigration vs. Assimilation: The Debate in the African American Press, 1827–1861, *first published in 1988 by McFarland.*

The poem on page xi is reprinted from *The Panther and the Lash* by Langston Hughes, copyright 1951, by permission of Alfred A. Knopf, Inc., and Harold Ober Associates.

LIBRARY OF CONGRESS CATALOGUING-IN-PUBLICATION DATA

Kinshasa, Kwando Mbiassi.
  Emigration vs. assimilation : the debate in the African American press, 1827–1861 / Kwando M. Kinshasa.
    p.   cm.
  Includes bibliographical references and index.

  ISBN 978-0-7864-6730-3
  softcover : acid free paper ∞

  1. Afro-Americans — History — To 1863. 2. Afro-Americans — Colonization — Africa — History — 19th century. 3. Afro-Americans — Cultural assimilation — History — 19th century. 4. Afro-American press — History — 19th century. I. Title. II. Title: Emigration versus assimilation.
  E185.K49 2012
  973'.0496073   88-42512

BRITISH LIBRARY CATALOGUING DATA ARE AVAILABLE

© 1988 Kwando M. Kinshasa. All rights reserved

No part of this book may be reproduced or transmitted in any form or by any means, electronic or mechanical, including photocopying or recording, or by any information storage and retrieval system, without permission in writing from the publisher.

Front cover image © 2012 PicturesNow; cover design by Matthew Simmons

Manufactured in the United States of America

McFarland & Company, Inc., Publishers
  Box 611, Jefferson, North Carolina 28640
    www.mcfarlandpub.com

To Mayme and Dad

Acknowledgments

Dr. John Henry Clarke, despite his own scholarly commitments and busy schedule, was gracious enough to advise me on the most salient aspects of my voluminous notes. His prodigious knowledge of work in my area of interest saved me inestimable time; his forthright and clear interpretation of the African's experience in the United States gave me enlightened inspiration.

I am likewise indebted for the critical supervision and support given me by members of my doctoral dissertation committee: Dr. Richard Sennett, Dr. Irving Goffman and Dr. Ruth Ramsay. This work emerged from my dissertation. I owe special thanks to Graham Dickson for his invaluable help with editing, and to Tania Kilpatrick-Bell whose typing skills transferred my difficult handwriting into a legible manuscript. I must disclaim any responsibility on their behalf for flaws which exist—these are of my own devising.

Donald M. Jacob's work, *Antebellum Black Newspapers*, provided valuable assistance in locating material about specific topics in the antebellum press. Unfortunately, his indexing of topics from *Freedom's Journal*, *The Rights of All*, *The Weekly Advocate* and *The Colored American* only extended to 1841; therefore, isolation of materials in areas of caste, education, emigration arguments and the American Colonization Society up to 1861 was solely my task. Martin E. Dann's book, *The Black Press, 1827-1890*, along with Floyd Miller's *The Search for a Black Nationalism* expanded my understanding of the social context from which the African American press emerged.

Much of the material on which this study is based was obtained from the microfilm library of the Schomburg Center for Research in Black Culture. This center is affiliated with the New York Public Library, and its original collection was donated to the NYPL by an Arthur Schomburg. Their holding, however, only contained about one-third of the newspapers printed between 1827 and 1861 (see Appendix B). Copies of newspapers, such as the Canadian Freemen's *The Voice of the Fugitive*, were located in the Boston Public Library. I am grateful to the University of Pennsylvania for access to *The Provincial Freeman* (another Canadian free black publication, and newspapers such as *Douglass' Monthly* and *Frederick Douglass' Paper*, which have been used in previous studies. Similarly, Howard University's Moorland-Springard Research Center was most helpful in this task; several rare issues were in their possession. The nature of this work required that I examine all available issues.

I must add that the labor of coping with semiobliterated print and nineteenth-century journalistic style was justified by my intense interest, and a personal belief that an understanding of contemporary African-American thought requires a thorough grounding in the very roots of our experiences and thoughts prior to the Civil War.

Finally, I must state clearly and unequivocally that without the love, understanding and forthright critical assessment of my wife, Imani, and my children's supportive interest, this work would have remained simply an idea, unfulfilled.

Kwando Mbiassi Kinshasa
September 4, 1987

Table of Contents

Acknowledgments vii
Preface xiii
Introduction 1

I. Caste and Class Structure of Free Blacks 6
    The Early Period 8
    Effects of Religious Orientation on
        Emigrationist Views 24
    Assimilation and Free Blacks 45
    Literary and Educational Societies 52
II. Emigration vs. Assimilation as Social Remedies 63
    Emigration and Colonization as Defined
        in the Black Press 73
    Emigrationist Press: Conflict in Approaches 89
    Colonization as Viewed by White Abolitionists
        in the Black Press 102
    The Black Press as a Forum for Leadership 110
III. The Black Press Examines Two Settler Movements:
    Liberia and Haiti 121
    Liberia and the Colonization Movement 121
    Emigration Movement to Haiti 133
IV. Evaluation of the Black Press 158
    Its Influence on Emigration 158
    The Rejection of Emigration 177

Epilogue 190
Chapter Notes 195
Appendices 207
Tables 213
Bibliography 225
Index 231

What Happens to a Dream Deferred

    Does it dry up
    like a Raisin in the sun?
    or fester like a sore—
    and then run?
    Does it stink like rotten meat?
    or crust and sugar over
    like a syrupy sweet?

    Maybe it just sags
    like a heavy load.

    Or does it explode?

              "Harlem," Langston Hughes, 1951

Preface

This book examines the social-political foundation of the African American press from its beginning in 1827 to 1861, and the position various editors professed on the issue of free blacks' emigration and assimilation.

Though the social status of Africans in the United States has been one of subordination since the 17th century, the issue of successful assimilation continually dominated the thinking of the African American press. Debates on the wisdom of these efforts by its editors can be found as early as in the first black newspaper printed in this country, *Freedom's Journal*. While emigration and assimilation were viewed as the two major alternatives for antebellum free blacks, this study indicates that *four* rather than two alternatives existed: Individual Growth, Universal Betterment, Resettlement, and Emigration/Colonization. The differences between these alternatives were strong enough to divide any consolidating of free blacks into a political force.

Early newspapers such as *Freedom's Journal, The Colored American, The Voice of the Fugitive* and *The Weekly Anglo African* neither hid their divergent political philosophies nor attempted to appear objective in their ideological positions. Consequently, conflicting political opinion and personal attacks in the press disrupted possibilities for unified social action beyond that of national and state conventions. However, the importance of the African American press was critical, as it provided a public forum for a populace which heretofore did not exist. While utilizing this forum in an often brusque manner, elite free blacks through their press were able to propagate concepts of individuality and entrepreneurship. Similarly, the creating of a consciousness favoring the American ruling class's ideology of material gain was paramount.

Using their newspaper as conduits to penetrate the minds of those they assumed influence over, black editors attacked the concept of emigration and colonization. In this quest, their methodology not only laid the foundation for an accommodationist rhetoric which underlined the powerlessness of their class, but successfully retarded any dynamic push for emigration or political sovereignty.

Introduction

Examination of the opinions about emigration held by the African American population of the United States during the years 1827–1861 is particularly problematic if one relies heavily upon the African American press of that period. It is possible to consider this press as representative of a general set of opinions and approaches to the issue of emigration, or one may choose to consider only the social status and cultural training of those nonenslaved African Americans who served as editors of the free black press.

The degree to which opinions articulated in this press reflected the social attitudes and decisions of the total black population can be judged by examining: (1) journalistic content which reflected particular social and political interactions between free blacks and whites, and (2) historical information from other sources which reveals caste and status conflicts within the free black community. Similarly, two major social views will be explored in this presentation; these may shed light on the social conditions which shaped the antebellum African American press and the extent to which this press spoke for all blacks in the United States. The first viewpoint was a developing belief, arguing that emigration was necessary as a solution to the social problems of slavery. However, emigrationists were divided as to their destination — some felt a return to the African continent was logical; others suggested that emigration to the Caribbean, Central America or Canada would be more practical. The second viewpoint was concerned with economic and political questions related to the United States as a slaveholding society. Consequently, those who wished to remain in the United States in order to change the fundamentals of American society were in opposition to the emigrationist.[1]

Economic and political beliefs underlay the fundamental differences within the free black community over what ideological stance should be expressed. In fact, emigrationist and abolitionist sentiments were to be found not only among the free black and white sectors of society, but within the enslaved black populace as well.

Understanding the viewpoints and positions supported or attacked by various black editors during the 34 years from 1827 to 1861 requires comprehension of the dual roles which burdened many free black editors. Although claiming to act as leaders of a "protest press" which attacked both the evils of slavery and their own socially ambiguous position as "free blacks," editors generally refrained from taking any position which would embarrass or alienate their financial supporters. This proved to be a major concern for publications such as *Freedom's Journal, The Colored American, The North Star, The Rights of All,* and *The Alien American.*

Literacy levels at this time were extremely low, thereby limiting any sustained support from free or enslaved blacks. Not surprisingly, this press was geared toward a readership who, if they were black and literate, valued their ability to read as a symbol of social achievement. However, sympathetic whites who supported this press were generally cautious in their public commitment to political alternatives presented by the black press.

It should be noted that efforts to compile exact circulation figures rely on a variety of sources, none of which are certifiably accurate. For example, Frederick Douglass' paper, *The North Star* (later renamed *Frederick Douglass' Paper*), reached a weekly distribution of somewhere between 2,700 and 3,000 papers. Douglass himself commented that his paper had five white subscribers for every free black subscriber. Of course, one copy passed through many hands besides those of the actual subscriber.[2] This is supported by Rollin Chambliss' 1934 statement that "the circulation of 3,000 weekly carried Douglass' paper to many corners of the land and its service in the Abolitionist cause was immeasurable."[3]

The opinions of free black leadership as expressed within the black press articulated various alternatives to the white social structure and its racially oriented press, which more often than not ignored the existence of their black professional counterparts. Thus, the emergence of the controversial, highly motivated free black editor not only created a platform for African American opinion, but shaped an opinion antagonistic to white asssumptions about free blacks as a subordinate class.

Coming from a religious background, or having acted as a schoolmaster, these inimical editors enjoyed a position of influence and power. In many cases their publications' strength exceeded that of the pulpit in shaping the outlook of this readership. Rashey B. Moten, in his study of "The Negro Press of Kansas," stated,

> The fact was that the Editor had power unequalled by any other person of his race. The minister, the lawyer, the orator, might have great influence, but this was necessarily limited in its sphere. The Negro Editor, through his paper, wielded influence limited only by the extent of its circulation. Here was a weapon that pushed the editor's influence beyond the narrow confines of the local community. Here was a power that might be despised and hated, but it must, of certainty, be dealt with.[4]

Further research also suggests a proclivity for religious advocacy by the African American press when considering problems of slavery and social inequality. Religious orientation, and the press's espousal of free black literacy, indicate a heightening awareness of caste and status polarizations within the press itself — especially when confronting issues of colonization, emigration or assimilation.

In view of the foregoing, the African American press can be regarded as an instrument for social interpretation and caste domination. It articulated the goals and interest of an elite stratum among free blacks. It is, then, not surprising that their interpretations of society took on aspects of class interest, and their values and expectations mirrored assumptions which reflected dominant white concepts: the possibility of social mobility, the virtues of education and material gain, and the philosophy of Christian obedience. Many editors viewed entry into the United States political structure as the major goal for the emerging stratum of free blacks. Men such as Richard Allen pursued this aim with vigor as they championed Christianity as a civilizing process, and formal education as a major instrument for social advancement. Such opinions resulted in a heavy emphasis on public discourse as a way of propagating demands for social justice.

Leading spokesmen who warned of the numerous dangers in any emigration scheme were also quick to claim that the only pertinent issue for free blacks was their improvement of social conditions within the United States. Essential to this position was the argument that an individual's *condition in life*, not *color*, was the chief cause of prejudice and racial conflict. The argument's extension was that free blacks would be accepted as equal partners in citizenship once given the chance to prove their ability to reach higher levels of financial success.[5] Consequently, the social premise that status in society is based upon Christian morality and not economic or political exigencies played an important role in free blacks' social philosophy.[6] This then becomes significant as it was further translated into notions of class responsibility by way of manuscripts and journals which advocated an onus to instruct and lead "the race" out of its social degradation. This reductionist construction of reality is a result of an analysis which suggests that the development of Christian deliverance and enlightenment is a historical imperative, that is, one opposed to African "heathenism."

This vision masks, in many ways, the daily conflict of choice between rejecting white values or accepting damaging social assumptions; between human solidarity and social alienation; between speaking out and foregoing any meaningful political leverage outside of that prescribed by antithetical segments of society. These dichotomies found explicit expression within the free blacks' own educational institutions as they became aware of the depths of their own negative socialization.[7]

Since many free blacks reconciled themselves to the range of choices as well as the possibility of being forever "quasi-citizens," it may also be enlightening to look at those who *did* view dominant United States values as conflicting with their *best* interest, and who found slavery so repugnant that they advocated open rebellion or emigration. There are indications that the ideological indecisiveness of editors retarded this development of racial consciousness and a sense of racial worth and social-political continuity. Data also suggest that later demands by many free blacks for a voice in the United States' political structure were influenced and accompanied by a high level of self-rejection as "Africans" or "persons of African ancestry," and this rejection affected how the debate on emigration and political sovereignty was expressed in their press.[8]

Free blacks also differed as to the value of colonization for improving their condition in life. While some regarded emigration as a default of obligation to their enslaved brethren, others considered a movement back to Africa as a process which would be civilizing and beneficial to the indigenous African. Many, however, criticized this position, holding that social, political, and cultural development for blacks had to evolve *away from* rather than *towards* Africa. This group of free blacks, who favored assimilation and renounced political sovereignty (which they symbolized by adjuring the racial term "African"), will be examined in this book as an attempt at racial-cultural purification through "Americanization."

Finally, the relevancy of these social associations, viewed within the context of the significant antebellum issues of emigration (voluntary withdrawal from society), and *colonization* (forceful removal), as proposed by the American Colonization Society are examined. The opinions, decisions, and ideological constructs which emerged from this issue received extensive coverage within the press. Further investigation and evaluation of the volatile nature of the issues and their social matrix must, however, be demanded of scholars when research reveals that these opinions were biased, often garbled expressions of a world outlook by an elite subset of the black population of the time.

The idea of an objective press is illusory at best. Consequently, any accrediting of the African American antebellum press as an accurate, impartial social organ is questionable. Nevertheless, the "reality" this press attempted to project will be assessed for its success in motivating blacks towards social excellence within the boundaries of an adopted political form.

I. Caste and Class Structure of Free Blacks

> *The idea of Christian brotherly love, for instance, in a society founded on serfdom, remains an unrealizable and, in this sense, ideological idea, even when the intended meaning is, in good faith, a motive in the conduct of the individual. To live consistently, in the light of Christian brotherly love, in a society which is not organized on the same principle is impossible. The individual in his personal conduct is always compelled—in so far as he does not resort to breaking up the existing social structure—to fall short of his own nobler motive.*
>
> Karl Mannheim, "Ideology and Utopia,"
> in *The Utopian Mentality*, pp. 194-5.

Emigration for the African American during the antebellum years 1830–1861 represented more than a choice of viewpoints in a passing social issue. It represented the quintessential issue of black political, social and cultural thought and expression. Questions pertaining to social identification and political affiliation were both meaningful and urgent at a time when the socially "free" African American struggled with obtaining minimal basic rights such as the franchise. The uncertainty over blacks' legitimacy as full members of society made them the objects of social interpretation rather than definers of themselves.

While racial and economic persecution functioned as a catalyst for desired social change, social position vis-à-vis the dominant white society became the criterion for development and social value. Within such a societal climate, concepts of class and caste were largely complicated notions of racial subordination. Congruences based on status ranking among free blacks became a pernicious reflection of white social values.

As a result, free blacks often appeared as paradoxical. Thus, the label "free black" in no way corresponded to one's social or political condition, nor did it in 1837 when the black editor Samuel Cornish raised the rhetorical question:

> What an empty name. What a mockery. Free men indeed. When so unrighteously deprived of every civil and political privilege. Free indeed. When almost every honorable incentive to the pursuit of happiness, so largely and so freely held out to his fairer brother, is withheld from him. A Freeman, when prejudice binds the most galling chains around him. Drives him from every mechanical employment, and situations of trust, or emolument, frowns him from the door of our institutions of learning; forbids him to enter every public place of amusement, and follows him wherever he goes, pointing at him the finger of scorn and contempt. Is this to be a Freeman? Is this to enjoy untrammeled, a Freeman's privileges? Is this to be a participant of the Freedom of a country boasting to be the freest under the canopy of heaven? What a sad perversion of the term Freeman. No man of color, be his talents, be his respectability, be his worth, or be his wealth what they may, enjoys, in any sense, the rights of a Freeman. That liberty, and those privileges which of right, and according to the principles of our constitution, ought to be his, he enjoys not. Persecuted and degraded, he wanders along through this land of universal liberty, and equality, a desolated being. His, no situation of honor, power, or fame. Too often the virtuous and intelligent man of color, must drag out an ignoble life, the victim of poverty and sorrow. Then unwept for by but a few of his persecuted race, drops into the grave.[1]

The appearance of a growing free blacks class during 19th-century America was largely unforeseen by the enterprising 17th-century slaver. Though free blacks constituted a social development which defied cultural practices of the day, the possibility that they might become an economic or political threat to white dominance was generally ignored. Not until their dramatic numerical growth became evident in the postrevolutionary period and the early 19th century, were assumptions of white racial dominance challenged. In a society otherwise gearing itself for a ground swell of egalitarianism, the simultaneous existence of free blacks and slaves challenged black and white beliefs about an expanding America, split the country intellectually, politically, religiously, socially and economically and, in the end, drove it into catastrophic civil war. The specter of an economically competitive, organized, nonwhite ex-slave as part of the fiber of America was too much for both southern and northern whites. In 1834 a group of whites explained to the Connecticut legislature why whites could not compete with free black labor: "Whenever they come into competition...the white man is deprived of employment, or is forced to work for less than he is required." The complainants went on to state that thousands of white men had been forced to flee the state, "for the accommodation of the most debased race that the civilized world has ever seen."[2]

Free blacks were indeed a special class of people who, through numerous strategies and situations of birth managed their lives in a way which, for the most part, circumvented the brutal world of slavery. They were people with skills, though relegated to a subordinate class and position in society.[3] Caught between the world of the slave and white America, free blacks began to forge a functional understanding of the social structure values, aspirations, and expectations of themselves as quasi-citizens. Consequently, views emanating from this class on issues such as colonization, emigration and assimilation become examinations of identity and definition in a society economically based on black subordination. Any sociological or historical examination of free blacks, however, must logically take into account not only assumptions made by them as to their role and status in society, but also those made or projected at them by whites.

The Early Period

Racism in 19th-century America fostered the socially agreed-to consensus that the the anomaly known as the "free black" should have a good deal less liberty than the laws of the land bestowed. Similarly, free blacks quickly learned that often it was not the stated position of law, but social practice which determined what would be. Moreover, the knowledge that one is the victim of social differentiation breeds social discontent and fosters the misery of comparison.[4] Free blacks were bound to make comparisons of themselves in a society that on the one hand proclaimed them free, yet restrained the practice of that freedom! For most, however, it was not their legal status which defined social relations, it was their skin color. Bitter experiences further suggested that, "In America, law and custom had identified freedom with whites. By definition, the virtues of a free human being—independence and self-reliance—were not the virtues of a slave; by law, blacks were presumed to be slaves."[5]

Social presumptions about race during the antebellum period held emphatically that color itself carried a negative value. Whites, for example, were assumed to be free, self-reliant, upholders of law and custom, and independent. Blacks were generally viewed as lacking any high level of purpose and as maintaining a very primitive social infrastructure; the "negative" pigmentation of blacks indicated that they were forever to be a dependent race of people.[6] While such radical assumptions aided whites in establishing attitudes towards blacks, claims that such a policy was unvaryingly implemented throughout the entire society cannot be supported. On the contrary, the intensity of racial attitudes correlated with economic conditions and the percentage of "free blacks" available for work.

For example, Carter G. Woodson has listed five sources which were influential in increasing the number of free blacks: Children born of free colored persons, mulatto children born of free colored mothers, mulatto children born of white servants, children of free black and American Indian parentage, and manumitted slaves. While it cannot be accurately determined how much of the population increase came from each category, the numerous offspring of white fathers and free colored mothers indicate that this relationship was a major source in the development of the free black population (especially in areas such as Louisiana).[7]

Like many other groups which did not fit into the traditional social strata of the United States, free blacks began to concentrate in the growing urban centers.[8] The existence of a large racial mixture (mulatto) among the free black communities is very evident (see Table 1, p. 213). Racial mixing also occurred between blacks and the indigenous nonwhite population (American Indians), which further made "free blacks" disproportionately a mulatto class. As a result, "By 1860 fully 40 percent of the Southern free black population was classified as mulattoes, with *only one slave in ten* having some white ancestry."[9] Interestingly, during this period, as black urbanization increased, the rate of racial mixing tended to decrease (see Table 1, p. 213).[10]

Nineteenth-century white America responded to this population growth with a variety of social actions aimed at restricting free blacks' development and competition in sectors of society deemed reserved for whites, particularly the economic sector. However, while much of the resentment felt by whites towards the free black was not the result of a sense of instant repulsion, its development was continuous as it moved from prejudice to racial discrimination to outright attempts of re-enslavement.

With the termination of hostilities at the end of the colonies' revolution against England and the exit of thousands of slaves along with the British, many slaveowners and supporters of slavery began to look askance at the rising number of free blacks; as a white Virginian in 1781 complained, "There is reason to believe that a great number of slaves which were taken by the British Army are now passing in this country as Free Men."[11] Undoubtedly, throughout this period, many blacks who participated in the Revolutionary War either on the British or the American side now attempted to exploit this transitional period for their own benefit. Thus, runaway slaves, when sensing the inability of slaveowners to pursue "their property, logically and quickly moved to pass over into a growing class of free blacks.[12]

While numerous states attempted to control this development by enacting legal measures, the institution of slavery began to fail in northern states. Revolutionary ideology, combined with a growing urban professional and mercantile class, began to bolster northern antislaverists' rhetorical attitudes. Blacks, numerically fewer than whites (see Table 2, p. 214), tended to further enhance this development by propagating antislavery sentiments through the formation of citizen societies. Much of this postrevolutionary activity occurred in such cities as Philadelphia, with the advent of groups such as "The Pennsylvania Society for Promoting the Abolition of Slavery," "Society for the Relief of Free Negroes Unlawfully Held in Bondage," and "The Society for Improving the Conditions of the African Race." Soon similar societies were being formed in New Jersey, Delaware, Maryland, Rhode Island, Connecticut, and Virginia. While this 18th-century attempt to destroy slavery was motivated by the religious conviction that slavery was a sin, "for which God would eventually exact retribution," slavery's seeming inconsistency with the philosophical premises of the American revolution was, for many, also a factor.[13]

The quaker David Cooper expounded vigorously upon this position, stating that:

> If these solemn *truths*, uttered at such an awful crisis, are *self evident*: unless we can show that the African race are not *men*, words can hardly express the amazement which naturally arises on reflecting, that the very people who make these pompous declarations are slave-holders, and by their legislative conduct, tell us that these blessings were only meant to be the *rights* of *Whitemen* not all men.

Cooper concluded with a caustic observation that, "We need not now turn over the liberties of Europe for authorities to prove that blacks are born equally free with whites: It is declared and recorded as the sense of America."[14]

In the southern states, such "revolutionary" or even religious idealism was met with stiff resistance. Much of this was directly related to the numerical proportion of free blacks in the population. In response to the perceived threat to a slaveholding way of life, antiabolitionists in southern states such as North Carolina, South Carolina, and Maryland stimulated various legislative measures aimed at retarding the development of a liberalized southern society. For example, in 1787 the North Carolina assembly passed the following act:

> Whereas divers persons from religious motives, in violation of the law that slaves are to be set free for meritorious services only, continue to liberate their slaves, who are now going at large to the terror of the people of this state.... Be it enacted by the General Assembly of ... North Carolina ... that if any slave hath been liberated contrary to the before recited act (and is known to be lurking about) the justice of the peace is impowered and required immediately to issue his warrant ... to the sheriff, commanding him to make diligent search and apprehend all such slave or slaves and to commit him, her or them to the gaol of the country....[15]

The concerns of southern legislatures about liberalization tendencies were by no means isolated attempts at holding together a dying social structure, for in many ways northerners, although less threatened by blacks, free or slave, also shared these concerns. At first, northern mercantile interests in southern slaveholding states were little affected by the early religiously oriented abolitionists, as the security of northern investments in servile labor was recognized. Consequently, the presence of a growing class of free blacks who *seemingly* advocated equal participation in the economic-political process convinced many whites that eventual emancipation of the slaves was a matter of time. Such a process, whites concluded, was a threat to their entire social fabric, and could destroy the fundamental structure of the American political system. Nowhere along the eastern coast of the United States during the latter part of the 18th century (with the possible exception of Pennsylvania with its strong abolitionist groups) were there slaveholders or mercantile interests that didn't recognize this possibility as a danger. Therefore, it was important for such interests to keep free blacks outside the political sectors of society. To not do so, it was argued, condoned the development of a class of nonwhites who would compete effectively with white skilled and unskilled labor.

At this time the number of blacks in slaveholding states was already ten times larger than those in northern states, indicating their relative unimportance as a threat to northern labor or social fabric. This changed as free blacks began to grow in number and became more mobile. However, in 1790, the urban mercantile elite of free blacks comprised less than two percent of the population of New England, a third of the population of Maryland, a percent of the population of New York, and nearly 44 percent of the population of South Carolina.[16]

Free blacks appeared in society as quasi-free beings, not connected to society by franchise, yet required to fulfill a social obligation above that of a slave. Their very existence was in many ways dependent on the will of others. Viewed as an unwanted variation of the norm, with pigmentation and its many hues signaling the status of their birth, blacks labelled as "Freemen," "Mulatto," or "halfbreed" attempted to structure an existence in a society which was becoming increasingly alarmed at their presence.

Arguments centered not only on the possible physical threat they posed to the institution of slavery, but on the belief that they were not citizens and if ever allowed to vote in any state, such a vote was probably illegal. This type of debate was pursued during the 1835 National Negro Convention with the claim that being called "Freeman" in the abstract did not confer on free blacks the dignity of citizenship. Furthermore, fighting in the Revolution did not make them citizens any more than it made citizens of the slaves who similarly fought in that war. Arguing this point, a North Carolina proslavery sympathizer observed that:

> A slave was not a citizen. When was a Free Slave naturalized? And until naturalized could he be a citizen? Citizens of one state have privileges of citizens in the other states, and yet (North Carolina) severely restricted their coming to this border, thus implying that they were not citizens.[17]

A delegate from Chatham, North Carolina, continued the argument, asking:

> Is there any solid ground for the belief that a free mulatto can have any permanent interest with, and attachment to this country? He finds the door of office closed against him by the bars and bolts of public sentiment; he finds the circle of every respectable society closed against him; let him conduct himself with as much propriety as he may, he finds himself suspended between two classes of society—the Whites and the Blacks—condemned by the one and despised by the other; and when his favorite candidate in the election prevails, it communicates as gratification in his breast, for the candidate will be a White man, and he knows full well that the White man eyes him with contempt.[18]

Therefore, the process of becoming "free," be it as a result of emancipation, manumission, or as a runaway, meant finding some form of physical refuge and psychological salvation. Practical considerations made it clear that if one was looking for employment, and was skilled as a craftsman, carriageman, housekeeper, dockworker, or similar occupation, the chances for employment were higher in the city than in a rural environment. For the fugitive slave, the least desirable place to seek employment was in rural or less populated areas; cities such as Philadelphia, New York, Baltimore, and Washington offered both anonymity and possible employment.

During the postrevolutionary years of 1790-1810, free blacks were able to establish surprising gains in spite of the increasing hostilities of whites. Much of the period was spent establishing the needed social infrastructure which would later act as a springboard for political demands upon the dominant society. In conjunction with this development, by 1810 the 108,000 free blacks of the South were the fastest growing segment of the southern population. In Virginia, the free black populace doubled between 1790 and 1810. Startling figures appear when we look at Delaware during this period. In 1790 about 4,000 free blacks were listed in the census; by 1810, this population had more than tripled to 13,136, just about destroying the existence of slavery in that state where slaves then numbered 4,177 (see Table 5, p. 215). Developments of this nature prompted many fearful whites to comment that, "The nearer [free blacks] approach numerical, social, or political equality, the nearer they approach that crisis which must drive one race from the field. It is the universal impression that something must be done."[19]

While census figures during this period suffered from severe inaccuracies, it can still be ascertained that from 1830 to 1860, cities throughout the northern, middle, and southern states became the major social, and then political, centers for the free black population (See tables 3 and 4, pp. 213-214). By 1830, the free black population stood at 137,000; at the same time there were over 2,000,000 slaves in the United States. Less than one percent of the slave population lived in New England and the Middle Atlantic states, and most of those lived in New Jersey.

This rapid growth of urbanized blacks served as a stimulus to the proliferation of a property-holding class which quickly sought not only the stability of community and the development of African free schools, benevolent societies, artisans, tradesmen, and the African church, but, more significantly, the ascendancy of individual accomplishment and prestige.

This attitudinal change did not occur simultaneously throughout the free black populace, nor did it correlate with whites' development during this period. It did, however, reflect the Jacksonian philosophy of individual merit, aptitude, competence, and responsibility as positive social values. It is evident that, by the beginning of the 1830s, the now increasingly urbanized free black was attempting to define his position in relationship to the large nonblack society. Aware that their rights of "citizenship" were as ambiguous as their social status, many began to view themselves as belonging to a *class* of people, apart from either the general slave or white society. The importance of this awareness is underlined by the myriad of daily abusive experiences which tended to shape and enforce a social-political attitude of imitation and subordination. Even though the vast majority of blacks in America during this period were enslaved, the merging political attitude among many free blacks (as expressed in journals and conventions) tended to reject race as *the* major factor of social condition, as opposed to one's individual capacity for social improvement. The issue was perceived to be: To what extent could an individual participate in American society, rather than to what degree must he withdraw. Antebellum Louisiana is a case in point.

As as result of French, then Spanish domination of Louisiana during the 17th and 18th centuries, much of the free black population reflected strong racial mixing. For example, in 1803 when the United States took charge of the Louisiana Territory, the free black population amounted to 1,566. By 1806, their number had risen to 3,350 and in 1810, there were 7,585 inhabitants classified as "Free Persons of Color."[20] While these figures *alone* do not indicate a strong propensity towards racial mixing, they do suggest the successful and continued growth of a populace whose racial allegiance or identification was questionable. Efforts to stop, if not reverse, this growth of "mixed blood" free blacks met with little success, as local and international events further stimulated this phenomenon. For example, during 1809, after Napoleon invaded Spain and they in turn declared war against France, an influx of "immigrants" arrived from Cuba. The number of French-speaking immigrants to this region topped 10,000; that is, slaves, free blacks and whites. By 1830, the Louisiana free black population came to 16,710 inhabitants which, when combined with the slave population of 109,588, constituted a majority, since whites numbered only 89,441.[21] The predominance of mulattoes among free blacks was most marked in Louisiana by 1860, when 18,647 free blacks and 15,158 mulattoes were listed by the census.[22]

For whites, these figures alone constituted a serious threat to continued domination. Legal and "extra legal" activities were begun to respond to this situation. Thus, in 1817 a variety of laws were enacted which made it unlawful for free blacks who had criminal records to come into Louisiana. All watercraft owners who knowingly carried black convicts were subject to having their vessels confiscated once in Louisiana waters.[23] On March 8, 1830, one Robert Smith was arrested and charged with selling David Walkers' controversial *Appeal to the Colored Citizens of the World*, an event which further intensified pressure on free blacks. The Louisiana press played on this theme as the seventh census confirmed the worst fears of Louisiana whites; it indicated that 17,462 of its inhabitants were free coloreds, 244,809 were slaves and 255,461 were whites.[24] Whites began to give vent to their fears in "letter to the editor" columns. One citizen called for regulation so severe it would make free black migrants "unhappy and discontented with their present condition" in Louisiana.[25]

By 1859, slaveholders in St. Landry Parish were recommending to the State Legislature:

> ...That if any Free persons of Color shall enter within the limits of the state he shall be sold as a slave at public auction, one half of the proceeds of which sale shall inure to the benefit of the informer, the remaining half deposited in the state treasury after paying all cost. That all Free persons of color who are now in the state in contravention of its laws shall also be sold as slaves for life at public auction and the proceeds to be applied as set forth in the foregoing....[26]

Though whites tended to feel that the growth of the free black as a distinct "class" was due to immigration, and that this "curse upon her population" must be removed, the sentiment was not by any means unanimous.[27] Other voices suggested that legislation be adopted that would elevate the status of the native free black and that slaves who evidenced *very little* African blood be "declared Freemen at a proper age," thereby demonstrating "our Christian mercy to the world."[28]

By the beginning of the 1800s, the fast growing, "urbanized" free black started to redefine his role in relationship to the larger nonblack society. Challenging whites' characterization of them as "roving the country in idleness and dissipation," they began to develop a political-class attitude based more on economic-cultural accommodation within the social system, rather than on an endogamous racial and political power outside of it.

This philosophy was articulated by Lewis Woodson, one of the first free blacks from the Pittsburgh community to espouse strong views on this issue. Writing under the pseudonym of "Augustine," Woodson declared:

> The observance of this fact, for the last fifteen years, has entirely satisfied my mind that *condition* and *not color* is the chief cause of the prejudice under which we suffer. I have noticed that the intelligent colored man of polished manners and pleasing address, is always received and well-treated while some others, who were even wealthy, but who had paid no attention to the cultivation of the manners and habits of polished society were rejected.[30]

In a supplementary and more explicit manner, J.R. Starkey's letter to an editor claimed:

> How differently would colored people be looked upon could our oppressors pass along the principal thoroughfares and read over the doorway of several first-class business houses the firm name of BLACKMAN & CO.? Or taking up the morning paper read the arrival of a ship consigned to NEGROMAN & CO.? Or a first class factory in operation, the door of which read BLACK, SON, & CO.? If this were so, Colored men would not be looked upon as a nation of steamboat waiters.[31]

However, for many free blacks, *color* was a significant factor in defining status and the notion of racial-cultural "purification" vis-à-vis European physical/cultural characteristics implying the diminution of African traits as a step toward social acceptance and higher status. Significantly, this establishment of hierarchical relationships of class and status had color as a major criterion for social mobility. Consequently, from the point of view of the individual, the class system in which free blacks existed may be viewed as a hierarchy of conceptual, social-status frontiers. While every antebellum American in this racial-class system vied for superior status, the ex-slave, as a nonwhite black, would be marginal on every level of society. Thus nineteenth-century American social classes may be thought of as nebulous social strata, varying in meaning and position with the status of the person seeking entry.[32]

For example, antebellum Louisiana, as well as most areas with a substantial free black and slave population living side by side, found "complexion" a determining factor in social relationships. An observer of this period in Louisiana noted:

> By 1830, some of these "gens of Couleur" had arrived at such a degree of wealth as to own cotton and sugar plantations with numerous slaves. They educated their children, as they had been educated, in France. Those who chose to remain there attained, many of them, distinction in scientific and literary circles. In New Orleans they became musicians, merchants and money and real estate brokers. The humbler classes were mechanics, they monopolized the trade of shoemakers, a trade for which, even to this day, they have a special vocation, they were barbers, tailors, carpenters, upholsterers. They were notably tailors, they were almost exclusively patronized by the elite, so much so that the Legoaster's, the Dumas', the Clovis', the Lacroix' acquired individually fortunes of several hundred thousand dollars. This class was most respectable. They generally married women of their own status, and led lives quiet, dignified and worthy, in homes of ease and comfort. A few who had reached a competency sufficient of it, attempted to settle in France, where there was no prejudice

against their origin; but in more than one case the experiment was not satisfactory, and they returned to their former homes in Louisiana....
In fact, the quadroons of Louisiana have always shown a strong local attachment, although in the state they were subjected to grievances which seem to be unjust, if not cruel. It is true they possessed as to the protection of person and property; but they were disqualified from political rights and social equality. But ... it is always to be remembered that in their contact with White men they did not assume that creeping posture of debasement nor did the Whites expect it — which has more or less been forced upon them in fiction. In fact, their handsome, good natured faces seem almost incapable of despair. It is true, the Whites were superior to them, but they in their turn were superior, and infinitely superior, to the Blacks, and had as much objection to associating with the Blacks on terms of equality as any White man could have to associating with them. At the Orleans theater they attended, their mothers, wives and sisters in the second tier, reserved exclusively for them, and where no White person of either sex would have been permitted to intrude. But they (men) were not admitted to the Quadroon Balls, and when White gentlemen visited their families it was the accepted etiquette for them never to be present.[33]

Free blacks' inability to directly influence their socio-economic condition in antebellum America forced them to continually evaluate their anomalous existence. This process frequently suggested accommodative development as a social remedy. As a result, those who were receptive to this approach often accepted the culturally debilitating Christian doctrine of being delivered from "the perils of African heathenism." This acceptance of their present condition as being superior to the past or even to that of the slave, meant adopting cultural and political assumptions of white Americans while disregarding those of their African past. Thus, the socialization of free blacks, in conjunction with the growing social-political institutions of an expanding America, became part of a value system shared by many, a value system laden with notions of class, though not without the more *socially instructive* development of caste.

There can be little doubt that early 19th-century social attitudes of most free blacks were not based on conscious ethnocentrism, but rather on a concept of active accommodationism with the hope of eventual economic parity and racial-cultural affinity with white America. Consequently, the social philosophy that individual success was not only paramount, but an expected occurrence among Americans, was vital to the manner in which free blacks began to view themselves. Just as success and social improvement were expected, failure was not. If failure occurred, it was an individual responsibility and was caused by some defect of character. Consequently, failure could only be remedied by stringent effort towards self-improvement, and any measurement of success became a judgment of how one elevated himself to the vaunted norms of the dominant culture. As one observer of the time noted, "A man in America is not despised for being poor in the outset.... But every year which passes, without adding to his prosperity, is a reproach to his understanding or industry."[34]

Though the existence of a large slave populace was a living denial of America's vaunted social principles of equality, there was some parallel in the roles of women and nonwhites (see tables 6, 6A, pp. 216–217), in that individual success was a validation of the essential qualities of intelligence, merit, and responsibility. But not political power. It was argued that the position of the slave was unalterable to any major degree so long as environmental factors favored one race over another. As a result, the notion of natural selection, based not on individual capacity but social order, was fashioned by the dominant white bourgeois class to proclaim inferiority, ignorance and servility as qualities of blacks, while intelligence, merit and responsibility, which the white bourgeoisie attributed to itself, were justifications for racial dominance.[35]

Concurrent with this spirit of individualism was the concept of land ownership, and its ability to define what some considered to be Republican individuality. Yet, few free blacks possessed land; in fact, with the exception of the states of Louisiana and North Carolina, most were connected to a more urbanized lifestyle (see Table 4, p. 215).

In the southern regions, this left a population of free blacks, which viewed from the perspective of fecundity, had a larger proportion of women than men, most of whom lived in cities. While emancipated women increased the southern urban free black population, males with a higher level of mobility could and eventually did leave the South. Thus, in border states and in slave-free territories to the west, a predominance of free black males tended to be the rule rather than the exception (see Table 6A, p. 217). This influence resulted in the establishment of male-dominated business enterprises, despite the enactment of a host of regulations attempting to prohibit or retard such development. Furthermore, the possibility of economic development helped to establish among some free blacks the concept of being tradesmen and, to a lesser extent, plantation owners.

Throughout the Louisiana region, and several other areas of the South, rural free blacks were economically better off, better trained and better prepared to secure an economic foothold than were other groups in society.[36] Their resulting conservative attitudes are significant when viewed in relationship to the condition of the enslaved. Yet, for many, this attempt at upward economic and social mobility was rationalized as being a blow against the stigma of racial inferiority as well as a demonstration of their claims for equality.

A case in point is Andrew Durnford of Placquemines Parish, south of New Orleans, who being a free black, was ranked among the largest planters of his class in Louisiana. By 1850 his estate was audited at $80,000. He owned 70 slaves (35 female, 35 male), 2,660 acres of land producing 1,000 bushels of Indian corn, 200 hogsheads of cane sugar and some 16,000 gallons of molasses. He was not alone. Adolph Reggio owned an estate valued at $70,000; Constance Larch owned a rice plantation valued at $25,000; James William, a mulatto woodyard keeper, was able to amass property holdings of $6,000 at this occupation. These were free blacks who reasoned that their likelihood of a better existence was greater as plantation owners than in other economic pursuits.[37]

Less fortunate, lower strata free blacks worked smaller amounts of land. For example, J.B. Read of St. Tammany Parish owned $740 in real and personal estate, yet he was self-sufficient. It was this type of individual who, experiencing less opposition than his skilled kinsmen, became self-sufficient and who could be found, not only in the Louisiana region, but throughout parts of the southern and Middle Atlantic states.

David Dodge's description of free blacks in North Carolina's rural Piedmont region is particularly informative. He observed that:

> A very few Free Negroes prospered, bought larger and better farms, and even owned slaves — as many as thirty — which they held up to general emancipation. But generally, when they bought land at all, the purchase was ludicrously small, and, in the country phrase, "so po' it couldn't sprout er pea dout grount'n." On these infinitesimal bits they built flimsy log huts, travesties in every respect of the rude dwellings of the earliest White settlers. The timber growth being often too scant to afford fence rails, their little patches of phantom corn mixed with pea-vines, or, rather stubs, their little quota of hulls akimbo on top — were encircled by brush fences, which even by dint of annual renewals were scarcely to be regarded by a beast of average hunger and enterprise.[38]

The movement towards North America's rural sectors for a livelihood was not simply a desire to find fertile soil. Critical to this search for land was the refusal by whites to tolerate free blacks as a competitive element in society. Maintaining interests which were intrinsically related to the economics and politics of slavery, they became apprehensive over related issues, such as free blacks' growing demands for civil liberties, property rights and their own felt need for stringent fugitive slave laws. Many feared a possible stimulation of antisouthern feeling among people who might otherwise be sympathetic to their struggle against abolition. Southerners in particular feared that the urban centers had become centers for abolitionist activities and asylums for fugitive slaves, that merchants and travelers would become emissaries for abolition and, worst of all, that the free blacks would begin actively to join in arms with their enslaved brethren in any major crisis.[39] Concomitant efforts by free blacks to establish separate communities, free from prejudice and the everpresent threat of re-enslavement, further threatened the prevailing social custom of black subordination. Consequently, for many whites, the concept of black settlers was unacceptable, and a dangerous example for the slave.

A major factor in this attitude was the problem of skilled free blacks competing with whites. Whites during this period carried on an unremitting effort to curtail or completely prevent any success by black artisans. Increasingly, white urban workers concluded that demonstrating their discontent with both slave and free black labor was the only way to survive what they considered to be unfair competition.[40] As a result, free black farmers in rural southern and Middle Atlantic states gained a substantial economic foothold, as opposed to those who migrated to the more heavily settled city areas. Thus, the free black farmer, living in the politically inarticulate and relatively sparsely settled countryside, rose in economic independence, while his embattled, urbanized kinsmen enjoyed less wealth but a more articulate existence.

The urban environment provided a central focus and organizational impetus for civic, political and cultural activities, which eventually structured questions and concerns into an articulate political framework. From this emerged the activities of black abolitionists, organized churches, schools, conventions and newspapers, all of which spoke to the difference between North and South, black and white, slave and free black, assimilation, colonization and emigration. It was also within the city that concepts of class and caste became highly developed as skilled, aggressive "individuals" began to assume influence and status over the unskilled, or those who were socially defined as undesirables. Among free blacks, such structuring systematically began to inflict social definitions of what was acceptable and what was harmful.

The ability to distinguish and correlate actions with socially acceptable ideas became the criterion for an emerging case of elite urban free blacks and their leaders. Yet, the experiential world of this caste presented distinct economic, social, and cultural relationships which continually reminded them of their "less than" status in society.

The American experience of racism and classism demonstrated that it was not possible to enslave men continually without logically making them feel thoroughly inferior.[41] Furthermore, neither could one race systematically enslave another for more than three centuries without acquiring feelings of racial superiority.[42]

Efforts by free blacks to establish a social position within the dominant culture became more prevalent by the mid-1830s. Conscious attempts to structure an internal set of principles, based on perceived requisites for becoming the "complete" citizens, were now in order. Social etiquette and political philosophies became reflections of one's "civility." *The Colored American* continually supported this attitude, as when its editor, Samuel Cornish, noted:

> They [freemen] would then find that elegant language and polished manners would give them greated currency in society, than a smooth beaver, or a golden headed rattan; and that a cultivated mind is of higher consideration than dollars and cents. They would cease to haunt our church doors and the corners of our streets, offending the moral sense of all who go in and out, or that pass by, and crowd into the lecture room or library; and instead of drinking grog or smoking tobacco, they would read the newspaper.[43]

In the rush to eliminate vestiges of an unwanted past many free blacks began to establish rationales for a social movement which would question their position in society and the institutions which assumed total authority over their lives. In a manner not uncommon to the politicalization process of many other social groups, this dominated class began to organize, petition and articulate grievances. When, in 1832, eight free blacks from Delaware protested to Governor Hazzard about regulations which prohibited them from holding religious meetings after 10 p.m., while also limiting their possession of firearms, they did so by emphasizing that they were conducting themselves peaccfully, were owners of real estate and personal property and had gained (they believed) the confidence and respect of their "superiors." Suppressing any presumptuous statements as to their rights under the Declaration of Independence or the Constitution, they did express a belief that the legislative powers would take their interests to heart. Attacking the regulations, they claimed:

> In addition to the many difficulties under which they labor [i.e., blacks], arising from their caste and color, being debased by slavery—this act appears to have visited upon them evils of the greatest magnitude—it has a demoralizing effect upon the Free people of Color, for by placing them under suspicion—making them feel that the eyes of the White

people are continually over them, whether for good or for ill—it is not for them to say—it takes from them one of the strongest inducements to virtuous actions: it interferes with their religious privileges, violates their right of conscience—and exposes them to all the horrors of perpetual slavery for the act of worshipping their creator, according to the dictates of their consciences.[44]

By the advent of the 1830s free blacks seeking salvation in a society bent on denying them any assumed rights sought the development of their own schools and churches as paths for self-improvement. Allied encouragement emanated not only from other free blacks but from white abolitionists such as William L. Garrison, who stated in his address to an 1830 convention in Philadelphia,

An ignorant people can never occupy any other than a degraded place in society; they can never be truly free until they are intelligent. It is an old maxim that knowledge is power: and not only power but rank, wealth, dignity and protection. That capital brings highest return to a city, state or nation (as the case may be), which is invested in schools, academies and colleges. If I had children, rather than that they should grow up in ignorance, I would feed upon bread and water: I would sell my teeth, or extract the blood from my veins.[45]

However seemingly sympathetic to the struggle of free blacks, Garrison's statement circumvented an equally controversial issue which he often attacked bitterly, one that raised the question of economic independence to the highest, if not ultimate conclusion: political sovereignty through emigration.

Though free blacks generally recognized the importance of education, acquisition of real estate and the development of business, they became divided over the intent of such a process. The premise that one could best assimilate into American society by cherishing the values of self-improvement became a point of contention, as it rationalized racial antagonism as the price for economic advancement. Conversely, arguments which asserted the futility of such a position were vigorously advanced by pro-emigrationists, who viewed the very structure and the United States Constitution as a pro-slavery instrument. Nonetheless, many free blacks saw the United States as a country of hope and promise. Such were the sentiments expressed in *The Colored American* when it printed the following:

...When we reflect seriously upon the treatment which the colored citizens of the United States have received at the hands of their White brethren, for fifty years, our soul is filled with amazement. We often in view of this subject, find ourselves involuntarily exclaiming, how can it be? Do not our White brethren know, that at least some of us, have as keen sensibilities as refined taste, and as good education as they have? That some of us were bred and born as respectably as they? That we have used the same industry and enterprise, and accumulated as much wealth as most of our fellow citizens, and yet have they no respect for our character and feelings?

Why should a colored man, who is equal in wealth, in education, in refinement and in taste, be subjected to legal disabilities—debarred [from] the institutions of this country—crowded into pews in the church, and into dog-cars on the railroad, or pantries on board the steamboats? Can anyone answer these inquiries? . . .

Some say, let the colored people leave the country! We reply, NO, BRETHREN. We would rather die a thousand deaths, in HONESTLY and legally contending for our rights IN THIS OUR NATIVE COUNTRY. We cannot act in this respect so IGNOBLY as our Pilgram fathers did. We will stay and seek the purification of the whole lump. With the character of the country we are identified, and with its character we intend to sink or swim. If the country sink in disgrace, we will perish amidst its ruin—yet seeking its regeneration and salvation...[46]

Consistent, articulate advocacy in the black press for the improvement of one's economic position *within* the United States was the benchmark for success. Similarly, the need for acceptance by whites was indicative of a keenly felt rejection by an aspiring class of free blacks who, to a large extent, accepted with question the values of American society. Ironically, the more they argued for social assimilation, the more they tended to express a pronounced feeling of insecurity, if not inferiority. This they experienced more vigorously than their power-class brethren, whose participation in the "white man's world" was more limited and conformed more to the standards of their own separate world.[47] However, while upper strata free blacks rejected the slightest aspersion directed toward them by whites, they often expressed feelings of subordination and inadequacy when comparing themselves to whites! In a sense, their striving to accomplish what they accepted as the proper goals for the "race" was influenced by a feeling of necessary separation from the vast, poor, uneducated and enslaved black populace. As a result, the higher they perceived their own rise within the social structure, the more they tended to view themselves as torch bearers, that is, facilitators of the race. One way to enhance this prospect, it was thought, was through increased education. Consistently, the black press pursued this as the most viable path for self-improvement, arguing that with increased education and exposure to business, social flexibility and business acumen would develop, thereby erasing the stigma of racial inferiority and social subordination.[48]

Effects of Religious Orientation on Emigrationist Views

Denied easy entry into American society beyond the status of slave, the African found it imperative to create a sense of local community where national community was lacking. A major step in this direction was the development and growth of the black church. Structuring a social and psychological escape route for free blacks, the church provided an early barrier to the insensitivity of the white church towards slavery.

By the beginning of the 1800s, free blacks were organizing the African Methodist Episcopal Church, African Methodist Episcopal Zion Church, the Protestant Episcopal Church, Congregational Church and Baptist denominations throughout both northern and southern cities. As a result, not only was an arena established for religious expression, but a forum was also established for the discussion of political ideas relevant to the welfare of free blacks. Though most free blacks were Protestant, some were attracted to other denominations (e.g., the Roman Catholic Church). However, these relatively few members usually came from the "privileged" stratum of those who constituted, for example, the Louisiana free mulatto class.

In this regard, class affiliations were noticeable; generally the lower economic brackets of blacks chose the less conservative Baptist and Congregational denominations for worship.[49] The implication of this was not wasted on some, such as the Reverend Cary Lott, who when asked about colonization, secularized his comments by stating: "I am an African, and in this country, however meritorious my conduct, and respectable my character, I cannot receive credit due to either. I wish to go to a country where I shall be estimated by my merits, not by my complexion; and I feel bound to labor for my suffering race."[50]

Intentions of this nature were continually articulated in the fledgling black press by religious personages as the issues of emigration and colonization stimulated thought on the duty of oneself to society. Expressing the need for social change, if their interests and those of "the race" were to be advanced, meant that issues pertaining to colonization and emigration were tested in the arena of public discourse. Such debates, while providing an increased level of information for free blacks and a sense of increased social awareness, also enhanced a feeling of political involvement that heretofore had been denied. Opinions once the privilege of a few to read and discuss now became the property of many, via the pulpit and the press. Religious education and social concerns were now expressive of local concerns and those of the larger national community. *Rights of All* editor and the Reverend Samuel Cornish's correspondence to the Trustees and Faculty of the African Mission School of Hartford, Connecticut, is a prime example of pulpit and press combining to articulate an opinion on the role and duties of a social organization:

> Ever since its organization, I have viewed your school with feelings of the liveliest interest—in its formation you seem to have touched the proper string. To introduce and extend civilization and religion throughout the vast continent of Africa is certainly the high privilege of the church of God. How pleasing in this way to be co-workers with the sons of God in carrying forward his meritorial purposes and extending his glory. Believe me, I feel a deep interest in your establishment at Hartford, and shall ever pray for its prosperity. Your efforts and plans are truly spiritual, they aim directly at the improvement and salvation of a numerous nation—they are not shackled with the political chimera of removing three millions of people from their country and their homes—neither are they calculated to waste the public effort and means by vain and fruitless attempts. The objects of your pursuit are in accordance the mandate of heaven, "Go ye into all the world, and preach the gospel to every creature." Experience has taught us, that missionary operations are the shortest, and most efficient means for the accomplishment of this benevolent command. The success of Dr. Cary's establishment of colonies and commerce in the attainment of this object, but that we would forthwith raise up missionaries and send mission families that perishing souls may immediately be supplied with the bread of life. We look, with interest, dear sirs, to your school, as being the most likely instrument in the accomplishment of this good work; you will therefore pardon me, as the conductor of a public journal, should I from time to time suggest to your better judgment, some ideas calculated to facilitate your noble object, and secure its greatest success. It cannot be expected that any body of men are so well calculated to judge in matters wholly confined to our coloured people, as those who, by the God of nature, are in every respect identified with them. You will therefore please to take it as no disparagement, should I presume to present for your consideration, some evils, which to my knowledge, blasted the prospects of the patrons, and destroyed the interest of a similar school, established by the Presbyterian Church. Such is the nature of things among us, that these evils will always present themselves under such circumstances. The Presbyterian school failed from an unhappy selection of its candidates, and the limited extent of its tuition. And I cannot help fearing should you not resort to different measures and be more careful in the selection of your candidates than they were, your labours of love will meet a similar issue, and your fair prospects a similar blight.[51]

Black editors such as the Reverend Cornish, who rejected negative racial aspersions were, however, not remiss in condemning what they perceived as negative race characteristics. Reflecting an awareness of their dominated position in society, they continually defined themselves within the imposed socio-economic constraints of American culture and discourse. Perceptions of strength were rarely extracted in print from the experiences of the lower, uneducated class, but from those who most closely resembled the dominant race and class of society. Thus, it appears that while whites never questioned their ability to "rise," dominated free blacks questioned the appropriateness of such an attitude unless preceded by formal religious/educational training. The Reverend Cornish concluded his article with:

> Pardon me in saying, that White men are not calculated to judge of the abilities and adaptedness of colored men for so responsible, so high, and so holy a calling—you know our coloured population but in certain sphere of life. The intelligent among us, can descend with them into their different walks and associations, and therefore can better estimate them under their various circumstances. A coloured man who has arrived at an adult state, should never be selected as a candidate for the responsible duties of a preacher or teacher, whose disposition, association, and talents are not peculiarly adapted to the work, whatever may be his moral and religious character. The case is very different from that of a youth, whose mind and habits are to be formed. I very much question the propriety of taking up young men who have spent twenty to twenty-five years as common servants. Their minds scarcely can have escaped the contracting influence of their brethren, and destitute of the nobler feelings of the soul. I have always found that when situations of trust and responsibility are offered, the more ignorant and unstable among us were generally foremost in their application. That some of these difficulties may be guarded against, I hope you will appoint some intelligent coloured man to select the candidates for your patronage—cannot this trust be confided to some coloured members of your church, whose situation renders them competent to the task?
>
> With these few hints, respected sirs, I submit this interesting subject to your consideration.
>
> And with deep concern for your health and prosperity, have the honor to be your humble servant.   -The Editor-[52]

In the mid–1830s, the Reverend Samuel Cornish, along with wealthy sailmaker James Forten and Bishop Richard Allen of the African Methodist Episcopal Church, scoffed at the very mentioning of the terms "emigration" or "colonization." For them, any departure from this society represented a betrayal of enslaved blacks. While this should not be surprising for men who saw themselves as the leading edge of their race, in many respects there existed an ideological inconsistency among free blacks who, in the 1820s, voiced acceptance of some forms of colonization (e.g., Haiti) yet by the 1830s voiced disapproval.

Colonization and religious separatism were two different reactions to the deeper social issue: To what degree should blacks' demand for social equality be respected by whites? Or, as Frederick Douglass succinctly asked, "What shall be done with the Negro?" His answer was:

> Already I am charged with treating this question in light of abstract ideas. I admit the charge, and would to heaven that this whole nation could now be brought to view it in the same, clear light. The failure so to view it is the one great national mistake. Our wise men and statesmen have insisted upon viewing the whole subject of the Negro upon what they are pleased to call practical and common sense principles, and behold the results of their so-called practical wisdom and common sense! Behold, how all to the mocker has gone.[53]

The intense emotions around the issue suggest that the strong assimilationist bent which surrounded free blacks' concepts of society was related more to the development of political-economic power than the notion of social morality. For example, among white abolitionists, the harboring of a racial bias was blatant. An address by the Reverend Theodore S. Wright of the First Colored Presbyterian Church, before Utica's New York Abolitionist Society, noted that, "This foul monster, which is at once the parent and offspring of slavery must be purged from the personality." Nathaniel Paul, a black Baptist clergyman, speaking before the Albany Anti-Slavery Society in February 1838, described another kind of abolitionist who despised slavery, "especially that which is 1,000 or 1,500 miles away," but hated even more, "a man who wears a coloured skin."[54]

Similarly, when abolitionist James Russell Lowell in 1849 encountered opposition to the proposal that Frederick Douglass be accepted as a member in the intellectually oriented Town and Country Club, the finger of suspicion pointed strongly to the allegedly high principled Ralph Waldo Emerson.[54]

In other words, rapport between free blacks and whites scarcely sustained a peer relationship, as paternalistic interactions continually reinforced dominant and submissive personality traits.[55] Therefore, it is not surprising to read that on September 15, 1837, a 31 to 21 vote by the Junior Anti-Slavery Society of the City and County of Philadelphia against free black participation in its activities was sustained, further indicating the importance of race within American antebellum society.[56]

Belief in emigration, as opposed to colonization, was strong among free blacks in Newport and Providence, Rhode Island, as early as 1787. Samuel Hopkins, a long-time minister of Newport's First Congregational Church, became involved in the idea of blacks returning to Africa, and was a founding member of the African Union Society of

Newport. Believing that a black Christian presence in Africa would help abolish the slave trade, Hopkins also contended that as "inferior creatures" blacks would never achieve equality in the United States. Therefore, he concluded, helping to Christianize the "African Heathen" was the only path open to free blacks in their search for freedom.[57]

His desire for a "black exodus" is of particular importance as it underlines a major point of disagreement when considering the different motivations of free blacks and whites. For example, minutes of the American Colonization Society's meeting in 1817, between its secretary, the Reverend Finley, and twelve Philadelphia free blacks, reveal some of the anxieties felt by blacks about colonization. If Finley's biographer's description of this meeting is accurate, "J.F." and "R.A.," later identified as James Forten and Richard Allen, rejected any establishing of free black settlements in "unoccupied" western land in the United States, yet favored African or possibly Haitian emigration!

Forten allegedly took the position that his people "would become a great nation ... " and "He gave it as his decided opinion that Africa was the proper place of a colony." Similarly, Richard Allen, who was one of the founders and first bishop of the African Methodist Episcopal Church in 1816, reportedly spoke "warmly in favor of colonization in Africa—declaring that if he were younger he would go himself."[58]

Dr. Finley is also reported to have said at the beginning of their meeting that he "found that they (at first) were considerably alarmed at the proposed plan of colonization, and strongly prejudiced against it, suspecting that some purpose injurious to their class of people was hidden in it." After spending nearly an hour conversing with them on the scheme, indicating "advantages to it," the biography states, "at length, they declared themselves fully satisfied as to this point, that the designs of the gentlemen who proposed and advocated the scheme were benevolent and good, and that the thing in itself was desirable for them."[59]

Speculation on Forten's and Bishop Allen's change of heart hints at what some free blacks considered to be the coercive aspects of colonization. Furthermore, for many, colonization represented not only a renunciation of choice and will, but also the odious notion of leaving their enslaved kinsmen to their own fate. As the *Anglo-American Magazine* noted,

> In 1829–30 the Colored people of the Free States were much excited on the subject of emigration: There had been an emigration to Hayti, and also to Canada, and some had been driven to Liberia by the severe laws

and brutal conduct of the fermenters of colonization in Virginia and Maryland. In some districts of these states, the disguised Whites would enter the houses of Free Colored men at night, and take them out and give them from thirty to fifty lashes, to get them to consent to go to Liberia.[60]

By 1824, both Bishop Allen and Forten were strong advocates of emigration, not to Africa, but to Haiti, and formed the Haytien Emigration Society of Philadelphia. Convinced at this time that only black men could help other blacks "leave a country where it is, certain the Colored man can never enjoy his rights," they further resolved, "that we do approve of the proposals of President Boyer [land offered by the Haitian president], also heartily agree with him in the belief that emigration to the Island of Hayti will be more advantageous to us than the colony in Africa."[61]

Throughout 1824, free blacks who advocated emigration in New York, Baltimore, and Philadelphia also emphasized a belief in an historical identification with Haiti. Bishop Allen planned to establish a mission station as early as November, and had even selected a missionary who was to establish several missions. Within a few years there were missionary societies throughout Haiti.[62]

The possibility of living in a black nation excited the imagination of many. Some sixty emigrants departed from Philadelphia in the summer of 1824 on the *Charlotte Corday*; ten days later the *De Witt Clinton*, with another 120 free blacks, left New York City. Prior to their sailing, the Reverend Peter Williams, addressing the Haytien Emigration Society of Coloured People, stated that they should "Go to that highly favored, and as yet only land, where the sons of Africa appear as a civilized, well-ordered, and flourishing nation. Go, remembering that the happiness of millions of the present and future generations, depends upon your prosperity, and that your prosperity depends much upon yourself."[63]

Throughout the rest of 1824, enthusiasm for Haitian emigration continued. In September, ships left from Baltimore with mechanics and a full load of cargo. In October, the *Concordia* left New York with a passenger load of 160, while another 280 emigrants prepared to depart from Baltimore. Within this period of time, an estimated 2,000 free blacks sought emigration to Haiti, via the Haytien Society. As far away as Cincinnati, blacks began to form similar organizations, such as the Cincinnati Haytien Union.[64] These efforts, though seemingly gathering support, were generally curtailed by a pessimistic attitude on the part of middle- and upper-strata free blacks. Confusion about the ideological differences between colonization and emigration undoubtedly acted as a hindrance as both the propertied and propertyless blacks struggled with questions of American identity and claims made for the Christianizing mission of colonization. Thus, by 1832, the American Colonization Society was only able to convince 2,638 out of 166,757 free blacks to leave America for Liberia.[65]

A significant amount of the urban, free black leadership who supported the colonization issue came from the religious sector of their communities. Following this lead, white abolitionists in the 1830s who earlier supported colonization as a way of reducing possible racial conflict, changed their minds as they followed the leadership of outspoken assimilationist-oriented black men of the cloth. The call for the immediate emancipation of slaves, under the banner of antislaverism, now excited the passions of both blacks and their white abolitionist supporters.

Interdenominational representation, not only in Philadelphia but in other cities such as New York, Baltimore, and Boston, provided an excellent structure for the development and propagation of opinions on this issue. Their continuous advocacy for moral improvement and self-help were the essential ingredients for the development of political concern, activism and ideas of self-determination. However, so sensitive were whites to blacks' increasing awareness, that any semblance of free blacks' *collectivity* was suspect, arousing uncomfortable feelings among whites.[66] *The Baptist Monthly Record* relates that:

> About the year 1806, the colored brethren and sisters of the First Baptist Church worshipping in Gold Street, for reasons unnecessary now to mention, respectfully proposed to the said church the expediency of a separation; seeing that the Colored Methodists and Episcopalians had made similar propositions to their respective churches with success, they humbly desired the same.[67]

Regarding this, Carol George suggests that, "forced to sit together, they may have appeared to be a larger group than they actually were: more than one White churchman testified that his members accepted the presence of a few Blacks scattered about the congregation, but grew uneasy when they appeared in a group."

Boston's situation was somewhat different. Though its black population was relatively small, segregation was enforced as white workers and the newly arriving European immigrants were protected from economic competition by free blacks. The resulting interest by blacks in the colonization issue was to be expected, especially with the settling of the militant David Walker and his subsequent organizing on January 6, 1832, of the city's first Anti-Slavery Society in the schoolroom basement of a church.

Further to the south, in Baltimore, the importance of community leadership and racial background played an important role in the development of issues around colonization and the episcopacy of the African Methodist Church. Unfortunately, division and rivalry forced the emigration of the Reverend Daniel Coker to Liberia with the blessing of the Maryland Colonization Society. Coker, an extremely light-skinned free black whose color and personality played a role in his accepting and then rejecting the episcopacy of the African Methodist Church in 1816, indicated in his diary some of the divisions which led to his departure for Africa:

> ... There is great work here to do. Thousands and thousands of souls here, to be converted from paganism and Mahometanism to the religion of Jesus. Oh! Brethren, who will come over to the help of the Lord? If you come as Baptists, come to establish an African Baptist Church, and not to make divisions. If you come as Protestants, come to support an African Protestant Church, and not to make divisions. If you come as a Methodist, come to support an African Methodist Church. We wish to know nothing of *Bethel* and of *Sharp Street*, in Africa—Leave all these divisions in America.... The Sharp Street Brethren will be to me as the Bethel Brethren; all will be alike. I wish to forget all such names and distinctions.[68]

Richard Allen was chosen to replace Coker as bishop almost immediately. Reasons as to the exact nature of the dispute are not clear, although some have speculated that Allen's unmixed African bloodline was a major factor.

Reverend Coker's decision to depart to Africa did not endear him to a leadership which viewed the "Christianizing" aspects of the American Colonization Society as simply a screen allowing slaveowning interests to separate what they defined as a "social nuisance": the free blacks from the slaves. Nevertheless proponents of colonization argued that the success of their proposal was contingent upon selecting those blacks who were properly educated. Implementation of this plan, they reasoned, must begin with the youth.[69] In 1825, the board of directors of the African School in Parsippany, New Jersey, noted that "the exigencies of the times demand an institution more enlarged and better endowed"; they suggested that the use of their graduates as "officers and civil servants in Haiti and Liberia" would be acceptable if support was obtained from the New Jersey Colonization Society.[70] Free blacks were to be educated in "mechanics, arts, agriculture, science, and Biblical literature," with exceptionally bright youths to receive training as "Catechists, Teachers, Preachers and Physicians."[71]

This plan, as with others, failed to a large degree because of active opposition by individuals such as Bishop Allen, who in a reversal of his pro-emigrationist sentiments, now advocated that:

> We are an unlettered people, brought up in ignorance, not one in a thousand has a liberal education. Is there any fitness for such to be sent into a far country, among Heathens, to convert or civilize them, when they themselves are neither *civilized* nor *Christianized?*[72]

Another plan in 1817 involving the estate of the Polish general Kosciuszko. The Kosciuszko Fund of $16,000 was adjudicated to Thomas Jefferson as executor of the estate, and earmarked for the African Education Society of the United States, so as

> To employ thereof in purchasing Negroes ... and giving them liberty in my name, in giving them an education in trade or otherwise, and in having them instructed for their condition in the duties of morality.[73]

Jefferson refused to act as administrator of the fund, after which a Supreme Court battle in the District of Columbia ensued as members of the Kosciuszko family filed a bill claiming that the fund was superseded by an earlier 1798 bill favoring their interest. This was enough to forestall any education plans of the African Education Society.

Undaunted by such developments, colonizationists arguing for educated free blacks in Africa continually found strength in religious rationalizations. The chief agent of the American Colonization Society, Jehudi Ashmun, spelled this out in an 1827 report on Liberia:

> To be civilized, a country must have religion, and this religion must be Christianity. Now where is Africa, dark degraded, ignorant Africa! Where is it to obtain this blessed gift? How shall we hear without a preacher, and how shall they hear without a preacher, and how shall they preach except they be sent by our exertions? ... But alas, ... we cannot obtain missionaries. The want is universal. It is felt sensibly in Great Britain as well as in our own country. But a short time since, letters were addressed to different persons from the church missionary society, stating that they had looked anxiously to this country for missionaries, catechists, and schoolmasters—they wished for pious, intelligent and active men of colour for this purpose, and stood prepared to give them ample support. The White man, as we are convinced from melancholy proof, cannot endure that climate, and besides, his colour, which is associated with the idea of disease, unfits him for usefulness among the tribe. The call is loud then for African missionaries throughout the Christian world.[74]

Though one major problem did revolve around the varying interpretations of Christian duty, for the vast majority of educated free blacks in the early 1830s, colonization did not inspire images of missionary zeal. The concept of having first to be "educated" in order to thrive in a country not of one's own choosing, such as Liberia, contradicted what many saw as the basic purposes of education. Some argued that if Christian education "promotes genius and causes man to soar up to those high intellectual enjoyments and acquirements which place him in a situation to shed upon a country and people that scientific grandeur which is imperishable by time, and drowns in oblivion's cup their moral degradation," why not here in America!75

William Jay, an intellectual abolitionist, attacked colonizationists by advocating the education of blacks wherever they were. He couldn't understand how a Christian could prohibit or put conditions on educating any individual. Furthermore, he argued, if Africans could be elevated in their native land, but not in America, it was the fault of Caucasians' sinful condition, for which blacks should not be penalized through extradition.76

During the 1835 National Negro Convention, James Forten helped to structure the charter of the American Moral Reform Society, a biracial assimilationist organization which had as its intended social policy the advocacy of Christian education, temperance, economy and universal liberty for all mankind.77 In pursuance of these aims, the society attacked all "those national distinctions, complexional variations, geographical lines, and sectional bounds that hitherto marked the history, character and operations of men ... [and] not boldy plead for the Christian and moral elevation of the human race."78 They proposed that vice, greed, corruption and slavery were all evils which must be eliminated from society. Christian virtues of meekness, humility and pleasantness were to be encouraged along with one's rights within society. Christian militancy was the watchword as this society attempted to influence not only free blacks but to elevate the entire human race.79

A major focus of their attack was directed at the black church for not being more aggressive in its fight against slavery, and its reluctance to assert that blacks should be in the forefront of any struggle against slavery. True to its mandate, the first annual convention in 1837 hailed the establishment of *The Colored American*; disapproved of the term "Free People of Color"; gave recognition to women's struggle for social participation; praised John Quincy Adams in his fight for the right of petition; opposed the annexation of Texas; and encouraged the development of agricultural and mechanical pursuits.80

Most of the convention delegates were in accord with actions approved by the assembly, with the noted exception of the Reverend Cornish, editor of *The Colored American*. Attacking the Moral Reform Society as being "visionary in the extreme," Cornish asserted that the society was uselessly "scattering its feeble efforts to the winds, as though unconscious of any definite objects of benevolence, or any responsibilities growing out of its circumstances, its location, its means and its talents."[81]

Frederick A. Hinton, another delegate at the convention, joined in with the Reverend Cornish, noting that the convention had earlier approved of the racial classification of "colored," and that only after reconsideration by its president, James Forten, was it reversed by the deciding presidential vote, as Forten stated:

> On the motion of William Whipper, seconded by R. Purvis, resolved that we recommend as far as possible, to our people to abandon the use of the word "colored," when either speaking or writing concerning themselves: and especially to remove the title of African from their institutions, the marbles of Churches, etc.[82]

Hinton, along with Junius C. Morel and Whipper, all advocates of the "color" designation, insisted that the Bible used color for identification; therefore, any reference to man's skin need not be derogatory. Cornish also claimed that the moral reformers were trespassing upon concerns which belonged only to the church. Only through this vigorous effort was the motion favoring the use of "colored" passed the following day. By the time the 1838 convention convened, others were attempting to use the term "oppressed Americans," and in doing so, caused Cornish to bitterly attack them by stating:

> Oppressed Americans! Who are they! Nonsense brethren! You are COLORED AMERICANS. The Indians are RED AMERICANS, and the White people are WHITE AMERICANS, and you are as good as they ... God made all of the same blood.[8]

Caught between the two goals of antislavery's reform for America, and an emerging racial consciousness, advocates of the American Moral Society found themselves torn between Christian rectitude, industry, thrift and temperance, while vigorouly rejecting any concept or idea which suggested racial or religious separation. One such member of this "reform society" was Lewis Woodson, who argued in *The Colored American* that the black church should maintain its independence from the white church, in that:

> The White Church will never relinquish her prejudices against color, until she has abolished her slavery — until she has cleansed her shirts of the blood and souls of men ... and until it is accomplished, it will be posi-

tively necessary for the colored people, wherever they exist in sufficient numbers, to have separate places of worship for themselves. And it is of the highest importance to our moral, religious and social improvement, that men identified with ourselves, and qualified with grace and knowledge, should be our pastors and teachers.[84]

Woodson's insistence on the moral function of ministers and the importance of moral responsibility by the laity tended to fix blame for a disorganized free black class upon the backs of black leadership rather than society. Charging elements in the black community with irresponsible conduct, Woodson suggested that only by adhering to Christian virtues of moral purity could free blacks lift themselves from a wretched condition, which, he added, could not be blamed entirely upon whites. While maintaining that "condition and not color is the chief cause of prejudice under which we suffer," Woodson's analysis stopped short of implying social integration. Separate development, via independent communities, was his solution.[85]

The major task, then, was how to steer free blacks away from abstract Christian morality. Martin Delany, a leading advocate of separation, stated in the *North Star* that "Among our people generally, the church is the Alpha and Omega of all things. It is their only source of information — their only acknowledged public body — their state legislature ... their only acknowledged advisor...." Advising that Christianity contained an insidious evil which taught free blacks doctrines of debasement and degradation, he argued that racial assumptions of prayer being sufficient for all things was misleading. "Prayer is a spiritual means," continued Delany, "used in conformity to the spiritual law, and can only be instrumental in attaining a spiritual end. Neither physical wants, nor temporal demands of man can be supplied by it." Moreover, he added, "prayer and praises only fill one's soul with emotion, but can never fill his mouth with bread nor his pocketbook with money."[86]

Arguments presented by white colonizationists tended to emphasize two aspects of the problem. The first was explained by the American Colonization Society's Robert Finley, in a letter to a New York friend. He explained in strongly benevolent and parental terms,

> The longer I live to see the wretchedness of man, the more I admire the virtue of those who devise, and with patience, labor, to execute plans for the relief of the wretched. On this subject, the state of FREE BLACKS has very much occupied my mind. Their numbers increase greatly, and their wretchedness too, as appears to me. Everything connected with their condition, including their color, is against; nor is there much prospect that their state can ever be greatly meliorated, while they shall continue among us.

> Could not the rich and benevolent devise means to form a colony on some part of the coast of Africa, similar to the one at Sierra Leone, which might gradually induce many Free Blacks to go and settle, devising for them the means of getting there, and of protection and support till they were established?
>
> Could they be sent back to Africa, a three-fold benefit would arise. We should be cleared of them — we should send to Africa a population partly civilized and Christianized for its benefit, and our Blacks themselves would be put in a better situation.[87]

A second view took into account the possible political and economic advantages gained by America, as a result of a colonization policy which put primary emphasis on the competency of free blacks as colonizers:

> The colonization society has done its work, private charity and Christian benevolence have performed their duty. Through their agency, law and liberty, religion and civilization have been carried into Africa and there embodied in Free national institutions. A new power and influence are now required to sustain and to accomplish the final and glorious result for which they were established. That power is national — that influence is commercial. It is our duty, as it will be our interest, to exercise that power and direct that influence. If we will do so, we shall accomplish the two grand results contemplated by the friend of African colonization — the civilization of Africa and the removal from this country of that anomalous class of men, called Free People of Color. I have already shown the mighty influence of commerce upon the first named object. I will now endeavor to show its efficiency to accomplish the latter. The Negro is a timid creature; he lives and moves more by sight than faith. He feels in his soul that he is an inferior being and therefore the subject of deception and wrong. Hence it is that so few of the Free People of Color have been found willing to leave even this land of their degradation for a better home and country in Africa.[88]

Regardless of the concern the American Colonization Society exhibited towards blacks, many free blacks came to their own conclusions about the viability of mass organizations for greater social advancement. Spurred on by the African Methodist Episcopal Church (AME), free blacks created their own benevolent and fraternal organizations to attack a variety of social ills. With the black church as an ideological center, clergymen of different denominations, such as Peter Williams, rector of St. Phillips Church in New York, argued that free blacks must be convinced that their best opportunity for a useful, intelligent and virtuous life was only possible within American society. He further charged that the Gospel of Jesus Christ and the Declaration of Independence were sufficient powers to raise blacks to the level of full citizenship. In 1834, the radical implications of remarks such as these were often sufficient to raise antagonisms, not only between the races but within the church itself. Williams' bishop asked him to resign from the Anti-Slavery Society if he hoped to continue at St. Phillips.[89]

The inability of free blacks to debate social issues within the white church led more free blacks to seek religious separation. Though this separation was based on resistance to white authority, many of the deep-seated values of white society found their way into sermons presented by blacks. Black ministers preached the values of family discipline, religious marriages, baptism and church burials and became the most important voices of black leadership. This leadership was endowed with the precepts of hierarchy and saturated with the pretensions and mannerisms of an elite class. While preaching against the ills of society and allowing itself to act as a haven from a hostile environment, the black church became a crutch to those broken in spirit, and compensated for the limited societal gratification afforded them.

The separation of blacks from white churches was not always accomplished without disorder and tension. As far back as 1815, freemen in Charleston, South Carolina, had a separate quarterly conference. Finding themselves harassed by the local government, two of its delegates went to Philadelphia to consult with Bishop Richard Allen. After being ordained by Allen, they returned to Charleston, whereupon the dispute was renewed, this time over a suitable burial ground for blacks. As a consequence of this dispute, over three-quarters of the 6,000 black Methodists withdrew from the white church and constructed their own. This structure was subsequently demolished by the city government seven years later, forcing many to return to the white church. An observer at the time commented:

> The bulk of the Blacks returned to the White congregation where they soon overflowed the galleries and the "boxes" which were assigned them at the rear of the main floors. Some of the older Negroes, by special privileges, then took seats forward in the main body of the churches, and others, not so esteemed, followed their example in such numbers that the Whites were cramped for room. After complaints on this score had failed for several years to bring a remedy, a crisis came up on a Sunday in 1853, when Dr. Capers came to preach. More Whites came than could be seated forward—sitting Negroes refused to vacate their seats for them, and a committee of young White members forcibly ejected the Blacks....

Subsequent criticism by a white minister on the conduct of the church's white members offended many members of the white congregation, who eventually withdrew from the church to form the Methodist Protestant Church.

The prospects of getting any large percentage of emigrants to Liberia was not only financially prohibitive, but also lost popularity due to the persistent efforts of influential free blacks to retard any emigrationist tendencies. The colonization societies' inability to provide for sufficient missionary schools to supply those schools already established in Liberia further hampered any serious progress by the American Colonization Society. This issue was further complicated when both the American Moral Reform Society and the American Colonization Society were attacked by Cornish in his newspaper for being too abstract and acting as a broker for slaveholding interest.

Cornish half-heartedly supported emigration efforts to West Canada and Haiti, but refused to accept the Christianizing assertions made by individuals such as the Reverend Lott Cary who, back in 1815, emigrated to Liberia. Cornish as well as others who were critical of the American Colonization Movement, was therefore not surprised by Cary's complaints to his sponsors, the Baptist Board of Foreign Missions, when he stated in 1821:

> If you intend doing anything for Africa, you must not wait for the Colonization Society nor for the government, for neither of these are in search of missionary grounds, but of colonizing grounds; if it should not suit missionary needs, you cannot expect to gather in a missionary crop. And, moreover, all of us who are connected with the agents, who are under public instructions, must be conformed to their laws, whether they militate against missionary operations or not.[91]

Nor was Cornish sympathetic to John Russwurm's decision to end his co-editorship of *Freedom's Journal* with Cornish and emigrate to Liberia, when he wrote:

> We have always been of the opinion, that slavery was an evil which yet would cure itself. There is no need for a Liberian colony, to induce masters to liberate their slaves—should the system continue a few years longer, slaveholders will be glad to say to their human stock, divide with us the spoil, that we may go to the north and leave you to possess the south.[92]

Characteristic of most anticolonization arguments during this period was the blending of political and religious doctrine aimed at securing a desired social goal. The expressing of views through the newly created African church further enhanced the impression that free blacks were not only educated enough to articulate opinions which they considered vital to their interests, but were now willing to create institutions separate from those of whites. It was the close relationship of the pulpit and the press, one with its congregational base, the other with a much larger community constituency, which raised the issue of colonization to the level of a public issue and heightened social tension.

Whites in general responded with mixed feelings to the African church. However, a significant number of them viewed this development with paternalistic amusement while also fearing the independence this church afforded its followers. Therefore, in a short period of time, the African church was viewed as a social imperfection.

Within the African church itself, social relationships reflecting the growing status levels of the free black community found expression in ideas of social obligation and caste. While the church was being an essential institution for black expression, it also strengthened concepts of social status, responsibility and political leadership. Essential to this development was the synthesizing of political opinions into an ideological structure which defined the outside world from the perspective of free blacks' interest. Once established, the African church functioned as a viable social institution which helped blacks recognize the need to control and develop organizations within their communities. For example, within the Methodist Episcopal Church, regardless of how much authority blacks were able to gain, repressive laws of the 1820s and 1830s negated any assumption of equality between the races. Religious worship was not an exception. As a result, between 1836 and 1856, the membership of the Baltimore Conference of the African Methodist Episcopal (AME) Church had more than doubled.[93]

The Reverend Daniel Payne's comments on this development are enlightening:

> These converts included all who are now called Negroes, namely all persons of African descent, from the Octaroon down to the ebony Black, if such can be found. These naturally joined the Methodist Episcopal Church. As long as this church were in number few, and in condition poor, its colored members were gladly received and kindly treated, but as soon as it began to increase in numbers and wealth, so it became elevated in social position — with this increasing prosperity, the enslaved and proscribed Free Negro became contemptible in its eyes. — This contempt culminated in such treatment of the colored members, as none but men robbed of true manhood could endure.... We say: all who believe in the power, divinity and binding obligation of these words withdraw from the Methodist Episcopal Church, and organize the African Methodist Episcopal Church.[94]

The black churches had constructed a platform on which free blacks confronted social conditions with increasingly militant appeals. To the distress of whites, "the African church, with its subsidiary schools, fraternal organizations and benevolent societies," was able to discern between a reality that often hid behind altruisms.[95] This is indicated in a resolution adopted at an 1830 Philadelphia meeting in the Wesley Methodist Church, which concluded that "we view with charity the national policy of the American Colonization Society; as one necessary to the interest of the white inhabitants of this country."[96]

Throughout this period, congregations were inundated with sermons advocating various positions on colonization. What emerged was not a unified response to the possibility of colonization, but an outlook which can best be described as a concept of "two-ness" as identified by W.E.B. Dubois:

> One ever feels his two-ness — an American, a Negro; two souls, two thoughts, two unreconciled strivings; two warring ideals in one dark body, whose dogged strength alone keep it from being torn asunder.[97]

Similar evaluations of the external world underline the problem of interpreting a conflict created by an oppressive culture and its "liberating" God. Consequently, the need to convert European-oriented religious practices into social experiences unique to the displaced African was indicative of free blacks' Africanization of Christianity and their search for deeper social meanings.

Sermons, whether they were presented orally to a local congregation or "nationally" through the black press, constantly addressed themselves to the perceived needs of the community and how these needs could be satisfied in one "idealized" society. For the black church, and specifically the black preacher, God, the Gospel and religion were an imminent force always ready to assist those in need, just as "the Jews were aided when they were in need."[98] Within this social framework, a rhetorical style emerged which viewed the essential question of antebellum America through moral rationalizations rather than political dialectics. Those who attempted to place political realities on a plane outside of religious constructs were viewed as agents of the devil or, at worst, representatives of the slaveholding interest of America.

An example of the two opposing appeals can be observed in the October 1858 issue of the *Anglo-African Magazine*, when the Reverend James T. Holly expressed his "Thoughts on Hayti." Subtitling his article "Wrong Conceptions and False Expectations to be Guarded Against by Emigrants to Hayti," Holly examined the social expectations Haitian emigrants were believed to possess:

> It may be set down as a truism, that slavery, proscriptions and oppression are poor schools in which to train independent, self-respecting Freemen. Individuals so trained are apt to have all their aspirations, aims, ends and objects in life on a level with the low, grovelling and servile place of a slavish and dependent mind; or if by chance that mind has grown restless under its fetters, and sighs for enfranchisement and liberty, it is

apt to push the other extreme in its desires, and is led to covet those positions for which it has no proper qualifications whatever. The bent of the slavery-disciplined mind is either too low or too high. It cannot remain in equailibrium [sic]. It either cringes with all the dastard servility of the slave, or assumes the lordly airs of a cruel and imperious despot.[99]

Attacking what he viewed as the essential weaknesses of the emigration "fever," the Reverend Holly asserted that the desire for "christianizing the heathen" did not in itself resolve the problem of physical survival in an alien, hostile culture: The emigrants needed a "noble daring and heroic self-sacrifice of independent self-respecting Freemen," and not "the expectation of finding servile employment, such as they had been used to in this country."[100]

Servile employment was not to be found in Haiti. The crudeness of the Haitian soil, the "strangeness" of the indigenous Creole dialect and the necessity for individual sacrifice without guaranteed success challenged the very mettle of this emigrating class, who themselves were not convinced of their "divine right" to settle, conquer and exploit this "new land." These were not the early North American Pilgrims who took over a hundred years to develop the rationale of ocean-to-ocean "manifest destiny." Furthermore, the Haitian emigrant perceived himself as an intruder, a seeker of a morality who claimed equality with all men. Obviating the role of superior people carrying out God's will to conquer, they sought for themselves a noncontroversial haven or, as Absalom Jones commented on possible termination of the slave trade, "a deliverance from their bondage at the pleasure of God."

This was not the fabric of a dynamic settler class, prompted Holly. However, he advised:

> Hence, then, let me say to those emigrants who would prove themselves to be worthy of their adopted country, go to Hayti neither with servile longings nor with inflated aspirations and pretensions after political power and place. Duty to yourselves in the matter of self-respect forbids the servility of the former, and duty to the native Haytians, in rendering unto Cesar the things that are Cesar's, forbids the assumptions of the latter. But let the American emigrants be content to be the industrial civilizers of Hayti. Let them be satisfied to occupy the same position as bourgeoisie do in Europe. Let them develop the natural resources of the country, and increase her wealth; and by so doing they will be able to keep themselves from sinking into domestic servility, by wielding a power behind the throne greater than the throne itself.[101]

Carefully divesting African American emigrants of any "rush" to power, Holly concluded:

Thus circumscribed, and thus divested of the wrong conceptions and false expectations of a fanciful imagination, Colored American emigrants will find among the Haytians the most favorable field in which to obtain their manly growth to the full stature of free and independent men; and thereby vindicate their capacity to be the architects of their own fortunes, the shapers of their own destinies, and equal in every respect to the demands of the nineteenth century of modern civilization.[102]

Though mobilization efforts in the 1850s by Holly and others were imbued with notions of racial separation, earlier leaders of this class, such as Bishop Allen, were very reluctant to adhere to any ideology of emigration. Asserting that free blacks' deficiencies prohibited any successful emigration, Allen claimed that an "unlettered people, brought up in ignorance; not one in a hundred can read or write, not one in a thousand has a liberal education," could not be expected to desire emigration. Then proceeding to renounce any historical similarity between the 17th century Pilgrim immigrants from Europe and African American emigrants to Africa or Haiti, Allen assailed any comparison as ludicrous, as free blacks to him were not only generally intellectually inferior, but culturally unfit for the task. He asked, "Is there any fitness for such to be sent into a far country among heathens, to convert or civilize them; when they themselves are neither civilized nor Christians?"[103] Moreover, Allen argued that great injustice would be rendered upon free blacks if given the responsibility of determining the future growth of a new society. Consequently, any comparison of the Pilgrim "fathers" and African American emigrants was bankrupt and full of contradictions. He noted:

America was colonized by as wise, judicious and educated men as the world afforded. William Penn did not want for learning, wisdom or intelligence. If all the people in Europe and America were as ignorant and in the same situation as our brethren, what would become of the world? Where would be the principles of piety that would govern the people?[104]

Anticolonizationists argued that any attempt to merge political independence and religious freedom in the form of colonization to Liberia or emigration to Haiti was a backward step from Christian deliverance. Strategies for political separation were considered not only a threat to the "civilizing" of blacks, but illogical and unappreciative of the "blood which has watered this land, our mother country."

Addressing himself to these issues in *Rights of All*, Cornish asserted that to then speculate on its (Liberia's) value to "ameliorate the condition of the vast body of our colored population, I never shall believe ... but make the master Christ's servant, and the slave Christ's Freeman, and even the southern sectors of our country shall become home for the oppressed, slavery will be but a name in our dictionary."[105]

Free blacks who rejected the role of Liberian "settler" symbolized the effectiveness of American socialization in two ways. First, inherent in this process was desire for social approval and equality with whites, while accommodating themselves to the established American social maxim of race, class and status. Similarly, Christianity with its rationalizations for internal moral development and patience was viewed as being synonymous with civilization and enlightenment. In addition, anticolonizationists argued that if any role in Africa was demanded of them, it would be to "bring the light of truth to that dark continent."[106]

Secondly, the forceful impact of slavery with its resulting social and religious framework reinforced free blacks' perceptions of themselves as the "lambs" of Christianity, rather than the "warriors" of God. As a result, Africans' "predisposition" to Christian humility is viewed within the context of a need to find meaning for their existence in America. Deprived of a cultural continuity built upon African religious orientation, which could have provided a mechanism for self-verification, the Christian church, borrowed from whites, enlisted blacks' deepest loyalties. Dislocated African deities were now replaced with new manifestations of the sacred.

Thus, the free black was socialized into a belief system which, once ritualized, became an overpowering rationale of intrinsic value. "His" God, who was a borrowed god, a God not of his own making, became one of increasing value as it helped to confront the negativity and skepticism of slavery and quasi-freedom: "The believer, who has communicated with his God, is not merely a man who sees new truths of which the unbeliever is ignorant; he is a man who is STRONGER. He feels within him more force, either to endure the trials of existence, or to conquer them."[107]

One, John Chavis, educator and "stump" preacher from the backwoods of North Carolina, agreed with this analysis expressing the sentiment that slaves should be thankful for their "importation" to America, otherwise they would have almost certainly been denied the blessings of Christianity. He also felt that abolition would add to the woes of his fellow blacks, and "that it is truly a matter of thankfulness to the black people, that they were brought to this country, for I believe thousands of them will have reason to rejoice for it in the ages of eternity."[108]

While free blacks' efforts for social survival and respectability constituted a major part of their daily activities, the belief that a supreme adherence to religion would alleviate any ambiguity about self also played a critical role. In this respect, religion assisted them in their *attempt* to become a voluntary segment of the American society rather than a dubious appendage. Ironic as it may seem, by separating from the Episcopal Church, the AME Church hoped to demonstrate that theirs was not a separation from America, but a movement towards separate yet equal status within the American church. As a result, colonization as pursued by the American Colonization Society or any outward movement of blacks was viewed as a threat which would atomize free blacks' ideas of social worth and advancement within North America. Bishop Allen of the AME Church chided colonizationists by asking:

> Is there any fitness for such to be sent into a far country, among heathens, to convert or civilize them; when they themselves are neither civilized nor Christianized? Is there not land enough in America, or "corn enough in Egypt?" Why should they send us into a far country to die? See the thousands of foreigners emigrating to America every year, and if there be ground sufficient for them to cultivate, and bread for them to eat, why would they wish to send the first tillers of the land away?[109]

The naivete of Allen's questions only barely suppresses the assimilationist desires of its author, as when he suggested that one's cultural origins were secondary to a recognition that Christian superiority over all nonbelievers was not only proper, but justified. For Allen, Christianity was a framework of thought which brought him into contact with other free blacks of similar belief. Within this context, Allen was convinced that the church provided the best structure for political collectivity. Religion (Christianity), he argued, was a needed extension of society into one's character. It focused on those aspects of American society endowed with sacredness. "Hence, the nearly limitless influence of religion on culture and personality, and even the establishment of the authority of reason," flowed from these religious beliefs.[110]

In accepting the "benefits and knowledge" of Christianity, while renouncing the past as a mosaic of heathenistic experiences, Christianized blacks increasingly struggled with the concept of cultural identity. Consequently, assertions by individuals such as Chavis as to the "blessings of slavery" suggested some kind of purification process, "as in initiation or eucharistic ceremonies, ... a means by which a person or thing passes from the profane state to the sacred."[111] Moreover, experiences in survival, now ritualized from values and norms inculcated from the dominant culture, enhanced the development of a social personality best described as imitative and accommodationist. This is evidenced by a growing acceptance of the descriptive terms: non-African, that is, Negroes or colored men. Furthermore, the discontinuance of traditional African customs, language, folklore, etc., which in most instances were rejected by white America as savagery, influenced many blacks to conclude that they had little recourse but to dig deep into the source of life in which they now existed. Being relieved of the physical necessity to confront and rebel by a Christian doctrine of morality, solace and comfort through the rites of cultural submission via religious rationalizations were pursued as social value. However, some, like Lewis Woodson, balked at such a response to American racism.

Woodson, in an article in *The Colored American*, attempted to delineate the ideological confusion of forceful colonization and missionary zeal. He suggested that colonizationists were obscuring their real intentions with the veil of Christian missionary work and that, "deprived of its missionary and benevolent features, and held up in its true colors, [colonialism] would be loathed and discarded by every follower of the meek and lowly savior."[112] A more separatist development appealed to him. Coming close to advocating a nationalistic orientation when "carrying out Gods' work," Woodson further stated that:

> Indeed, if we had no love for Africa, love for ourselves and our children should prompt us to engage in this cause.... But I feel satisfied that we may safely appeal to our brethren in behalf of this high and holy cause, upon higher and holier principles than mere selfishness, I believe that hundreds of them stand ready to perform their duty, as soon as they know it, from the love they have to the blessed redeemer, and his kingdom on earth.[113]

Free blacks such as Woodson held on to the belief that eventual equalization between the races could occur if separate settlements were established *within* the American society. Explaining further, he asserted: "we should be all on perfect equality ... free from the looks of scorn and contempt ... free from all the evils attendant on practical and unequal laws."[114]

Assimilation and Free Blacks

With the advent of the 1830s the concept of separate free black settlements, isolated from influence or threat by whites, dominating land

and developing the rudiments of self-sufficiency, contrasted dramatically with the goals of an increasingly urbanized free black. Though Jacksonian values of an independent, self-reliant, agrarian man as the backbone of a growing America were still popular, the realization that these values were not intended for a competitive free black agrarian population forced many free blacks to seek their success within an urban environment. Accommodating themselves to this social reality was the benchmark for their success.

Acknowledgment of possible growth within societal norms as opposed to a forceful, dramatic change of society became the major form of appeal by educators and preachers such as John Chavis and free black slaveholders like Andrew Durnford. Identifying with the contemporary values of America, each in his way sought a further measure of respect at the price of an accommodating lifestyle. Establishing a social identity which denied them any sense of recognition as citizens except as "pariahs," free blacks found themselves blocked by social inequalities, limited in social mobility and, as we shall see, ideologically hampered by a need to fulfill notions of an ideal world.

If one views this process of "assimilation" as a ritual of passage, then the idea of it being completely realized is a question of time. For some it is a question of faith which in turn ties material accumulation with class advancement. The ability to compete at the expense of another became the essential qualification for survival. One's inability to prosper meant being labelled as inferior and incompetent, the stereotype view many whites maintained towards blacks. As a result, Darwinian concepts of "survival of the fittest" were not lost in antebellum rationalizations about relationships between the races. Nevertheless, the concept of competition for free blacks was not politically innovative, but rather, geared to learn the "rules" of society, as opposed to the rules by which to run society. While such a structure intensified ideas of class and caste among blacks, interracial interaction was characterized by diffused, intimidating, noncompetitive, asymmetrical relationships.

As a result, black slaveholders such as Andrew Durnford in 1835 concluded that society was "made up of two distinctive parts; on the one hand, wolves and foxes, and on the other hand, lambs and chickens to provide food for the former." "In the forest," he added, "a lion recognizes another lion, a tiger does not make another tiger its prey."[115] Durnford's analysis provides us with a good example of free blacks' accommodation in the extreme, as one emigrationist complained:

...too many of them aspire no higher than the gratification of their passions and appetites, and cling with deadly tenacity to a country that hates them and offers them nothing but chains, degradation and slavery.[116]

Indicative of such a personality is the individual's willingness to participate in the most immediate trends of his or her time, regardless of societal efforts to hinder or retard the person. This suggests not only an intense faith and belief in the ongoing institutions of society and their resulting political and economic characteristics, but that the eliminating of social inequities, no matter how confining, by *direct subversion* was not supported by this class of free blacks.[117] Herein lies a critical point as free blacks, seeing themselves as assimilating into society through a process of accommodation, minimized the historical significance of what the dominant sectors of society considered as absolute; that is to say, the significance of naked violence in defense of economic and political advantage. Resorting to a narrow philosophical interpretation of society, they seized upon the notion of Christian morality as the essential element of society, not fully realizing the antithetical aspects of antebellum Christianity and the underdevelopment of its "quasi-free" populace.

Not unlike other segments of society, a belief in the social process itself convinced free blacks that their condition would improve if they would simply emulate the values of white America. Part of this emulation was the negation of any segment of the human population which was not Christian. Since most 19th-century Africans were not Christian, the process of slavery, it was argued, facilitated both their Christianization and civilization, and brought them into contact with the economic values of enlightment via American power. Incorporating these values into everyday practice presented a serious obstacle in that essential to this process was the development of and use of social institutions and reference groups which would insure and sanction social input. Lacking this, existing social mechanisms were borrowed and subverted to insure social viability. In this regard, the black church filled a void by developing social networks while cementing institutional relationships with the black community. But in areas such as economics and political representation, free blacks tended to imitate rather than conflict with white society.

For example, an observer of Philadelphia's elite class in 1841 noted that:

> Among the very erroneous opinions that are formed respecting the people of color, is the one that supposed them indifferent to the state of things

by which they are surrounded, and that they make little or no effort for their relief.... It should be kept in view, that in Pennsylvania, particularly, and also in some other of the non-slaveholding states, they (Freemen) are almost, if not entirely, deprived of political rights and powers; and that, consequently, in all matters relating to their interest, which involve legislative action, they must appear altogether in the attitude of suitors; and show themselves very humble in the exercise of even that prerogative. They cannot say to legislators, "If you fail to act for us, we shall not fail to act against you when called to exercise the functions of electors"; they expect not, as yet, to be called to that exalted purpose; and this the former being well aware of, they take particular care to proceed in such a manner only, as they deem best calculated to further their popularity with those who do possess and exercise that power. It is then opined that when legislatures are asked, "Why do you not act for colored men?", they answer, "Because colored men do not act for me!" Thus it is necessary for the people of color to keep up an incessant BEGGING of their RULERS to legislate in their behalf; and with what effect is well known to all.[118]

While this accommodative attitude by free blacks was never total, it was a reactive response to the conflict involved in contact with white America. On this point, Gunner Myrdal, in his *An American Dilemma*, suggested that "every Negro has some sort of conflict with the white world." That is, his conflict is essentially with the social stratum whose power is inherited from its position in the existing order. From this position, the dominant group is able to master the subordinate stratum, first unconsciously and then through rational calculations. Consequently, enjoying neither the immunities of "freedom," they were subjected to the incapacities of a despised, poverty-stricken class ... "only a glance away from chattel slavery."

In spite of this, racist hegemonic power bases were not totally outside the pale of the free blacks' activities. Internalization of clothing styles, "proper" linguistic forms, social etiquette and attitudes signaling advancement in society eventually became more than imitation, but rather conscious attempts at accommodation, the effects of which were forms of social control embodied in behavioral patterns. These patterns became the foundation for establishing acceptable social behavior. Subsequent awareness of the social attributes associated with color further suggested a necessity for group coherence and an acceptable self-image. Social restrictions and cues quickly engulfed free blacks with the preferred attributes of the dominant society.

Though free blacks' acceptance of this relationship was contingent upon their level and frequency of contact with whites, among the elite or upper-strata the process included being educated, Christianized or marrying lighter than one's own color. These were attempts to escape what society deemed were inherent negative African characteristics. As a result, self-categorization in relationship to white America induced many free blacks to transfer white characteristics to all blacks. It was further deduced that only in this process of "purification" could the problem of accommodation with the hope of assimilation be reached.[119] This process of purification requires of the individual an awareness of the effort needed to successfully negotiate situations, and the dependency of his or her efforts upon the reactions of a judgmental audience. Critical in this process is the individual's awareness of assumed self-limitations, which when overcome, will reflect successful elimination, that is, purification of less desired characteristics, thereby raising one's position in society.

Free blacks' assimilation can be linked with an accommodationist behavior if one examines their relative proximity to whites in the economic sectors of society. Similarly, acceptance of existing norms which dictated social-economic distance between the races was predicated upon the rationale that parity was only possible when familiarity with an accommodating consciousness was practiced and maintained. The ability to effect this type of assimilation was obviously contingent on whites' continual highlighting of differences based upon color and cultural characteristics. Furthermore, free blacks' correlating of economic development with a renunciation of African characteristics became an increasingly recognizable occurrence in the process of social purification.

One is reminded of Ralph Ellison's *Invisible Man*, Dr. A. Herbert Bledsoe, who explained emphatically to a young black college student his perception of reality, and, in doing so, illustrates the ongoing conflict between the aspiring black and his alienating environment:

> You're nobody, son. You don't exist—can't you see that? The White folk tell everybody what to think—except men like me. I tell *them*; that's my life, telling White folk how to think about the things I know about. Shocks you, doesn't it? Well, that's the way it is. It's a nasty deal, and I don't always like it myself. But you listen to me: I didn't make it, and I know that I can't change it. But I've made my place in it and I'll have every Negro in the country hanging on tree limbs by morning if it means staying where I am ... I mean it son. I had to wait and plan and lick around.... Yes, I had to act the nigger ... yes!

The struggle to attain a level of "passable assimilation" involved the problem of creating within the individual or group a sense of self which would arouse belief in one's appearance among a milieu of strangers, both black and white. Free blacks' adoption of the accommodationist role was in fact an attempt at achieving a social image believable enough to convince others of its viability. While it did not represent totally the feelings of blacks who accommodated themselves to a hostile reality, it did provide a shield against societal condemnation of their race. Richard Sennett notes that "the knowledge on which belief can be based is confined to the frame of the immediate situation. The arousal of beliefs, therefore, depends on how one behaves—talks, gestures, moves, dresses, listens—within the situation itself."[120] Among free blacks, this was true not only in relationship to interracial interaction but free blacks' intergroup relationships.

Whites in most cases maintained a generalized stereotyped opinion of blacks; they assumed blacks to be of an inferior race, whose enslavement and social regulation to a lower echelon of society was necessary. Difficulty in judging a particular black was resolved by imputing limited knowledge of the group to the particular unknown element. Thus, once objectified and stripped of any individuality, blacks were labelled with attributes which satisfied the needs of a racial characterization within a societal context requiring their domination and suppression. Inside this social environment, free blacks were continually involved with attempts at successful presentation of self. "Passable assimilation" became the enactment of separate yet imitative aspects of the macro-white structure. In this process, the negotiating of oneself occurred in deference to whites, with the hopeful destruction of perceived negative characteristics as the goal.

Resulting intergroup concepts of status tended to reflect macrosocietal beliefs of upward mobility and improvement of one's condition through Christian education, tolerance and morality. Moves toward accommodation became the tacit acceptance of society's alleged capacity to bring equality and civilization to all. Thus, Augustine's comment in *The Colored American* suggested that the moral, social and aesthetic uplift of the race would aid dramatically in improving free blacks' condition:

> If we have the capacity to devise the means and prosecute the end of our moral elevation, what but the want of a right and noble mind could hinder us from doing it? What better argument could our enemies desire, to establish the doctrine of our intellectual inferiority, than this, that when we ourselves acknowledge, and even feel, our present low undesirable condition, we make no general effort on our part, to rise above it.[121]

Efforts to free onself from the insularity of racial characterization and economic stagnation without the desire to advocate Africanism as positive values resulted in many free blacks viewing societal practices as the only viable social criteria. Therefore, from a social psychological perspective, the free black was in fact a colonized individual, whose needs for social recognition were inextricably tied to his economic condition of dependency. Many could claim, as did William W. Brown in his cynical observation on colleague Lenox Remond, that blacks had a burning conviction that they were in a crusade that encompassed the salvation of white as well as black Americans.[122]

A classic example of the social attitudes of this class are contained in an 1841 article titled *Sketches of the Higher Classes of Colored Society*. In describing Philadelphia's elite free black class from a 19th-century perspective, the author states that:

> Their churches embraced nearly all the Christian denominations... the Methodists are by far the most numerous, and next to these, in numerical order may be named the Presbyterians, Baptists and Episcopalians.... Mutual relief societies are numerous. There are a larger number of these than of any other description, in the colored community.[123]

Though it was in the area of education that the "upper class" sought the tools for advancement and possibly assimilation, this observer saw the problems involved as those which defined *distinctions* between free blacks:

> I am to present a boundary between a class of persons whom the great body of public have been accustomed to consider so closely allied to each other, as to render it very improbable, if not impossible, that any social differences could be held in recognition among them. This is a great error, it is true, but it does not much lessen the difficulty.[124]

He then proceeded to claim that:

> The chief grounds of distinction among men are founded upon wealth, education, station and occupation.... But here [i.e., among Freemen], are none of these, to an extent which would warrant their, or either of them, being made the point of departure. I have not the foundation of wealth; because the number who may be permitted to come under that denomination are too limited to be justly made the standard of the men and manners of the whole body... neither may I erect upon education nor occupation; as among the higher classes—unless an unjust and illiberal contrast is sought—there is no very remarkable difference anywhere to be found.[125]

In a similar manner, Lewis Woodson, writing under the pen name of Augustine, argued:

> The general character of any nation or class of men is determined by the private character of a majority of the individuals who compose it. A few individuals of any class of men, being civilized, enlightened and refined, does not procure for their class such a character.... The few who have risen above the condition of the many, are not regarded; will never be fully appreciated, until the majority of the class with whom they are identified have risen to something like a level of themselves. Hence the necessity of making an adequate effort for general moral improvement.[125]

Literary and Educational Societies

Endeavoring to escape the conflicts of a marginal existence, "higher class" free blacks resolved that, "Order is Heaven's first law, and in this context, some are and must be greater than the rest — more rich, more wise," as they sought to establish a social position within the dominant society, which would facilitate mechanisms for assimilation. Primary in this effort was the development of committees and societies which would strengthen "their intellectual faculties and cultivate a refined literary taste," which in the final analysis was geared to demonstrate to whites the free blacks' capacity for self-improvement.[127]

The establishment and support of these literary associations and debating societies were, to a large degree, the result of rigid social norms which limited free blacks' activities, especially those which threatened whites' economic well-being.

As early as 1787, Absalom Jones and Richard Allen established a beneficial society in Philadelphia called The Free African Society, which had as its stated purpose a desire to give mutual aid to members in distress. Soon after, blacks organized themselves into beneficial, missionary, temperance, tract, educational, welfare and moral reform societies, most of which were located within the eastern and Middle Atlantic states.[128]

Since the large urban areas were also the economic nexus for the society at large, laws limiting these activities were often not enforced to the extent they were in rural areas. Consequently, blacks found themselves exposed to newspapers and journals whose interpretation of local and national events provided a basis for their further understanding of society. Undoubtedly, these "liberties" convinced many blacks that compared to the southern region of the country, northern blacks were closer to achieving the ideals of freedom than anywhere else. For example, a free black in Mississippi in the 1830s publishing a newspaper or pamphlet concerned with the condition of slaves or free blacks was not only unlawful but "seditious." To cite an instance, in 1835, Amos Dresser, an active member of the Ohio Abolition Society, was arrested in Nashville, Tennessee, and charged with circulating pamphlets among slaves to incite them to insurrection. The committee of vigilence, consisting of fifty-two citizens, found him guilty, sentencing him to a whipping and forcible ejection from the city.[129] Since these "efforts" by whites to control blacks were not isolated, they generally spurred blacks to create libraries, reading rooms and channels for publication and public debate within northern urban centers. A list of the more important free black societies (see Appendix C, pp. 210-211) suggests a growing preoccupation with their image within the larger society.

Finally, assimilation between equals suggests the willingness of both parties to negotiate mutually acceptable terms for cultural, political and economic exchange. The exchange is not merely limited to such items as dress, language, food and sports—which are fairly easy to acquire and appreciate—but includes less tangible items such as values (beliefs), memories, sentiments, ideas, and attitudes. However, the unequal, dominant-subordinate relationships between cultures, as in antebellum America, represented for blacks an unending struggle for acceptance on any level. While many blacks thought assimilation was a justifiable goal and structured organizations to facilitate this process, whites' fear of amalgamation with an "inferior race" (who, it was generally believed, would also threaten their economic security), prompted many blacks to attempt alleviation of these fears by developing more "acceptable" images of self. This process of "Americanization" prompted the following response:

> I care not how many societies, whose objects are moral or mental improvement are raised up. They will tend to clear us from the charge of indolence or indifference, to our own welfare, which has been heaped upon us, and also, from that foul asperation [sic], as to the inferiority of our intellectual capacities, with which many have been pleased to brand us.... They show, too, that we are not a people, wholly given up to revelry and licentiousness, as we have been basely misrepresented, but that the leisure hours of many are devoted to thought and literary advancement.[130]

Within these societies lay the conscious attempt by upper-strata free blacks to structure a socio-economic belief system which would guide them towards value definitions established by the white world.

Vestiges of African tradition or culture, which had somehow survived the process of enslavement, were displaced with distinct white moral, social and aesthetic codes. The de-emphasis on color, that is, racial awareness, became a rhetorical cue as it was suggested that blacks were really like whites only a little darker! Cultural heritage was viewed as beginning with Christianity (slavery), while African history, language, music, art and aesthetics were related to as artifacts of a heathenistic people. Thus, the literary society, acting as a social bridge for a people living in a hostile environment, was in fact the public expression of elite free blacks who concluded quite openly that, "He who implanted the mind and endowed it with certain capabilities and faculties of development, hath also placed in our power the *means* thereof; and happy is he who makes the best use of them."[131]

Yet, their reality in 1840 precluded any notion of the "happy man of color." Education and moral codes were not sufficient to influence or convert the growing walls of political and social indifference through which white America viewed all Africans. In a soliloquy on the "colored society," an author posited that:

> The educated man of color, in the United States, is by no means, so far as he may be affected by exterior circumstances, the happiest man. He finds himself in possesssion of abilities and acquirements which fit him for most of the useful and honorable stations in life, where such qualities are requisite; but does he find — can he even with reason anticipate — their ever being in like manner appreciated and rewarded?

He then concluded, "but education possesses its own intrinsic worth, which it imparts to those who enter its pursuits."[132]

In a smilar vein, M.H. Freeman succinctly explains in an article in *The American Magazine* that:

> The education of the Free Colored man is one of the most prominent measures proposed for the alleviation of the ills which Black humanity suffers in this country.... We need the educating power of wealth, of civil and political honors and offices for our children, for these are the means that first develop in the *children of the other race*, that due self-respect and self-reliance which must lie at the foundation of any just and harmonious development of mind.[133]

With this as a philosophical framework, the increasingly urbanized free blacks began to incorporate into their value system social goals, structures and attitudes which were best represented with the creating of educational societies which were to facilitate the assimilatory process.

The efforts of these literary societies deserve examination, for while they were shortlived, their influence and prestige were influenced by the material and class realities of the dominant slaveholding society. Though their assumptions about quality education were based on eventual ethnic pluralism and the equalization of material goods for free blacks, evidence indicates that social assimilation in this manner occurs slowly, as does identity assimilation. Thus, the literary societies were essentially a mechanism for *acculturation* but *not assimilation*. Notwithstanding this, free blacks, convinced of unlimited social possibilities via education, assumed that in everything, merit alone must triumph.

Discussions pertaining to public matters of immediate concern, as well as issues within the free black community, found their way into associations such as "The Philadelphia Library Company of Colored Persons." Instituted in January 1833, its membership consisted of individuals who pursued a career up the social ladder via the church and educational circles. The company was basically established to collect useful works of every description for its membership. In connection with this a debating society was formed with the intent of "stimulating the members to historical and other researches, and for practicing in the arts of elocution and public speaking." By 1836, this library company was incorporated and growing in membership, and "many a young man of color in this community, who previous to the establishment of the 'Philadelphia Library Company of Colored Persons' never dreamed of rising before a public auditory to make an address, or engage in a debate, is now enabled to do so with little or no embarrassment, and in a manner highly creditable."[134]

Other societies, such as the Rush Library Company and Debating Society of Pennsylvania and the Demosthenian Institute, basically fulfilled the same purpose. One society, the Minerva Literary Association, which consisted of thirty women, formed "a school for the encouragement and promotion of polite literature." The order of their exercises was reading and recitations of original and selected pieces, "together with other appropriate matters." Another female society, calling themselves the Edgeworth Literary Association, being similar to the Minerva Association, was described by a contemporary observer: "It is sufficient to say that the ladies consider them both (the two societies) worthy of being cherished, which is a sufficient guaranty that they are not wanting in importance and usefulness." The Gilbert Lyceum, composed of both sexes, at this time was the first and only society "established by the colored classes of Philadelphia, for both Literary and Scientific pursuits." Numbering forty, its members hoped to "encourage and promote among the colored classes, literature, science and the arts; and to embody all the good features of those now in existence, while it will be the aim to avoid such as have proven disadvantageous."[135]

In New York, societies propagating similar values flourished, the Philamathean Society and the Phoenix Society being the largest and most influential. Both societies were dedicated to the "improvement of literature and useful knowledge." The Philamathean Society in 1837 decided it would have an open door policy to all members of other free black societies. Hoping to facilitate a wider influence, the Phoenix Society maintained a policy which allowed both black and white to hold leadership positions, and among the leaders were Arthur Tappan, a white philanthropist and the Reverend Samuel Cornish, editor of *The Colored American*. This society established a network of ward societies whose members were required to visit various families within the ward vicinity and make a registry of every free black, ascertaining their age, sex, occupation and ability to read and write. The major focus was to induce the old and young to become members of the society. Furthermore, efforts were made to "seek young men of good moral character" as members who would ultimately be expected to obtain a good liberal education. It soon became evident that in addition to literary societies, other means of advancing their interests and elevating them as a class were needed. Schools for the educating of children were considered essential to this task.[136]

Cornish's plea for donations to the Phoenix Society's library underscored this need when he berated the free black community for not "turning their attention to their education and to the improvement of their condition." His concern was, to a large extent, in response to a growing awareness among blacks that the process of education alone would not resolve the conditions which plagued them, especially when white philanthropists such as John Jay expressed patronizing attitudes towards free blacks' education, such as:

> They [Freemen] should not be left entirely either to themselves or to their parents, it being difficult to give them good morals, manners or habits in any other way than by placing them under the care and direction of persons better qualified than their parents generally are.[137]

Examples of the ongoing contradiction between free blacks' and whites' philanthropic views on education surfaced as early as 1818 when the trustees of the African Free School in New York City reported to parents that "There is no disgrace incurred in the pursuit of any calling, however humble. It is the duty of every one to do all the good in the sphere in which providence has placed him."[138] Although blacks increasingly expressed the belief that education would insure their respect and prestige, and that emancipation was a crucial step in this process, some whites, such as Dr. Orville, suggested that "Blacks [in the free states] are worse off than the slaves of the south, not being so well fed." While many agreed with this assessment, others, such as Dr. James M. Smith, disagreed. In a series of letters to *The New York Tribune*, Smith explained that as a student of the African Free School in 1826–27, and later, a graduate with a medical degree from the University of Glasgow, Scotland, he felt more than competent to compile and assess statistics pertaining to free blacks' institutions in the North. From this perspective, he directed his conclusions to Dewey, asserting, "In view of the schools, churches and benevolent institutions, under the genial smile of emancipation, may not the north affectionately, earnestly and reasonably call upon the South to follow example."[139]

As revealing as his statistics were, reactionary forces within society continually opposed the educational assimilation of free blacks in the North. Many white citizens opposed it on the grounds that such mental improvement was inconsistent with blacks' position as persons held in service. A persistent hope existed that if the slave were deprived of intellectual advancement, those emancipated would be so dependent upon whites that economic and political control would be simple. This situation, prevalent in many parts of the South, was best described in the 1832 Virginia House of Delegates:

> We have as far as possible closed every avenue by which light may enter their minds. If we could extinguish the capacity to see light, our work would be completed: They would then be on a level with the beast of the field and we should be safe! I am not certain that we would not do it, if we could find out the process, and that on the plea of necessity.[140]

Supportive material for Smith's argument, however, not only suggested the growing educational advantages of northern urban lifestyles, but conversely indicated a growing inferiority of southern blacks in the valued area of educational attainment. For example, in 1850 there were 4,354 children of free blacks attending schools in the South, but by 1860 the number had decreased to 3,651. The states of Georgia and Mississippi at this time had practically deprived all blacks of educational privileges. However, in the free states there were 22,107 children of free blacks in schools by 1850 and 28,978 in 1860, mostly in New York, New Jersey, Ohio and Pennsylvania. Illiteracy figures for adult free blacks further indicate divergent educational policies within the two sections.

In this same ten-year period, illiteracy figures rose from 58,444 to 59,832 for slave states, while the situation in the northern states was just the opposite.[141]

Free blacks found such statistics clearly indicative of caste status as well as general social cultivation. Environmental factors in slave states were translated into dispositional characteristics which stereotyped the southern black, free or slave. Social advancement, through education, social mannerism, color or business attainment became the primary social indicator of personal motivation. As explained by "Sidney" in *The Colored American*:

> The correctness of our views will further appear from a consideration of the essentially peculiar ability of the oppressed, and the necessary incapability of all others, even the best of friends.... The elevation of a people is not measurably dependent upon external relations or peculiar circumstances, as it is upon the inward rational sentiments which enable the soul to change circumstances to its own temper and disposition.[142]

Viewpoints such as this tended to limit rather than expand the responsibility of free blacks to each other by viewing the individual's thrust of personality as solely significant. Advancement, such authors claimed, "must exist in the man. The spirit that would elevate him above his circumstances, and gain him respect and manhood, must have all the strength of personal character."[143]

In an editorial comment, *The Colored American* narrowed this individualized effort to the more utilitarian aspect of personal growth, by implying that a more productive use of energy could be obtained by encouraging students to study mathematics, chemistry, botany or commerce. They further claimed that "in this way we shall succeed in their elevation, and in making them important and honorable constituents in society." Caution was exercised when it came to women: "As to our daughters, let us give them a solid education, and whatever else we neglect, let us not neglect to teach them the use of the needle, housework and domestic economy generally."[114]

The propagating of individual achievement as a necessary goal in the black press, regardless of its cost in personal alienation, is evidenced by an occupational statistical table that was published by *The Weekly Anglo-African*. Though the study was limited to the New York City area, its conclusions were salient enough to conflict with an earlier study published by *The Herald*, a nonblack New York–based paper.

The reasons behind the discrepancies in the reports are indicative of northern bigotry as well as free blacks' attempt to surmount these obstacles. For example, *The Weekly Anglo-African* asserted that *The*

Herald's statistics were incomplete due to a high level of blacks registered as whites, and that, "One of the largest grocers and one of the best merchant tailors in our leading thoroughfare are among this class, to say nothing of banking clerks, park porters, and at least one enormously shrewd and exceedingly wealthy black broker."[145] Presenting strong examples of social negotiation by free blacks caught within the quasi-free world of white ethnocentrism, the article asserts that:

> Another constantly increasing drain on the count of the colored population in one metropolitan city, is the number who from year to year turn White and are counted as White. No matter how dark a man's complexion may be, if nature, or art, give him a crop of straight hair, he may, and in many instances does, count himself White—that is, not of African blood. And furthermore, if a man be in the combined with a dark complexion, and still the individual "Pass for White".... We think it a moderate estimate to say that in the ten years ending June, 1860, at least one thousand colored persons turned White in the city of New York.[146]

Another reason for *The Anglo-African*'s conclusions about the variations in free blacks' occupations was the inaccuracies of the latest census, which was taken during the months of June and July of the previous year. Being the "high season of steamboating, watering places and country migration" to places such as Maine, the capes of Delaware, Saratoga Springs, Catskill Mountains, Newport, Rhode Island, New Haven, Connecticut, Long Beach and Cape May, if the number of free blacks traveling to these places were included, the census alone would become higher by some fifteen hundred."[147]

Clarifying what they perceived as erroneous impressions, *The Anglo-African* explained:

> The article in the "Herald" states that there are 7,270 colored persons over twenty years of age in this city, and that there are 1,200 families of the same class. Of these 7,270 people, it is seen that over 5,000 or five-sevenths are engaged in honest occupations, three-fifths of them menial. Of all these, only 24 are engaged in liquor selling or 1 in 208. In our German city population, there is one in every 17 engaged in the rum traffic. Our people, therefore, compared favorably with the best class of citizens in the innocent nature and useful character of their occupations.... It is true we do not occupy the first rank in wealth and show; But of this we are assured, that we have advanced more in the last quarter of the century than any other class in New York.[148]

Herein lies an example of what Dubois described as the "two-ness" of blacks' existence. Laden with the ambiguous social position of quasi-citizenship, free blacks utilized the few organs of expression in the black and abolitionist press and attempted to develop and articulate ideological positions which would validate rather than negate their presence in America. Essential to this process was the political dilemma of whether blacks should concern themselves with the prospects of individual growth—a position many viewed as the abandonment of the slave—or strive for universal betterment.

Those who favored individual growth also fell into two categories in that, for some, any possible improvement of social condition could only occur within the context of what was generally perceived as Western enlightenment, Christian tolerance and economic growth. This moral suasionist ideology predicted full social integration as inevitable and desirable. A second group, no less determined to obtain and improve their condition, saw the likelihood of this occurring within America to be slim, if not impossible. *Resettlement in Canada* or *outright emigration to the Carribean* or *Africa*, they argued, was preferable. Though both groups professed contrasting ideological positions, only upon examining their rhetorical appeals for individualistic attainment do we uncover factors which indicate numerous ideological similarities.

For example, while the former group of free blacks resolved to become "Americanized," it was their social-economic relationship to the overall society, not the ability to simply mimic social practices, which determined their level of successful assimilation. As a result, the essential question for this group was whether racial unity should be exclusive or inclusive of white endeavors for the amelioration of blacks' social condition. As one observer put it, "The issue is not what can be accomplished for blacks, but what can they do of themselves and by themselves."[149] Literary societies, free African schools, development of the separate African church, blacks' predominance in lower-skilled work areas, all tended to constitute a series of factors militating against assimilation. As Martin Delany observed, "Our degradation being once—as it has in a hundred instances been done—legally determined, our color is sufficient, independently of custom, education, or other distinguishing marks, to keep up that distinction."[150]

For those who advocated *universal betterment* the factors of time, fortitude and education were to ease free blacks' entry into mainstream America. Allied to this philosophy was the establishing of political institutions which would first insure political cohesiveness and refute any claims of blacks' inferiority. As a result, pragmatic arguments by writers such as "Augustine" assserted, "Without a national institution of some description our affairs can never attain any degree of consistency or permanence." And that:

> There can be no HEAD or CENTER around which we may rally. Our numbers, MEANS and CAPACITY will remain useless, for want of something to combine and concentrate them. The high intellectual powers must diminish, if not become entirely extinct, for want of the means of their development.[151]

Essential to this vision of a better society, it was argued, was their ability to demonstrate in a materialistic manner their "equality" with whites, *within* the American system. Thus, in a unique manner, what might be viewed at first glance as black nationalism—the striving for social integrity, economic proficiency and political acuity—was in fact a move towards a desired eventual absorption of blacks within the American system. Conclusion of this sort, positing the necessity of a national movement, tended to minimize the importance of color in the black community in deference to class oppression, as "Sidney" explained in *The Colored American*:

> Whenever a people are oppressed, peculiarly (NOT COMPLEXIONALLY), distinctive organization or action, is required on the part of the oppressed, to destroy that oppression. The colored people of this country are required to act in accordance with this fundamental principle.[152]

Nationalism in the form of separatism, as advocated by free blacks during the 1850–1860 period, contained major justifications for separate development, many of which were not primarily based on race although race was not totally discounted. It was articulated that, with the termination of the legacy of blacks as a pariah class, a continued state of social and political improvement would ensue, as would their rapid inclusion into American society. Among those free blacks who rejected emigration, persistent identification with in-group social links also tended to exist even when they were forced economically or by direct physical measures to move from one area to another. Hardening social attitudes of most whites further enhanced racial-class differences, that is, the Fugitive Slave Act of 1850, the Dred Scott decision of 1857, as well as caste stratification within free black communities. Delany, in attempting to alert blacks to the vulnerability of their situation, cautioned:

> Were we content to remain as we are, sparsely interspersed among our white fellow-countrymen, we never might be expected to equal them in any honorable or respectable competition for a livelihood. For the reason that, according to the customs and policy of the country, we for ages would be kept in a secondary position, every situation of respectability,

honor, profit, or trust, either as mechanics, clerks, teachers, jurors, councilmen, or legislators, being filled by White men, consequently our energies must become paralyzed or enervated for the want of proper encouragement.[153]

Underlining his concern was the fear that whites' political and economic control of society would increasingly translate itself, at best, into paternalistic considerations on the issues of emigration, emancipation or abolition. Such a development, he concluded, would further hamper the political progress of an already highly acculturated class of people. Though this struggle was a battle for national identity, it was not limited to allegiance to American ideals. It *was* a move towards racial awareness and a certain validation of heritage; however, it was clearly based upon one's *individual awareness and motivation* as opposed to a *collective response to the unique condition* of the quasi-free.

It is from this framework that the African American press began to emerge as a vehicle for political expression. Created in an atmosphere of racism and oppression, it began to reflect the sentiments and aspirations of those who either sought social redress via assimilation, colonization or emigration to the Caribbean or Africa. In a unique manner, these early participants in the black press exhibited strong perceptions of individuality as they laid the groundwork for black political development and articulation on a a national scale. However, a more collective response to racial oppression waited offstage.

II. Emigration vs. Assimilation as Social Remedies

> *Here I have dwelt until I am nearly seventy years of age, and have brought up and educated a family, as you can see, thus far. Yet some ingenious gentlemen have recently discovered that I am still an African; that a continent, three thousand miles, and more, from the place where I was born is my native country. And I am advised to go home. Well, it may be so. Perhaps if I went I should recognize all I might see there, and run at once to the old hut where my forefathers lived a hundred years ago.*
>
> James Forten, 1859

Free blacks' leadership was generally disposed to emigration or colonization and, as a result, premised their social and economic needs primarily on the interests of the educated, business-oriented class, one which to a large degree considered the desires of its nonliterate, lower-strata brethren to be similar to its own. Efforts to diffuse information on this issue were more reflective of publishers' class affiliations and their financial backers than of any varying perspectives among the populace. Eventually, the phenomenon of an audience talking to itself became a politically limiting expression and the privileged "duty" of a few.[1] Furthermore, editors' reluctance to project Africa in a positive manner severely retarded any possibility of Africa being viewed as a "promised land." Social elevation was viewed *only* within the context of the United States. However, with the implementation of the Fugitive Slave Acts in the 1850s, which threatened to strip free blacks of their "assumed" northern sanctuaries, analysis on emigration began to gain popularity. A comparison of viewpoints on the issue of emigration from 1827 to 1861 clearly suggests that the reality of its being a viable alternative increased only when free blacks viewed their own enslavement as being imminent (see tables 7 and 7A, pp. 218–221). In this regard, the African American press played a major role as information drawn from social analysis in the press enhanced blacks' ability to make predictions about their condition. Similarly, any altering of their environment or social condition precipitated either a readjustment or reinforcement of viewpoints held.

While examining this early period of the black press, it is interesting to note that a dysfunction occurred affecting the transmitting of information and its interpretation, once editors and publishers charged with this responsibility became concerned with their own image, rather than the social impact of their publications. In a press which lacked any real sense of bipartisanism on the issue of emigration, concerns about maintaining one's publication as a beacon of social morality and political justice not only indicated an exaggerated concern with precepts of "American" morality, but also an intense preoccupation with the presentation of self.

As noted earlier, disagreements in the press on emigration did not preclude adherence to Christian American beliefs, nor the social norms which emerged from them. Instead, examination of the social arena as defined by class interest was the prime factor in making causal inferences on emigration.

Generally, articles either attacking or supporting emigration attempted to separate the individual from the broader aspects of the issue. Consequently, any concept of "mass" movement, even when referred to in connection with numerous national emigration conventions, quickly specified the importance of individuals as the motivators of events. For example, one reads of "delegates" at freemen conventions but not who they represented or how they became representatives, not to mention their specific relationship to a constituency. In one publication, failure of the Haitian emigration movement in 1824 was vividly enunciated in personal terms by a writer as he complained of the emigrants' inability to "communicate" and their "dissimilarity of manners and morals" as major areas for conflict and failure.[2] As a result, critics of emigration and colonization tended "not to be as concerned with those collective behaviors which vary in relationship to the established social system," but with the individual's analysis. Yet, it was precisely this collective relationship between individuals and the group which should have concerned the contemporary observers of antebellum African American society.[3]

Though later appeals in the press suggested "to all proposing to emigrate to look upon the cause in which they are engaged," and not the individuals involved, most appeals stated: "We call especially on *you* in view of the subject, what position *will ye take*? Why stand *ye* idle all the day?" Or, more disparagingly, "What will *you* do ... when surrounded by big spiders, lizards, snakes, centipedes, scorpions and all manner of creeping and biting things?"[4] It is also interesting to note that neither the leading proponents of emigration nor their supporters in the press strongly advocated *mass emigration*, preferring instead a more *selective* approach to any outward movement of free blacks. As a result, propagandistic efforts along these lines failed to elicit any meaningful response.[5]

Consideration must also be given to free blacks' perception of their press as knowledgeable and objective on the issue of emigration. Journals such as *Freedom's Journal, The Colored American, Voice of the Fugitive,* and others not only became sources of information, but critical factors in themselves. Their visibility and range of influence, regardless of a low subscription rate, was significant enough to affect secondary avenues of information diffusion within the free black communities. Similarly, their presence evoked a response from white abolitionists who previously found few, if any, avenues open for public expression with free blacks, notwithstanding the existence of William Garrison's abolitionist paper, *The Liberator*. Furthermore, a major characteristic of the black press was its parochial nature, which often based its policies on an "assumed power base" which, in reality, was narrow in political scope and shallow in financial support.

Realization that the use and processing of information are extremely important in making causal inferences on social attitudes is now noted. It is further suggested that, if free blacks' attitudes on emigration were based on a particular situational perception—that is, their class position, any change in their situation might signal a corresponding change in their perceptions. Secondly, any manipulation or slanting of information will, in turn, affect their view of society and themselves. As a result, free blacks' social attitudes were contingent upon the saliency of information received. A reprinting of a "Letter to the Editor" in *The Pennsylvania Inquirer* by *Frederick Douglass' Paper* provides a succinct example of the extent to which selectivity and class-oriented appeals were aimed at the potential emigrant:

> The truth is, we want FEW AND CHOICE emigrants for the present, to go to Liberia; Those who go should be persons of practical education, industry, intelligence, and possess a little money, at least. Ignorant, worthless colored persons from the Free states are not wanted in Liberia, and even the great mass of the slave population to-day, had far better remain in slavery, than to be emancipated on condition of their being sent to Liberia. A few strong and good persons are wanted, and should only be sent, for the purpose of making an introduction of our civil and Christian institutions more in the interior of Western Africa.[6]

It now appears that the transmitting of national or local events to a readership first had to surmount the gatekeeping processes of editors, whose perceptions of social reality were premised upon what they judged was valid or needed information. Correspondingly, an understanding that information does relate to the transmitter's attitude and that any manipulation on the part of the transmitter can evoke a change in the receivers' interpretation of the message is important. An example of this can be found in Samuel Cornish's efforts to eliminate, slant or censor any positive references to emigration in *The Colored American*. While this decision on his part negated alternative points of view, it also suggests that he considered some of this information too dangerous to print. Yet Harold Kelly argues that individuals (i.e., a potential readership) are undoubtedly affected by information intended as well as that which is not intended. To assume that individuals, such as those who read *The Colored American* on emigration, would only be affected by stated opinions and not those ignored neglects to take into account the influence of face-to-face communication, some of which transcends class as well as racial barriers. Thus, the attempt to enhance selective perception on emigration in the antebellum press was not a total success, as the populace's ability to make causal inferences was not limited to the black press.[7]

Attempts to exclude the free black populace from publicly expressing an independent opinion on issues pertaining to its acquisition of full citizenship, the franchise, colonization, slavery and their general state of social ostracism came to an abrupt halt on March 16, 1827, with the publication of the first free black journal, *Freedom's Journal*. Until this moment, despite the efforts of the African Church and numerous long-titled, abolitionist societies such as the Pennsylvania Society for Promoting the Abolition of Slavery—The Relief of Free Negroes Unlawfully Held in Bondage—And for Improving the Conditions of the African Race; and The American Convention for Prompting the End of Slavery—Improving the Condition of the African Race, advocated, rejected or accepted thoughts promoted within the confines of the African Church or the more socially selective literary societies.

The advent of *Freedom's Journal* becomes significant when one considers that within three years of its inception, the first of a series of national and state freeman conventions were held and attended largely by delegates who were either editors or major contributors to the few existing black newspapers. Though these conventions were composed of leading businessmen, educators and religious leaders, the disseminating of information as it related to the free black populace had the specific effect of enhancing the prestige of various "spokesmen for the race." The significance of this is critical as these individuals saw it as their duty not only to facilitate a level of communication which inculcated a sense of racial solidarity among other free blacks, but to propagate a visceral conviction that free blacks belong in America due to a cultural and intellectual attachment with the ideals of the United States.[8] Consequently, these conventions and the black newspapers' response to them were a major factor in the development of strategies aimed at forming a consensus of thought, regardless of existing notions that blacks were a largely uneducated, undisciplined, loosely aggregated populace.[9]

While the black newspapers of antebellum America provided a major tool for obtaining information, issues such as fugitive bounty hunters, free African schools, commercial interests and the latest in social etiquette were topics which were targeted towards the upwardly mobile, educated, city-oriented free black. Thus, the opening of this "channel of communication for the interchange of thought ... through which light and knowledge may flow to instruct," was viewed as a major focus to "enliven and fertilize all."[10] Cornish succinctly explains that:

> Because our afflicted population in the Free States are scattered in handfulls over nearly 5000 towns, and can only be reached by the press— A public Journal must therefore be sent down at least weekly, to rouse them up. To call all their energies into action—and where they have been down-trodden, paralyzed and worn out to create new energies for them, that such dry bones may live.[11]

Notwithstanding some concerns of editors toward the living conditions of lower class free blacks and their perpetual threat of being kidnapped, attention was directed in African American newspapers through the antebellum period to the issues of colonization, assimilation and emigration. How these issues were presented to their readership was as reflective of the editors' values as it was of the socio-political situations which they attempted to analyze in the press.

Most free blacks in the 1830s were not open to the possibility of eventual emigration or colonization. In fact, many viewed assimilation as the primary duty for a "Christianized" American. However, for others there was recognition and acceptance of the proposition to voluntarily separate and seek political sovereignty *outside* the United States. This, they argued, was the only viable path for full equality, if it could be accomplished *without* support from the colonizing desires of the American Colonization Society. Rationales behind these positions were indicative of the intensifying clash of interest between free blacks' professing indifference to any notion of American nationalism, and others who saw their presence in America as a providential blessing, if not a mission. Regardless of the position adopted—assimilation, resettlement in western territories, colonization or emigration—nearly every strategy had as its central supposition an eventual socio-economic parity with the United States. Consequently, ideological paradigms constructed by advocates for assimilation emphasized a political analysis that implied that economic parity equalled social and political equality, regardless of one's previous racial or social status in society. From this it was argued that the elevating of one's social condition determined one's status in society.

The attempted enactment of this belief and the resulting intransigency of white America crystallized free blacks' strategies into philosophies which suggested survival and the development of moral suasionist tactics. Militants such as Henry H. Garnet, in an appeal for slave revolt, made it clear that he thought racism would be eliminated once blacks demonstrated a capacity for economic elevation: "We speak of prejudice against color, but in fact nothing of the kind exists ... the prejudice is against condition alone, and were not this the case, the American feeling would pervade the whole earth."[12]

Garnet was not alone in this view, as arguments positing a more accommodative morality suggested that the improvement of one's social condition was the primary motivation of life. Assimilationist editor of the *Right of All*, Samuel Cornish, explained:

> To talk about prejudice against color is nonsense; but raise up sons learned and enterprising with offsets of 20 or 30 thousand dollars—but rear daughters intelligent and polished heiresses to their tens and hundreds of thousands, and the fair sons and daughters of Columbia will forget the law of lights and shades—It will be expunged from our system of philosophy. And as should be, merit from the estimate of character and respectability....[13]

Martin Delany, emigrationist and editor of *The Mystery*, in an incendiary attack on the status of free blacks also viewed social condition as a critical factor:

> What is necessary to be done, in order to attain an equality, is to change the condition, and the person is at once changed. If, as before stated, a knowledge of all the various business enterprises, trades, professions, and sciences, is necessary for the elevation of the White, a knowledge of them also is necessary for the elevation of the colored man: and he cannot be elevated without them.[14]

On this point, both emigrationists and assimilationists found common ground, agreeing with the basic economic assumptions of America and at the same time professing moral indignation with American racism.

Excluding the few free blacks who participated in the slave trade or who held slaves, free blacks who professed an abhorrence of slavery did not necessarily reject the concepts of class interest. Nor was there any major desire on their part to depart from the implied, if not explicit, assumptions of Western, Christian superiority and the economic assumptions at its roots. By the 19th century, no one, black or white, seriously questioned the conviction that God had uniquely entrusted America with the mission of spreading Christianity and democracy. Black leaders instead found themselves enmeshed in the more philosophical question of why God had permitted slavery to be inflicted upon Africans by the allegedly "chosen people," the white Americans.[15] This question led some Christian emigrationists—missionaries—to conclude that although God had not destined Africans for slavery, he had destined them "to be given up to the English language and hence to the influence of Anglo-Saxon life and civilization."[16]

Here lies the contradictory nature of the antebellum free blacks who, while sanctioning the economic goals of the United States, found themselves subject to social practices which defined their level of participation in America. The varying expectations of American culture that defined the accomplished and successful citizen completely eluded their grasp as it became evident that for blacks, to be dominated *was* the norm. There could be no such thing as an accomplished free black. Thus, the arbitrariness of his status, neither slave nor free, eliminated him from any significant power base. Regardless of the resulting accommodative strategies which emerged from this situation, stringent attempts by free blacks to identify with American values became increasingly objectionable to fearful whites. These attempts at integration and their subsequent denial precipitated and nourished in-group social links among blacks regardless of their geographical dispersion. The resulting rise and proliferation of formal associations, business and labor associations, and education and charitable associations further underline the political effects of societal rejection upon the oppressed segment of America. While leading black businessmen such as Sailmaker, James Forten and William Whipper (lawyer and editor of *The Northern Star*), along with the separatist religious leaders of the African Methodist Episcopal Church (Bishop Richard Allen and Daniel Payne), differed on the desirability of institutional separation, their strategies of survival and growth in the American society were along the lines of capitalist development. This was indicative of their increased economic and social identification with America as well as an antagonism towards any concept which threatened the class values from which this commitment came.

This is evidenced by the 1835 convention of free blacks in Philadelphia, where delegates under the leadership of William Whipper and participants from six states issued a declaration of sentiment aimed at clarification of the convention's anti-emigrationist stand. Proclaiming a determined desire to "struggle not for blood, but for right," they declared:

> It is our fortune to live in an era, where the moral power of this nation is waking up to the evils of slavery, and the cause of our oppressed brethren throughout this country. We see two rival institutions (the American Colonization Society and the American Anti-Slavery Society) invoking the benevolence of nations to aid in changing our condition. The former proposes an indirect action on the sin of slavery by denouncing its guilt, while it pleads for the elevation of the Free Colored man in the land of his nativity. The former we reject.[17]

Notwithstanding the fact that no blacks, slave or free, enjoyed the status of citizen, this emerging class of businessmen and educated professionals clearly saw a functional relationship between a stable community and the development of its market potential. This point was emphasized by Frederick Douglass in his journal, *The North Star*, when he appealed to free blacks that it was their duty to combat and destroy any concept which suggested that they were a blight upon American civilization. Reasoning that a common bond existed between all blacks, Douglass suggested that to "help free their brethren, rather than leave them in chains, to go and civilize Africa" was not self-defeating. He appealed, however, for his brethren to "stay where you are, so long as you can stay. Stay here and worthily discharge the duties of honest men, and of good citizens."[18]

Subsequent evolution of accommodationist analysis further reinforced this process, as class interest favoring the protection and development of entrepreneurs within the black community secured firm support and encouragement from a press sorely in need of consistent financial incentive. As a result, imitative gestures within the hierarchical structure of this class were propagated in its press, which proclaimed responsibility and social etiquette for self-improvement. With demands for entry and parity within a political system whose very existence was predicated upon the assumption that racism and social inequality were justified by law and God, any attempt at upward mobility was severely conditioned by explicit class-race considerations which limited economic, political or social development.

As a result, spokesmen and community leaders found it prudent to continually make demands upon their constituents to develop a sense of public responsibility, frugality, racial pride and self-help.[19] In accordance with these efforts, leaders—church hierarchy, store owners, printers, carpenters, blacksmiths, wheelwrights, barbers, grocers, dentists, tailors, newspaper editors—ventured to take advantage of and exploit the market potential within their community. This attempt at creating a functional bond between business leaders and their community was premised squarely upon historical circumstances which defined their lives. Once this bonding was established through the successful linguistic socialization and transference of roles from white America, an accompanying mixture of market-community relationships was to develop. Efforts to propagate and legitimize most of the dominant cultural values of America were then eagerly pursued by free black journals. Justifications for economic survival were extracted from an ideological framework that enslaved millions of Africans yet provided an arena for their "quasi-free" representatives to articulate grievances and develop an infrastructure which would support a level of economic growth. In this regard, Frederick Douglass supported the need for this type of bonding when he stated:

> For in the proportion which we shall rise in the scale of human improvement, in that proportion do we augment the probabilities of a speedy emancipation of our enslaved fellow-countrymen. It is more than a mere figure of speech to say, that we are as a people chained together. We are one people—one in general complexion, and one in a common degradation, one in popular estimation.[20]

Loyalty to an American credo adhering to the notion that everyone receives what they deserve did not, however, insure eventual assimilation or economic parity for free blacks.

Evidence does suggest that ideological development rooted in material and social exigencies did provide the leading economic and religious elements of this class with a social philosophy geared towards social survival rather than political dominance. The structuring of free black communities into what the leadership perceived were progressive self-help programs was, in fact, instrumental in the growth of both assimilationist and accommodationist philosophies. In turn, the advocacy of these dual policies in the black press was as much determined by the editors' social experiences and class interest, as was the reluctance of white America to entrust blacks in critical sectors of the political and economic structure. Thus, many blacks argued that the development of self-improvement agencies and businesses could only help strengthen the race in the face of increasing social antagonism. Subsequent development, they concluded, must first flow from this realization.

However, emigrationists argued that herein was an important perceptual difference as free blacks were confronted with alternatives of possible political sovereignty outside America or questionable economic dependence inside its borders. Within this context, the black press became a battleground for free blacks' allegiance.

Nearly every action taken by free blacks during the 1830s and 1840s, whether separatist or assimilationist, was directed toward the goal of national assimilation.[21] In a paradoxical manner, attempts at separatism and quasi-nationalism were indispensible to assimilationist assertions of American nationality, as they provided the creative thrust for free blacks' demands for full recognition as a distinct political entity within the American sphere of influence. It is only with the question of separation outside the United States—emigration to Haiti, Central America or West Africa—that arguments were formulated on the premise that political sovereignty and geographical separation of the races were necessary. Even then, however, Christian missionary emigrationists such as Alexander Crummel felt it necessary to propagate the thesis that the English-speaking culture was a perfectly adequate synonym for civilization. Moreover, he asserted that among the other providential events, an adequate compensation for African enslavement was the possession of the Anglo-Saxon tongue.[22] Bishop Allen, who by 1827 was severely critical of any form of colonization by blacks, also attacked the idea that blacks would make effective colonizers or emigrants, in that they were:

> ... an unlettered people, brought up in ignorance, not one in a hundred can read or write; not one in a thousand has a liberal education. Is there any fitness for such to be sent into a far country, among heathens, to convert or civilize them, when they themselves are neither *civilized* nor *Christianized?* See the great bulk of the poor ignorant Africans in this country; exposed to every temptation before them: all for the want of their morals being refined by education, and proper attendance paid unto them by their owners, or those who had charge of them.[23]

Emigration and Colonization as Defined in the Black Press

Regardless of the attitudes professed in newspapers, blacks' acceptance of middle-class American standards was activated by every major institution within and outside of their community. Black newspapers of the antebellum period were, by and large, a prime example of this. Attempting to neutralize racism while espousing self-determination, the black press acted as a conduit for white middle-class cultural values in the black community, rather than a screen intended to preserve intrinsic African characteristics.

Moral suasion and self-improvements, by-products of the accommodationist philosophy, were, therefore, vigorously pursued by the black press. However, with the introduction of separatist or emigrationist arguments, tensions of enormous importance escalated these issues from lengthy philosophical treatises into proposals for immediate application.

For *Freedom's Journal*, the controversy was strong enough to cause the demise of the partnership between the paper's co-editors, Samuel Cornish and John Russwurm, after six months. Resigning his position as senior editor, Cornish worked as general agent for the paper until Russwurm discontinued its publication on the 28th of March, 1829. Their disagreement, centering around conflicting viewpoints concerning political alternatives available to free blacks, was clear evidence of the volatile, highly controversial nature of the issues of assimilation, colonization and emigration.

While *Freedom's Journal* generally maintained a neutral stance on the policy of the American Colonization Society, which advocated the removal of free blacks to Liberia, continual publication of articles on this subject made it difficult for the paper to maintain an appearance of editoral neutrality. For example, Russwurm's sensitivity towards perceptions of Africa was forthrightly expressed in the paper's first issue, when he asserted that "useful knowledge of every kind and everything that relates to Africa, shall find a ready admission into our columns: and as that vast continent becomes daily more known, we trust that many things will come to light, proving that the natives of it are neither ignorant nor as stupid as they [have] been generally supposed to be."[24]

While Cornish maintained a pronounced dislike for any position advocating colonization or emigration, his co-editor, Russwurm, Jamaican-born and the second free black to graduate from a college in America, became increasingly interested in the possible benefits available outside America. Upon termination of *Freedom's Journal*, he departed for Liberia, whereupon he became editor of the *Liberian Herald*, superintendent of public schools, and later, governor of the Maryland Colony at Cape Palmas, Liberia, until his death in 1851.

The disparity in their opinions underscored many of the ideological conflicts surrounding the African-American's social condition. In this regard, it was thought that the articulation of these views on a "national" level would enhance the possibilities of collective rather than individual response to opinions and proposed solutions. Though this basic concept of information dissemination was theoretically reasonable, the idealistic nature of this attitude belied the fact that the free blacks' "community" was not socially uniform in character but had differences which periodically divided rather than increased the notion of community.

The existence of social stratifications within the free black community further suggested the presence of power groups, one of which was the small but influential group of black journalists. It was hoped that the dissemination of information through the black newspapers would not simply consolidate lines of communication between dispersed communities, but inculcate and strengthen belief in social elevation under the leadership of an elite entrepreneurial class. It was further believed that with the elevating of the illiterate, noneducated segment of this populace, an identification with the values and norms of American society would occur. This transferring of one's class interest was in fact an attempt to mobilize blacks into an effective consensus. Therefore, the black newspaper, largely in the hands of anti-emigrationist editors, became a major factor in assimilationist opinion formation as it mediated between the demands of an elite, urbanized class and the wants of the growingly recalcitrant black populace.

Presuming themselves endowed with "enlightenment" and "virtue," elite spokesmen for the race also saw as their duty the unification of the black community *in* America. While the struggle for political development leaned away from, rather than towards political sovereignty, a concerted effort was made towards institutional independence within the framework of America. Regardless of its alternatives, inclusion or exclusion, the black press existed as a prime tool for socializing free blacks along lines of Christian morality and capitalist politics. As one analysis in *Freedom's Journal* explained to its readers:

> For a community to become eminently virtuous, it is highly essential that there should be a general dissemination of knowledge, and for the

attainment of this, the press is a powerful auxiliary in the hands of enlightened and virtuous men.[25]

Any understanding of the exclusionary issue of emigration requires first separating and then clarifying its political and social implications and their relationship to the equally controversial concept of colonization. Efforts towards this analysis by *Freedom's Journal* and other journals encompassed a range of positions which more often than not demonstrated similar rather than dissimilar goals. Though some fundamental differences existed about the practicality of assimilation as opposed to emigration or colonization, it was the defining of the exclusionary option and its implications which provoked vigorous attacks by free blacks who espoused a strong attachment to the ideals of "Americanism." Thus what some editors labelled racial-cultural purification was in fact the negation of Africanism.[26]

From 1827 to 1861, the black press functioned as a social thermometer, as radicalization of free blacks over the concerns of the franchise, slavery and emigration were debated throughout its pages. Viewpoints about a need to be the definers rather than the defined proliferated, indicating a growing sense of social consciousness. Though these efforts often resulted in the publishing of contradictory opinions within a single editorial page, by the mid-1940s four basic alternatives had emerged: Individual growth, universal freemen's betterment, resettlement, and physical separation via colonization or emigration. While these four major positions were considered to be definitive by their advocates, their rhetorical developments often make it possible to place individuals in more than one category while not seriously invalidating their basic belief in moral elevation and self-improvement for free blacks (see tables 7 and 7A, pp. 218–221).

A closer look at these positions is helpful:

Individual growth, meaning elevation within the context of the American political system. Moral suasion was used as a rhetorical appeal.

> *My Brethren in the Free States*: The position we hold in the community is a prominent one—all eyes are upon us. Many philanthropic minds are waiting the results of the measures of our improvement before they enlist in the holy cause of the slave. And many tyrants are waiting and praying for our deeper degradation as an opiate for their consciences and an extenuation for their guilt.
>
> How then ought we to occupy this important and responsible position? "What manner of people ought we to be?" Feelings of this kind should abide in every breast; for vain will be all our theories about respectability and elevation, unless it becomes a practical subject with us ... each one

for himself, must commence the improvement of his condition. It is not in mass, but in individual effort and character, that we are to move onward to a higher elevation. I cannot do the essentials for my neighbor, nor he for me—but each can do them for himself....

We verily believe that God's set time has come for restoring Africa and her descendents to their former elevation in the scale of being. And making her a great and holy nation. And should any of our brethren be found in the way, or be as dead branches, God will remove them, and their place will be filled with fit materials.[27]

Universal betterment, the development of political and cultural influences through the establishment of separate social institutions within the United States.

Nothing is more apparent at the present time, than the want of union and concert of action among us—We are scattered over a vast surface of country, and settled in small communities at a great distance from each other, and feeling but little interest in each other's welfare. While at the same time, that prejudice which is the offspring of slavery, and is equally our enemy in all places, unites its votaries to cut us off from all privileges in the society by which we are surrounded, whether civil, social or religious. It separates us into a distinct class; not for the purposes of elevating and doing us good, but for the purpose of degrading and doing us evil....

We should form an institution that will bring the most distant and detached portions of our people together, embrace their varied interests and unite their whole moral power. Our collected wisdom should be assembled, to consult on measures pertaining to the general welfare; and so direct our energies, as to do the greatest amount of good to the greatest number. Thus UNITED, and thus directed, every weapon that prejudice has formed against us, would be rendered powerless; and our moral elevation would be as rapid, as it would be certain.

Without a national institution of some description our affairs can never attain any degree of consistence of permanence. There can be no HEAD or CENTRE around which we may rally. Our numbers, means and capacity, will remain useless, for want of something to combine and concentrate them. The high intellectual powers must diminish, if not become entirely extinct, for want of the means of their development. The noble and praiseworthy efforts of the FEW, must continue to be partial and imperfect, and unsuccessful, for want of the support and co-operation of the MANY. I have already expressed myself in favor of a convention....[28]

Resettlement, or Quasi-emigration. Development of separate communities within the states and territories not having slaves. Some considered movement to Canada not emigration, but resettlement:

In relation to the scheme of ... systematic colonization in Canada West, there are some fundamental objectives that we should all have in view, besides the chief idea of the renovation of our race, set forth in my previous communication: and which should be most deeply impressed upon the minds of those that shall take a leading part amongst us as public men.

1. We should be moved with a deep sense of gratitude towards her majesty's government for the untiring exertion it has made in various ways on behalf of the African race. Such as the magnanimous West Indian Emancipation Act, by which 800,000 human beings were disenthralled; —the vast expenses annually incurred for the suppression of the slave trade, by negotiating treaties to that effect with all the maritime powers of the earth, and supporting a large squadron on the coast of Africa,— The discouragement it gave to slave labor, by sustaining the differential duties up to 1846 in favor of free labor;—and finally, the secure asylums it offers to the fugitive slave in all parts of the imperial dominion, on which the sun never sets.

2. The second object we should have in view, ought to be the determination to add our might to sustain the impregnable barrier that Great Britain must ever oppose to the rapacious territorial aggrandizement of the United States, so far as her own dominions are concerned on the American continent.

3. The third object we should have in view ought to be to develop ourselves morally, intellectually, and industriously on the American continent, in the north temperate zone, and side by side, with the Anglo-American.... This is one of the great essentials that must demonstrate the unity of the human race, and prove the superiority of man over the brute creation —and when we, who were exclusively surrounded by the progressive influence of the Anglo-American, shall demonstrate this point in ourselves, by an equal development in all these respects, we may logically conclude that the white race transplanted to Africa would not only become physically adapted to the soil and climate, but being continually and exclusively surrounded by the deteriorating circumstances that exist there, they who in the course of generations degenerate to the same standards as that exhibited by the native Africa....

These are the noble inspiration which the subject opens before us, and with which it invites us on to a glorious destiny. Nothing grander was ever presented in a political sense, to engage the human mind, heart and hands. Will we avail ourselves of this opportunity with a noble enthusiasm? Or will we stand mute and motionless, until the ceaseless march of time shall overwhelm us in our inertness, and bury our memory in an infamous oblivion? On the solution of these questions hangs our destiny. May God inspire us in the right direction.[29]

Others considered the possibility of resettlement within the United States:

That our colored population are, and ever have been deficient in enterprise and policy, none can deny. It may be pled in extenuation of this defection, that it grows out of the peculiarity of their circumstances—yet the fact is the same, and the importance of their rousing up and making changes and improvement in equally treat.

Had the Free Colored people of our country, instead of flocking to the cities and larger towns, turned their attention to farming fifty years ago, a vast proportion of the farms of the middle states, at least, would have ere this, been owned and occupied by them. They would have been among our most efficient producers—the principle suppliers of our large markets and the furnishers of provisions for our alms houses, hospitals, hotels, etc. etc.

This would have given us long ago, an importance and prominency in society, which all the menial services of an hundred generations will fail to procure, however important those services may be. And it is to us a matter of surprise, that blindness prevails over our breathren still. A menial obscurity, darker than midnight, seems to hold a majority of them spell-bound, and to keep them back from everything beneficial, WISE and POLITE.

Why have we not two thousand colored voters in this city? Is it because we have not so many colored people worth 250 dollars? No, we have more than thousand, we think, worth that sum. It is because we are BLIND IN POLICY, AND DEAD IN ENTERPRISE. When we get money, we are like the animals in the woods, instead of planting it, we hoard it in a "hallow," or sew it up in a bag....

Our poverty and degradation is one half, and may we not say that the other half, too, is our own fault. Had we taken our rusty dollars, which we have been compelled to eat up in these late hard times, twenty years ago and purchased lots when we might have got them for, from two and sixpence, to 90 shillings a foot, half of us might ere this, have been rich— in possession of wealth as well as political rights. And brethren, this would have done more ... to elevate our character and standing in the eyes of this guilty nation, than all the virtue of the bible. For it has been too justly said of our countrymen, that "money" is their God.

The same folly and imbecility govern our middle, northern and eastern colored communities still. While thousands of our White fellow citizens are selling out their all, in populous cities, and dense states and counties, where competition has broken down enterprise and begged the inhabitants, that they may go west, get government lands at low prices and become rich, we are selling our country patrimonies, our goods and chattels, that we may crowd into the cities and towns, pursue the lowest occupations, and live in the meanest places. My heart sickens at the thought.

Why do we not, thousands of us, go west and become farmers, avail ourselves of the low price of lands? Why do we not scatter out through the various settlements and fertile regions of our cultivated country, where provisions are cheap, and occupations abundant? Brethren, our lack of policy and enterprise is blasting our character and entailing poverty, degradation, and misery upon our posterity.[30]

Colonization and Emigration. While colonization generally referred to Liberia, West Africa, emigration referred to Haiti, Central America and Africa. The following was written by Henry Highland Garnett in *The North Star*:

You demand of me an explanation of the "change" which has taken place in my mind in reference to the American Colonization scheme ... but first allow me to say, by way of preface, that my opinions of the Hon. Henry Clay, and other colonizationists of the same stamp, has undergone no change. I have no reason to believe that he is now different from what he has been during his whole life—that is, a hardened sinner—a cruel and murderous persecutor of my people, and of late, a baptized and confirmed hypocrite....

I have experienced no change of mind as to the possibility of our enfranchisement in this the land of our birth, all this can be done by patient labor, frugality, education and pure religion. But on the following points my mind has changed. New devleopments have been made in relation to the descendants of once glorious but now fallen Africa, and these have changed my mind....

1. I believe that the Republic of Liberia will be highly beneficial to Africa in a commercial and political point.

2. I believe that the new republic will succeed—and that its success will curtail the slave trade on the coast, by diffusion of light and knowledge, and by turning the attention of the Black traders to some other and honorable business, and by sweeping off the Whites once as with the hands of an avenging God.

3. I believe that every political and commercial relation which President Roberts (Liberian president) negotiates with European powers goes far to create respect for face throughout the civilized world. The walls of that infant republic may now indeed be insignificant, so much so, that you may leap over them as the founders of Rome did over the first bulwarks of that city, yet it is my firm and sober belief, that Liberia will become the empire state of Africa.

I am in favor of colonization in any part of the United States, Mexico or California, or in the West Indies, or Africa, wherever it promises Freedom and enfranchisement. Other people became great and powerful by colonization. Our cousins, the children of Shem and Japhet, spread over the world voluntary emigration; but we want till we are "forced from home and all its pleasure," and then refused to remove from our prison-house.... In a word, we ought to go anywhere, where we can better our condition.[31]

In a letter to *The Colored American*, J. Holcomb expressed his concern and dismay over what he perceived was confusion in the interpretation and differences between emigration and colonization, in that:

The time is not far distant when many who now support the colonization scheme will see the vast difference between that and ours, established on an entirely different foundation. The one sending out "the most vicious and degraded" and illiterate class, to enforce their religion at the cannon's mouth, and establish a government under the control of White-men, in the midst of Africa;—the other, going prepared to instruct the natives on the great principle of the gospel, and to enforce them by the great powers of persuasion, without establishing a separate government.[32]

Though Holcomb did not foresee the development of the Maryland Colony into the Republic of Liberia, his comments reflected the frustrations and indignation felt by many free blacks as they attempted to resist further manipulation of their lives. The gravity of this dilemma intensified as blacks struggled with the conflict between becoming settlers, motivated by the desire for self-fulfillment abroad, or becoming indebted colonials, forced out of a society in which they were socially despised and legally exploited.

Paralleling others, Holcomb's appeal for African emigration was encased in religious phrases which masked deeper political considerations. The religiously motivated emigrant was in fact a political missionary, one whose presence "would soon exert a renovating influence that would tell on the whole land," and whose "sciences and arts would return to her dark abode, which would tell on the whole land of Africa."[33] Annoyed at this interpretation of colonization, Cornish, himself a minister as well as editor of *The Colored American*, appealed:

> Brethren, but be true to your text, and colonization may go to the winds, Only treat colored men as you would have them treat you, were your circumstances changed with theirs, and righteousness and the *Bible* for it, you will have no need of a colonization society.[34]

While Cornish proclaimed an "unceasing, uncompromising war against colonization as is understood among us," he also suggested that "we are not so hostile to *voluntary* emigration," in that:

> Communities, like gardens, occasionally require culling: They become too luxuriant, and overgrown and then judicious selections should be made, taking the most vigorous and healthy plants, those whose culture and growth will bear removal, and transplant them in a soil, which although at first foreign to their nature, will eventually prove as congenial as their native soil.[35]

However, the foreign soil Cornish had in mind was the more rural farm areas of Indiana, Ohio, Iowa and West Canada—an internal migration and exodus from the crowded urban areas of the East.[36] Other free blacks, such as Lewis Woodson, viewed internal continental migration as the basis for separate black settlements in or outside the existing borders of early nineteenth-century America:

> Too many of my brethren, are just beginning to live happily in the West Indies, and in Canada, for me to think of dying just now. I had

rather be a LIVING FREEMAN, even in one of these places, than a "Dead Nigger" in the United States.[37]

Cornish chided his colleague's viewpoint, replying: "Alas! Alas! Has the expatriating spirit got hold of good brother? If it has, would to heaven he had gone to his rest, before his seduction and the promulgation of views so monstrous."[38]

Another concern of Cornish's was his insistence for "great care" when selecting volunteering emigrants, a concern which masked the pronounced class interest of his paper, *The Colored American*. Asserting that urban free blacks need not emigrate to the West Indies, for the "West Indian Islands want LABORERS, with capacity and willingness to work in the field with the hoe," he was in fact implying that the emigrants sent were not of this type. In a similar fashion, he proclaimed an objection to any emigration to the West Indies due to the "unhealthiness of the climate, and the customs of the people which are different from our own."[39]

While Cornish's dislike for emigration was based primarily on social conditions which he questioned as being advantageous for "American Blacks," he reserved a special abhorrence for any movement towards Africa as "an obstinate wickedness in men suffering from a terrible strong delusion." Cornish even assailed the incentive for land in Africa.

> They [free blacks] need not go to Africa for SOIL. The land they own here is their soil, and the country they are born in is their NATIVE COUNTRY.... No American, United States born man can have TWO NATIVE LANDS, or can have one without the limits of America. He can no more be born here and have him a NATIVE LAND in Africa, than an African, born on the Gold Coast, can make him out a native land here in New England.... This is a cardinal point, and it ought to be settled and made clear to the minds of our colonizationist brethren.[40]

The assertiveness of Cornish's remarks was buttressed by the fact that he was editor of the only consistently published black-owned newspaper at this time. Preachers, businessmen, civic leaders and educators no longer kept their views to a select few, but shared their thoughts with an audience which could now be reached relatively quickly. Through *The Colored American*, it was hoped, the thoughts of a few would become the possession of the many. Not only was righteous indignation towards a hostile society available to the reader, but also the awareness that only limited sources of information were available to free blacks. As a result, the use of subjective, highly opinionated consensus appeals by editors on race, class identity, economics and political responsibility became the rhetorical exigencies of a people striving for social entry. The ability of the press to create a feeling of consensus, whether valid or not, was not only feasible but actual. In this regard, assimilationist journals such as *The Colored American* had a point of view which stressed the free blacks' right to the label of "American" and a natural claim to citizenship. Yet, even the title of Cornish's journal provided stimulus for controversy:

> Many would gladly rob us of the endeared name "Americans," a distinction more emphatically belonging to us, than five-sixths of this nation, and one that we will never yield. In complexion, in blood and in nativity, we are decidedly more exclusively "American" than our White brethren.[41]

Armed with this belief, the role of martyrdom seemed not too improbable for Cornish by mid-1838, when he exhorted:

> The secret views of the colonizationist always have been, to make a furious onset with ripened purposes and ripened means, and to DRIVE us out of the country. We exhort every Colored American to die by his birthright, and his "inalienated rights." If we must be removed, let it be as martyrs—go directly from America to heaven.[42]

Comprehending the various definitions applied to emigration and colonization in the black press requires recognition of often overlapping and contradictory positions on these issues. For example, many free blacks severely criticized the forceful colonization to Liberia, while sanctioning the development of "Christian missions" in "heathen Africa." Similarly, support for emigration in the western hemisphere, for example, Nicaragua or Haiti, did not necessarily imply sanctioning emigration to Africa. Still others, rejecting emigration and colonization as a "regressive, outward" policy, supported the migrating of settlers to western territories, labelling these settlers emigrationists.[43] What *was* consistently demonstrated in blacks' newspapers were the numerous rhetorical appeals developed by contributors and editors alike, as they attempted to dilute and redirect, if not nullify, the various social/racial exigencies facing them on a day-to-day basis.

The possibility of forceful colonization and the discourses which emerged around this issue influenced many editors such as Martin Delany, Samuel Cornish, James Holly and Frederick Douglass to develop a *responsive* rhetorical style. In this regard, the dissemination of views on this issue by the press functioned as a social barometer for an audience which it was hoped would become a conscious agent for change.⁴⁴

While mobilizational appeals by James Forten, Bishop Richard Allen and Samuel Cornish in the press were aimed at destroying free blacks' feeling of isolation and inferiority and limiting the influence of the American Colonization Society (ACS), the propagating of social and political tension was also an essential element in this mobilizing effort. Insisting that the struggle was a moral conflict and not simply based on the alienation of free blacks, the black press crystallized a rhetoric proclaiming that a new order, the more perfect order, must now be enacted.⁴⁵ This rhetoric of assimilation spoke not about racial amalgamation, but rather the processes which suggested blacks' social incompetence. This emerging rhetoric was in fact a testing ground for the larger arena of social intercourse, a rhetoric which would clearly underline class relationships.⁴⁶

From this perspective, rhetorical strategies became revealing exercises in appeals for motivation and mobilization of free blacks.⁴⁷ For example, the use of rhetorical questions to examine and define were employed by "The Colored Baltimorean" when he asked:

> Why this strong aversion to being united to us, even by soil or climate? Why this desire to be so remotely alienated from us? Is it to extend to us in the hour of danger, the friendly hand of assistance? Or rather, is it not to get effectively and forever rid of that "heterogeneous" or supposed "dangerous element in the general mass of Free Blacks," who it is said, are a greater nuisance than even slaves themselves?⁴⁸

Still another writer expounded a belief in morality and justice by advocating that colonizationists would do better if their mobilization efforts were structured to minimize rather than flee the conditions of America:

> Colonizing the Free people of color in Africa is never going to facilitate emancipation, but rather retard its progress. Let the friends of color endeavor to make an intelligent and respectable community of colour in this country, if they wish to facilitate emancipation; This will appeal to the hearts of slaveholders, and do more in breaking the bands of slavery, than a thousand colonization schemes.⁴⁹

Anger and frustrations over the ACS's presumptuous attitude about what was beneficial for free blacks resulted in the publishing of long and detailed articles expressing a variety of emotions. Abolitionist writers such as Forten took leading white politicians to task, while defining an anticolonizationist policy. A major target of Forten's remarks was Henry Clay, speaker of the House of Representatives, slaveowner and founding member of the American Colonization Society (ACS). Attacking Clay's enthusiastic desire "to force Free people to emigrate, particularly those in southern states," Forten explains:

> It should be a matter of no small concern to the Free people of color, to perceive the rapid progress of the colonization society: Its increase cannot be viewed in any other light, than a desire to get effectively rid of the Free people. Mr. Clay particularly informs us, that it is to have nothing to do with the delicate question of slavery: It is, say he, intended to be exclusively applied to the Free people. I am aware that many philanthropists have become converts to the colonization scheme; Many I doubt not, who have at all times espoused the cause of the oppressed, and imagine that it will ultimately prove beneficial to them; others think that it is the only means by which Africa can become civilized, and "Ethopia stretch forth her hands to God," but they do not penetrate the real views of the colonization society, who have carefully disguised their intentions.... The colonizing plan, as exposed by Mr. Clay, is intended indirectly to force the Free people to emigrate, particularly those in the southern states, where they are so much oppressed by prohibition and taxation. It cannot but be warmly patronized by slave-holders. Mr. Clay contradicts in the most positive manner, those advocates of the colonizing system who have so repeatedly assured us that it is the only way by which the nation can get rid of that curse to the country.... Mr. Clay's proposal is to remove annually six thousands of those persons, and thus he says keep down their alarming increase: This he avows to be the Grand object of the society.[50]

However, a persistent attitude existed among many free blacks who, while not agreeing with every aspect of colonization, felt compelled to admit that "a well-regulated colony upon the western coast of Africa will be productive of great good," as it would dramatically "exterminate the foreign slave trade, and open an asylum for those slaves that may be manumitted in this country: and above all, be instrumental of introducing the light of science and religion into a portion of that vast and benighted continent." Nonetheless, they emphatically rejected any mobilization appeal towards Africa, denouncing it as "utterly chimerical and absurd."[51]

Through most of the antebellum period, prominent free blacks such as Cornish, Frederick Douglass, David Ruggles and Phillip Bell attacked any and all forms of "outward" movement by blacks, with the possible exception of limited resettlement in the western United States territories during the 1850s. It was their effective use of existing journals and their publishing of a number of treaties on relevant issues which established parameters for social debate and discussion. One such pamphlet by Samuel Cornish and Theodore S. Wright in 1840 attacked Theodore Frelinghuyser's and Benjamin Butler's assertion that colonization was "received with great delight" by the "Colored People," and that they "yearned in their hearts for Africa."[52]

In answer, Cornish and Wright elaborated on the falsity of such an allegation while presenting their own historical analysis of the relationship between the "yearning" assertion, their supposition that the free blacks who viewed themselves as American nationals rejected any notion of inferiority or a forced role as colonizers was essentially a desire to define emigration as speculative, detestable and traitorous.[53] The determined advocacy on this issue cannot be minimized when taking into account the fact that editors not only shaped the reporting of events, but in many cases were active participants in events themselves.

An interesting example of how vitally antebellum editors viewed the contents of their paper occurred in 1839 when a group of young men from Cleveland, Ohio, calling themselves the "Young Men's Union Society," managed to get their pro-emigrationist and separatist views published in *The Colored American*. Cornish, who was absent from the paper's office when the communication was published, was furious when he realized what was printed. He deliberately garbled the content of the report in the following week, and admitted he would not have published the original had he been present. His confession stands as an example of how the reporting of events pertaining to emigration and colonization was often censored or slanted to fit the particular views of the editor, in this case, an anticolonizationist[54] (see Appendix A).

Considering the long-range effects such editorial prerogatives had on the opinions of readers, along with the fact that from 1837 to 1841 only *one* major black journal was being published, it is not surprising that emigration was viewed unfavorably. Major editors such as Cornish, William Whipper and Frederick Douglass maintained this rejectionist stance up until the mid–1850s. Even when faced with the repressive mandates of the Fugitive Slave Acts of 1850, arguments pursuing William Lloyd Garrison's philosophies of the free blacks' duty to the slave could be read in the press.

A break with this philosophy did occur as early as 1837 with Russwurm's emigration to Liberia. There was also Phillip Bell, who edited two ephemeral newspapers, and for a brief period, *The Colored American*. However, for Bell, emigration did not imply West Africa or the Caribbean region, but California, where he later edited *The Pacific Appeal* in 1857.

In this light, Africa, missionaries and separatists were often viewed with contempt as editors found it necessary to warn their readers of the "death-camps of Africa under an equatorial sun—their own morals, and those of their children, (and their exposure) to the influence and temptations of the most treacherous and sin-sunken heathen that live...."[55] Thus, the attempt to explain away any assertion of emigrationist yearning was approached by presenting readers with an historical account geared to reflect unity of thought and a semblance of free black purposefulness. As Cornish and Wright began to warm up to their task, an analysis of the role of the settler-missionary began to emerge, defining emigration from the perspective of the colonized contemplating their role as future colonizers:

> The colonization society was scarcely known to have been organized, before its object was protested against, in a public meeting of the Free colored people in Richmond, Va. Not long afterward (in August 1817), the largest meeting ever yet held of the colored people of the Free states—The number being computed at 3000—came together in Philadelphia to consider the colonization scheme. Mr. James Forten, a man distinguished not only for his wealth and successful industry, but for his sufferings in the Revolutionary War, presiding at its deliberations. After ample time allowed for duly considering every benefit which colonization held out to the colored people, there was not a single voice in that vast assembly which was not raised for its decisive and thorough condemnation.
>
> Meetings of a similar kind were held in Washington city, in Baltimore, New York, Providence, Boston—indeed, in all the cities, and in most of the large towns throughout the free states. The abhorrence which was generally expressed of the whole scheme proved, that those to whose acceptance it was offered regarded it but as little more merciful than death.[56]

Rejecting emigration as a positive role for free blacks, Cornish and Wright hinted at deeper, more substantive factors which come into play between the settler and the colonized, factors which they felt would, in time, lower the moral standards of the emigrant to that of a brutish colonizer. The authors then suggested that complexion issues are of secondary importance, in that:

> The difference of complexion is not to be numbered among the primary causes, why the aborigines of all countries have uniformly dwindled away, or disappeared, before a successful scheme of Christian colonization. These causes, lying deeper than the skin, and having no relation to it, may be embodied in this principle—The Christian form of society is one in which the aborigines have no place and act no part.[57]

Viewing the indigenous population as "heathen or pagan" and in many ways "incompatible," the authors noted that:

> This society [the colonizers] at once assumes, as is unavoidable, superiority. It becomes the upper caste. A consciousness of inferiority soon takes possession of the natives. The colony extends itself, or, at least, its jurisdiction, over a large scope of country, from which it is unnecessary, whatever it be, they see overshadowed by that of the newcomers, and daily withering away under it.[58]

Viewing the settler-colonizer as an overpowering interloper, possessing superior culture, force of will and material goods, the authors suggested that the process for "inferiorization" was only a matter of time as the "native" possessed little to retard its progress. Expounding further, they claimed that:

> The spread of the colony—a mark of prosperity—circumstances the hunting-grounds, diminishes the quantity of game, and makes the substance of the native more precarious. The colonist, intent on their own concerns individually, or as a community, have but little intercourse with their rude neighbors, except as interest or convenience may from time to time call for it. In trading, they over-reach them; — A thing as certainly to be looked for, as it is certain that they are superior to them in the knowledge of values. They lose the confidence of the natives; the latter become suspicious—and, at last, *hate*, because they are too weak to enforce retribution or inflict punishment. Thus, they resort to cunning and sinister devices. They see their own social organization crumbling to dissolution, and know that they are unqualified for any other. Old stimulants to high achievements have passed away—no new ones are supplied; and unsupported by religious principle of hope, they inevitably sink down in the abjectness of those who, having lost all respect for themselves, feel, that they have no title to the respect of others. That such a people must eventually perish everyone is prepared to believe.[59]

The strength of these views was the result of their own experience as a colonized people in the United States. Thus, while Cornish and Wright were specifically referring to colonization and emigration in Liberia and Central America, they were speaking as *educated* free blacks who not only professed a profound respect for the intelligent black who viewed education as necessary for moral uplift, but one who had a foreboding about the abilities of the "uneducated settler."[60] Consequently, their mistrusting of a personality influenced by enslavement was pronounced, in that, "it is from this class that the colonists have, for a long time, been mostly drawn." Furthermore, they posited that an erroneous assumption is made by colonizationists when assuming that ex-slaves coming from an experience of degradation, "as well as other ills of slavery," would be the last to inflict the same ills on others.[61] Suggesting that free blacks are more aware than whites about the personality created by enslavement, they explain:

> DRIVERS selected from slavegangs are proverbially cruel. Slaves, of any color, becoming free in countries where their own race are in bondage, show as much, if not more eagerness (when they possess the means) to become masters, than such as are born free.[62]

Moreover, Cornish and Wright underlined the complicity of economic agreements between colonists who "not having been taught the more recondite mysteries of slaveholding casuitry," are unable or unwilling to comprehend the concommitant relationships of "slaveholder Preston or slaveholder Calhoun, and any poor tar burner," with that of "King Peter or King Boatswain, and Palm-Oil, Ivory or Gold dust on the coast." In this respect, their definition of the free black colonist as a pawn in an economic-political conspiracy not of their own making, not only implies unworthiness of character, but gives little encouragement that "the needy, ignorant, and uneducated settlers, exposed to the malignant influences of every kind . . . will ever contribute either to putting down the slave trade, or to christianizing the aborigines."[63]

By stripping the potential colonizer of any positive virtue as a colonist, and suggesting that they would be an uniformed usurper of the "native" by affirming oppression and injustice, the writers implored Frelinghuysen and Butler to review the weakness in arguments favoring colonization as:

> Unreasonable and unchristian prejudice — which persuades legislatures to continue their unjust enactments against us in all their rigor . . . which cuts us off from employment, and straitens our means of substance which afflicts us with the feeling, that our condition is unstable, and prevents us from making systematic efforts for our improvemnt, or for the advancement of our own usefulness and happiness and that of our families.[64]

As in other articles and journals berating the ills of colonization and emigration, the protagonist rejects any acceptance of colonization, regardless of existing political, theological or economic rationales. Caught between the chaotic world of white America and the enslaved and oppressed, free blacks could not establish unity due to an inability to reject all direct or partial compliance with the values and political aspirations of white America. The rejection of colonization and emigration was often prefaced by platitudes about American nationalism, rather than any appeals to political sovereignty outside America's borders.

While the social and political mutilation of free blacks tended to retard any development of an effective national voice, indications of a stronger unity did appear once a specific opposition was "discovered," as in the collusion of slaveholders and the American Colonization Society. Even then, the response was not total. Any suggestion of outward movement was attacked as a dysfunction response to white racism rather than as a functional alternative aiding political growth. Because they did not control the legislative or economic life of their community, and realized that no guarantee of equality was forthcoming, free blacks concluded that claims by colonization societies were little more than political distractions which de-emphasized any immediate need to reshape the structure of American society. The "escapism" of emigration was a step backwards, away from a reciprocity which bound the colonized to the colonizer, the oppressed to the oppressor.[65]

Emigrationist Press: Conflict in Approaches

As Cornish defined "acceptable" emigration within the context of the United States' western territories and West Canada, Henry Bibb, editor of *Voice of the Fugitive* in West Canada, rejected both emigration to Liberia and settlements in U.S. territories. In an article titled "Colonization or Slavery," Bibb advised free blacks not to accept *any* form of political accommodation with America, but "to run away from the tryant who holds them, and settle in Canada, where all men are protected in the enjoyment of freedom by the laws of Great Britain."[66]

When it came to the issue of emigration, Bibb's *Voice of the Fugitive* was less philosophical in its approach than most black journals. Choosing to deal directly with the problems of the 25,000-34,000 blacks who had taken refuge in Canada, he claimed that, "We shall endeavor to examine the subject in a commercial, agricultural, social, mental and political point of view."[67] Defining emigration from a much broader perspective than Liberia or the West Indies, he explained:

> The world is the Colored man's home, and any attempt of human legislation to restrict his boundary, or circumscribe his field of locomotion, is a gross violation of the fundamental principles of justice, and he who tamely submits to such a state of wrong ... is fit subject only for slavery.[68]

A leading contributor to the *Voice of the Fugitive* was James Theodore Holly. Holly, who in later years was a strong advocate of the Haitian emigration movement, lived in Canada where he emerged, along with Martin Delany, as a forceful propagandist for Canadian emigration. In a series of four letters published in the *Voice of the*

Fugitive from June to July 1851, he carefully distinguished between voluntary emigration and white-controlled colonization efforts to Liberia. Writing on the importance of avoiding the nullifying "anarchy of individual isolation," which too often perpetuated a state of political anarchy, Holly suggested that Canadian blacks were in need of "an organization in which the central authority was based on a just dependence to each of the individual parts." Stating that the problems involved for such an authority were the result of the first two hundred years of "enslavement, tyrannical persecution and bloody cruelty," he foresaw the necessity for mutual cooperation in the crucial struggle for racial survival. Trusting that recent history had given blacks enough incentive to choose between "everlasting slavery, expatriation or annihilation," he asked: "It remains to be seen, if a sufficient quantity of the instinct of self preservation remains in us to adopt the necessary step towards a unitary organization."[69]

Holly, as well as Bibb, called for several things. Viewing the *Voice of the Fugitive* as a catalyst, a "centre of unity" which would "mould the destiny of the whole Afro-American race," their journal attempted to transcend local rivalries and jealousies which, they believed, marred free blacks' organizing efforts in the United States. To a degree, they were successful. On September 11, 1851, a convention was held in Toronto, Canada, on the "central authority for Canadian and American Blacks," encouraging the emigration of free blacks from the United States. A major concern of this paper was the helping of settlers to establish themselves in Canada by erecting mills for the manufacturing of exportable goods.[70]

Though the *Voice of the Fugitive* would eventually get involved in issues which affected its credibility as a reliable journal, its major influence on the lives of Canadian blacks was its orientation toward fugitive blacks. Their concern was with fleeing American blacks whose anxiety about the fugitive slave laws made them very concerned about personal safety. Addressing this point, an editorial inquired of blacks:

> We call especially on you in view of the subject what position will ye take? Why stand ye here idle all the day? There is no permanent stopping place in the United States upon which the hunted fugitive can stand — Three millions and a half of our own brethren are in chains, the slaveholders of the south with American Colonization Society are striving to prevent us from settling in Canada, on the one hand, and to induce the Free people of Color to Africa on the other — was ever there a time in this country when the state of our cause called more loudly on us for united and preserving action today![71]

A second influential paper, *The Provincial Freeman*, appeared in March 1853 in Windsor, Canada (later moved to Chatham). Published by Mary Ann Shadd, Samuel R. Ward and several other blacks at a time when the *Voice of the Fugitive* was losing influence, *The Provincial Freeman* took the editorial position that blacks fleeing to Canada should not consider themselves as transient refugees but as British subjects. Defining emigration within the context of its fugitive population, *The Provincial Freeman* maintained that if Canadian blacks were to develop any nationality, they would have to be part of the British nation. Exalting the virtues of a possible "colored nation" within Canada, its editor, Mary Shadd, claimed that the journal was of vital importance as thousands of free blacks trapped by "Yankeedom with disfranchisement and oppression" needed to be informed about "a land of impartial laws and a constitution having no distinctions of color."[72]

Considerable concern was expressed in *The Provincial Freeman* for the integrating of its growing "fugitive" class into Canadian society as a whole. Devoting a significant amount of energy in its beginning years to attacking the idea of separate black settlements and the societies which supported them, such as the Refugee Home Society and its white philanthropic sponsor, the American Missionary Association, an editorial comment explained:

> The government has lands quite as good (if not better than) that owned by the Refugee Home Society, for sale at a lower price that the Refugee Home Society will sell, and the purchaser can obtain them with equal (if not greater) facility, and hold them by a much better tenure.... Fugitives who choose to be farmers, can find abundant facilities for acquisition of land in Canada, without the aid of the society in question.[73]

The *Freeman* argued that 40,000 blacks in Canada could be a significant and influential element *within* the "body politic," if they were continually informed of the political issues which affected them as a class in the country. In this endeavor to be the mouthpiece for Canadian blacks, *The Provincial Freeman* suggested that its forerunner's (the *Voice of the Fugitive*) support for separate development ignored the intelligence of blacks living in Canada. Noting the emigrationist and nationalist tendency of several settlements, Mary Shadd charged the *Voice* with corruption and general misuse of finances in the operating of settlements. The charges were also leveled at the *Voice*'s supporting agency, the British American Institute. These attacks became more expansive when Shadd realized that the proposals of emigrationists such as Delany and Holly included areas outside of Canada, such as the Caribbean:

> What will you do ... when, surrounded by big spiders, lizards, snakes, centipedes, scorpions and all manner of creeping and biting things? Do you want to be sun-struck? Do you court yellow fever and laziness, haughty employers, and contemptible black prejudice? If you do, go in peace.[74]

Despite the cynicism of the journal toward fugitive settlements of western Canada and their white philanthropic supporters, *The Provincial Freeman* abandoned, by late 1855, its hostility toward emigration and joined the camp of nationalist emigrationists Delany and Holly. Precise reasons for the *Freeman*'s political reorientation remain unclear, though increasing attacks by abolitionists on movements of blacks out of the United States or Canada might have pushed Shadd in this supporting direction. By mid-1856, the journal was being used by Delany to attack Frederick Douglass for his "vacillating" comments on the issue of Liberian colonization. In an article titled "Canada—Liberia" Delany berated Frederick Douglass' ability to first praise Canadian emigration, then subtly make supportive references to slaveholders' colonization efforts in Liberia.[75] Rhetorical jostling of this sort committed *The Provincial Freeman* to the cause of emigration and provided supporters with a platform from which to rebuke any challenge to their leadership.

Despite *The Provincial Freeman*'s move towards an emigrationist perspective, their concern and class interest for the more prosperous and better educated emigrant was evident throughout the journal. While the *Voice of the Fugitive* was clearly oriented towards support for the "twenty-five to thirty-five thousand" blacks in Canada who were escapees from slavery, *The Provincial Freeman* advocated a more selective, if not critical, approach to blacks' emigration to Canada. The difference in approach was reflected in the middle-class orientation of *The Provincial Freeman* as it berated fugitives for their lack of influence and their tendency to become divided in adversity. Shadd explained:

> Take a retrospect of the colored people of Canada for the last thirty years. Their institutions—their divisions—their knots and "squads"— their White and Colored beggars ... The quarrels of these beggars ... The contentions about their land ... The caucuses, conventions, resolutions and after all, the return of the pretended leaders of the people, "like a dog to his vomit ... "[76]

The remedy offered by *The Provincial Freeman* was the replacement of free black leaders with men of "confidence, intelligence [and] independence," who could help them to "become British at heart in reality."[77]

A major influence in the shaping of anti-emigrationist and colonization thought during this period was Frederick Douglass' editorship of three periodicals, *The North Star, Frederick Douglass' Paper* and *Douglass' Monthly*. Though the limits of white abolitionist influence upon free blacks was severely tested by the growth of free black national and local conventions, it was the development of the black press which shaped and developed the militancy of these conventions. For example, the extent of paternalism in the relationship between white abolitionist and black leaders is evidenced by an 1848 letter sent by a free black, Dr. James McCune Smith, who found it necessary to report to Gerrit Smith, a white philanthropic landowner, about Frederick Douglass: "You will be surprised to hear me say that only since his editorial career has he seem to become a Colored man!"[78]

Even Douglass' self-admitted mentor, the outspoken white abolitionist William Lloyd Garrison, was extremely "troubled" by Douglass' decision to start a newspaper without his blessings, so much so that in complaining to his wife, Garrison said:

> He [Douglass] never opened his lips on the subject, nor asked me advice in any particular whatever! Such conduct grieves me to the heart. His conduct about the paper has been impulsive, inconsiderate, and inconsistent....[79]

Ignoring the advice of Garrison and other abolitionists, Douglass wasted no time in making it clear that *The North Star* would vigorously denounce colonization and whites who questioned Douglass' initiative. Attacking Henry Clay's attempt to revive the now struggling American Colonization Society, Douglass warned in *The North Star*:

> We see in it a revival of that second enemy of the Colored people, the colonization society which next to slavery, is the deadliest foe to the Colored man, — unsettling his plans and improvements, by teaching him to feel that this is not his house; disheartening and subduing his enterprise, by causing him to feel that all effort at self-elevation is in vain; that neither knowledge, temperance, patience, faith nor virtue, can avail him anything in hand.[80]

Fully convinced that an individual's worth cannot be measured by complexion, Douglass argued that facts in this age of scientific discovery constantly prove that "when circumstances and education favor him," a free black is as fully "capable of brave and manly deeds as his white despisers."[81] Douglass vigorously defined issues independently of Garrison's influence. Challenging racism and slavery as the twin evils of American society, articles in his journal asserted "his American rights." Insisting that a black man's "attachment to the place of his birth is stronger than iron," and having fought, toiled and bled for America so that whites could loll in ease, he had no intention of leaving; nor would he accept advice to emigrate, advice which he believed came from "his worst and most deadly enemies."[82]

For Douglass in the late 1840s colonization as a viable alternative for free blacks was an inexcusable, traitorous and "imprudent proposition of the U.S. Senate, via Henry Clay." Nevertheless, he did find it necessary once to qualify his paper's position. He gave nominal support to colonization, reasoning that it was valid for blacks to make choices based on self-interest:

> We say they may go if they are so minded, just as white men go. So we say, they may go to California or to Nova Zembla, but they ought also to be allowed, as White men ask, to consult their own interest, and stay at home, if they happen to have formed an opinion that neither Liberia, California nor the North Pole is precisely the best place suited to their tastes and constitution.[83]

Incensed by any attitude which suggested paternalism, Douglass attacked a speech by Henry Clay on the colonization issue in *The North Star*:

> It is an insult, an insult and tyrannical assumption on the part of Mr. Clay, or anyone else, to tell us, or any part of the Colored people of this country, that he wishes us to go anywhere. We are at home here; and our staying here is evidence that we wish to stay here; and to tell us that he wishes us to go is an insult, which if offered to Mr. Clay instead of the despised Blacks, would subject the perpetrator of the insult to the indignation of the community. Our right to stay here is as good as that of Mr. Clay or any manstealer in this land; and God helping us, we will maintain this right before all the world.[84]

When the 1847 National Colored Convention was held in Troy, New York, the free black community could boast of a small number of newspapers, among which *The Ram's Horn, The National Watchman, The North Star, and The Mystery* were endorsed by the convention. There was much debate about the formulation of a national press:

> If a press be not the most powerful means for our elevation, it is the most immediate necessary. Education of the intellect, of the will, and of character, is doubtless, a powerful, perhaps the most powerful means for our advancement: yet a press is needed to keep this very fact before the whole people, in order that all may constantly and unitedly labor in this, the right direction.[85]

Being skeptical about the proposal, Douglass took the position that such a development would hinder the growth of ideas, sorely needed in the black community. However, by the time of the 1848 convention in Cleveland, *The North Star* had gained such prominence among free blacks, that the convention resolved:

> That among the means instrumental in the elevation of a people there is none more effectual than a well-conducted efficient newspaper; and believing *The North Star*, published and edited by Frederick Douglass and M.R. Delany in Rochester, fully to answer all the ends of purposes of a national press, we therefore recommend its support to the Colored people through-out North America.[86]

Interestingly enough, the same delegates also resolved that:

> Among the many oppressive schemes against the Colored people in the United States, we view the American Colonization Society as the most deceptive and hypocritical—"clothed with the livery of heaven to serve the devil in," with President Roberts, of Liberia, a Colored man, for its leader.[87]

It wasn't until the publishing of the *Frederick Douglass's Paper* in 1853 that Douglass' remarkable skill as a journalist emerged. In the paper's Rochester, New York, office, Douglass had all the latest equipment needed for quality printing on a weekly basis. For example, a published letter from Douglass to Harriet Beecher Stowe in 1853 examined and articulated many of the fears, anxieties and feelings of social inadequacy felt by Douglass on the question of emigration. Lamenting blacks' inability to fulfill the responsibilities of citizenship, Douglass speculated that education and emigration would coalesce as free blacks lost faith in the American society. Asserting that "Poverty, ignorance and degradation are the combined evil . . . the social disease of the free colored people in the United States," he suggested that it would be imprudent to hope "that in a single leap from our low condition, we can reach that of MINISTERS, LAWYERS, DOCTORS, EDITORS, MERCHANTS, ETC." However, it "will doubtless be attained by us; but this will only be when we have patiently and laboriously, and I may add successfully mastered, and passed through the intermediate gradations of agriculture and the mechanical arts."[88]

Douglas was sympathetic to those free blacks who did emigrate, or aassociated with the American Colonization Society, and who were educated far beyond most free blacks. He warned of a "brain drain" effect upon the black populace, in that:

White people will not employ them to the obvious embarrassment of their causes, and the blacks, taking their CUE from the Whites, have not sufficient confidence in their abilities to employ them. Hence, educated colored men among the colored people, are at least at a very great discount. It would seem that education and emigration go together with us; for as soon as a man rises amongst us, capable by his genius and learning, to do us a great service, just as soon he finds that he can serve himself better by going elsewhere. In proof of this, I might instance the Russwurms (Liberia), — The Garnetts (Jamaica-Liberia), — The Wards (Canada), — The Crummells (Liberia), and others — all men of superior ability and attainments, and capable of removing mountains of prejudice against their race, by their simple presence in tthe country; but these gentlemen, finding themselves embarrassed here by the peculiar disadvantages to which I have referred — disadvantages in part growing out of education — being repelled by ignorance on the one hand, and prejudice on the other, and having no taste to continue in a contest against such odds, they sought more congenial climes, where they can live more peaceable and quiet lives. I reject their election — but I cannot blame them; for, with an equal amount of education, and the hard lot which was theirs, I might follow their example.[89]

For Douglass, the essential burden of proof as to one's worth in society rested on the individual. One either "elevated" himself in society or fell by the wayside. On the question of emigration this was translated into an analysis asserting that free blacks lack the attributes needed for successful emigration — farming and husbandry. Douglass alluded to this when he claimed that Gerrit Smith's gift of 120,000 acres of New York State land to free blacks was a futile gesture as:

Agricultural pursuits are not, as I think, suited to our condition. The reason of this is not to be found so much in the occupation (for it is an ennobling one) as in the people themselves.... We cannot apply it, because it is almost impossible to get colored men to go to the land. From some cause or other Colored people will congregate in the large towns and cities; and they will endure any amount of hardships and privation, rather than separate and go into the country.[90]

This viewpoint not only suggests Douglass' own anxiety about the urbanized free blacks' character, but also their having the essential prerequisites for emigration — self-reliance, determination and industry — even for a migration into western territories:

Another consideration against expending energy in this direction is our want of self-reliance. Slavery more than all things else, robs its victims of self-reliance. To go into the western wilderness, and there to lay the foundation of future society, requires more of that important quality than a life of slavery has left us. This may sound strange to you, coming as it does from a colored man; but I am dealing with facts, and these never accommodate themselves to the feelings or wishes of any.... It is a fact, then, and not less so because I wish it were otherwise, that colored people are wanting in self-reliance—too fond of society—too eager for immediate results—and too little skilled in mechanics or husbandry to attempt to overcome the wilderness; at least, until they have overcome obstacles less formidable.[91]

Concluding his remarks to Stowe, Douglass claimed that there was little hope that any significant number of blacks could be tempted to leave America, even it it was desirable. Positing that the "blackman—unlike the Indian—loves civilization," he suggested that blacks do not progress unless living in an urban environment with all its good and evil. Similarly, the idea of uneducated, illiterate blacks providing the backbone of pioneers for a separate nation or settlement, seemed extremely unlikely. Consequently, throughout his editorship of *The North Star* and *Frederick Douglass' Paper*, Douglass advanced the position that emigration and colonization could only elevate blacks' condition if a capacity for independent work as opposed to servile labor were developed—development predicated upon eliminating the legacy of slavery. However, he also felt that this was unlikely, in that, "We do not take a firm hold upon the advantages and opportunities about us."

Thus, his rejection of emigration *was* tied to a desire to enhance blacks' economic stability and political growth in the United States, in that "permanent location is a mighty element in civilization."[92] With this thought firmly implanted in his readers' minds, he appealed for racial and national unity:

Then the love of country, the dread of isolation, the lack of adventurous spirit and the thought of seeming to desert their "brethren in bonds" are a powerful check upon all schemes of colonization which look to the removal of the colored people without the slaves. The truth is, Dear Madam, we are HERE, and here we are likely to remain. Individuals emigrate—nations never. We have grown up with this republic, and I see nothing in her character, or even the character of the American people as yet, which compels the belief that we must leave the United States.[93]

Interestingly enough, while sanctioning the emigration of "individuals," Douglass' rejection of mass emigration remained firm, though his paper in 1854 published opinions by missionary colonizationists such as Alexander Crummell, who were more sympathetic to Liberia.

Pro-emigrationists found their greatest literary appeal outside the constraints of the weekly journal, as editors reflecting more the will of a conservative professional class found mobility of of the population unsettling to their economic interest. Nevertheless, advocates of emigration, such as Martin Delany and James T. Holly, circumvented reluctant editors by publishing emigrationist pamphlets.

For example, though Holly in 1859 was able to have his "Thoughts on Hayti" published in *The Anglo-African Magazine*, it was his treatises on Haiti, "A Vindication of the capacity of the Negro Race for self-government and civilized progress," which established a possible rationale for voluntary emigration to Haiti. Asserting that it would act "as a means of removing the national disabilities of the Haytian people," Holly interpreted the successful Haitian struggle against France and its subsequent rule of "popular despots" as "evidence of their capacity for self-government." And in a challenging manner proclaimed:

> Having now presented the preceding array of facts and arguments to establish, before the world, the Negro's equality with the White man in carrying forward the greatest principles of self government and civilized programs; I would now have these facts exert their legitimate influence over the minds of my race, in this country, in producing that most desirable object of arousing them to a full consciousness of their own inherent dignity; and thereby increasing among them that self respect which shall urge them on to the performance of these great deeds which the age and the race now demand at their hands.[94]

Pursuing the dreams of developing a powerful sovereign nation in the western hemisphere, Holly envisioned Haiti as "the keys to the commerce of both hemispheres." It would also resolve all questions of respect for blacks. However, any emigration would necessitate "essential characteristics" in its participants. Considering the *Anglo American Magazine*'s neutrality on the issue of emigration, Holly was still able to have printed his four-part article, "Thoughts on Hayti," in which the criteria for emigration emerged. In an attempt to ease the process of assimilation among "native" people, he insisted that emigration movements must consist of a "homogeneous branch of the human family." Holly further proposed that the emigrants should come in contact with a people who have developed a civilization which is superior to the one they have departed from. This, he concluded, would facilitate a "wider more unrestricted field of useful activity and progressive development among the people where they migrate, than in the home which they leave."[95]

Clarifying his remarks, he posited that if the colored race in the United States, finding itself in a unique position of not having a strong material base nor political leverage for effective advocacy of its rights, would emigrate to Haiti. Success which comes with numerical strength would then be theirs. Whereas, if they chose to stay "in the United States, the numerical weakness of the colored people; the public sentiment of the dominant race against them, stronger than laws; and the social repellancy which whites manifest toward the blacks, stronger than the attractions of Christian love; place the black man under such obvious barriers of caste as he will never be able to surmount."[96]

Explicating African history in terms understood by most Christian-oriented free blacks, Holly asserted that the race must first:

> Escape as Lot from the guilty and doomed cities of the plain, not even looking back upon this accursed land—lest like the wife of Lot they should be turned into signal monuments of divine vengeance; or like that slavish generation of Israelites, who harked after the flesh pots of Egypt, be doomed to wander in the wilderness of darkness and error until they are all slain by the avenging hand of God, with but two left to bear witness that such a degenerate race ever existed.[97]

Acknowledging that voluntary emigration was not accepted as a legitimate concept by free blacks, Delany pursued this idea noting that "this objection is at once removed, when reflecting on our condition as incontrovertibly shown." Attempting to establish a discourse which placed the African's experience in America within an historical context, Delany claimed that the necessity for emigration was in conjunction with an historical process, in that:

> The time has now fully arrived, when the Colored race is called upon by all the ties of common humanity, and all the claims of consummate justice, to go forward and take their position, and to do battle in the struggle now being made for the redemption of the world.... For God himself as assuredly as he rules the destinies of nations, and entereth measures into the "hearts of men," has presented these measures to us.[98]

To the question of where and how such a movement should take place, Delany answered "Central and South America MUST BE OUR HOMES," but specifically, "Nicaragua and New Grenada." Explaining further, he stated:

> -In the first place, they are the nearest points to be reached, and countries at which the California adventurers are now touching on their route to that distant land—and not half the distance of California.
> -In the second place, the advantages of all kinds of enterprise, are equal if not superior, to almost any other points—the climate being healthy and highly favorable, and

-In the third place, and by no means the least point of importance, the British nation is bound by solemn treaty, to protect both of those nations from foreign imposition until they are able to stand alone.[99]

Reminding free blacks that the governmental structures of these two countries would be congenial to free blacks' political, social and economic aspirations, he elaborated:

> We shall not go there to be idle — passive spectators to an invasion of South American rights. NO — go when we will, and where we may, we shall hold ourselves amenable to defend and protect the country that embrace us. We are fully able to defend ourselves, once concentrated, against any odds, — and by the help of God, we will do it. We do not go, without counting the cost, cost what it may; all that it may cost, it is worth to be free.[100]

Committed to emigration as a means of establishing a political base, Delany fully accepted the role of a nineteenth-century settler, who, motivated by racial and economic justifications, claimed that Africans in the diaspora not only have the ability "to stand warm climates better than Whites," but "according to our oppressors' own showing, we are a SUPERIOR RACE, and being endowed with the properties fitting us for ALL PARTS of the earth, while they (whites) are only adapted to CERTAIN parts." However, in a seemingly contradictory observation, Delany divests free blacks of these "superior" qualities when he claims they are an assemblage of "the poorest people, as a class, in the world of civilized mankind — abjectly, miserably poor, no one scarcely being able to assist the other ... who too often cling to the oppressor as the objects of love," not recognizing that "a new country, and new beginning, is the only true, rational, political remedy for our disadvantageous position."[101]

Consequently, for Delany, emigration was a process of extreme importance, and one which not only must be voluntary if possible, but selective. To insure that "no mis-step" occurred, or "fatal error" was "committed at the commencement of emigration," Delany proposed that, as Holly proposed for Haiti and Mary Shadd for Canadian emigration, a vigorous selection process must be established for Nicaragua and New Grenada; screening for a specific class of free blacks with "a good business practical education," who would play a leading role among settlers. Delany noted:

> In our selection of individuals, it will be observed that we have confined ourselves entirely to those who occupy or have occupied positions among the Whites, consequently having a more general bearing as useful contributors to society at large.[102]

Though this suggests that if this proposal were enacted, only a very narrow segment of the free black community would be eligible, Delany's appeal was fashioned to motivate only the segment of the populace he considered to have the highest combination of entrepreneurship, educational skills and social dissatisfaction. Yet subsequent comments by Delany also reveal his concern with this class and its apathetic anti-emigrationist rhetoric which he saw as indicative of an "adaptation, and reconciliation of mind" to the conditions of quasi-freedom.[103]

Annoyed by their proclamations of "standing by the slave," Delany responded, "We believe it to be the duty of the free, to elevate themselves in the most speedy and effective manner possible: as the redemption of the bondsman depends entirely upon the elevation of the freeman." Because free blacks, Delany argued, could not possibly hope for such elevation in the United States, the slaves' hopes must also be dismissed. Thus, by strong motivational appeals, he attempted to convince this growing class of professionals that "if speedy redemption" of the slaves is desired, then "let us apply first, the lever to ourselves; and the force that elevated us to the positon of manhood's consideration and honors will cleft the manacle of every slave in the land."[104]

Efforts by Delany and Holly to propagate a movement in journals, pamphlets and books were more than equalized by the anti-emigrationist efforts to define emigration as an affront to the race. Similarly, responses to assimilationist arguments of Christianization, economic elevation, acculturation, responsibility to the enslaved, and loss of African language were difficult as most editors of journals were themselves convinced of the inadvisability of emigration. However, the few thousand blacks who did choose to emigrate to Africa, the Caribbean or other areas in the Western hemisphere, did so in response to the Fugitive Slave Acts, European emigration to America, lack of the franchise and societal racism, rather than in response to effective mobilization appeals. In this historical context, whether for or against emigration, the black newspaper did establish a line of communication between the immediate community and the processes surrounding them. However, the essential message which emerged from the press was a persistent effort to reform rather than confront physically the "absurdity and injustice" of racism in America.

In a sense, the views of the black newspaper on the question of emigration represented a belief that through discourse, a development of political structures (such as the National Negro Conventions) would eventually emerge to challenge blacks' negative "social image." Secondly, it was hoped that by emphasizing the importance of education and business as a means of modifying social-political constraints, economic gain and the skills required for social equality would be attained, thereby eliminating any need for emigration. Ironically, while the development of the press as a mouthpiece for the race clearly defined the opinions and abilities of most educated free blacks, it also underlined a move towards "separateness" from institutions which attempted to establish a preconceived role for blacks. As a result, aggressive proclamations by spokesmen such as "The Colored Baltimorean" and "Augustine" in the press represented an awareness, and to a degree, acceptance of a differentness between the races. Thus, the use of assimilationist appeals aimed at modifying social exigencies were checked by a heightening sense of class consciousness and ethnocentrism by free blacks. Again, the need to be viewed as political and economic equals with whites motivated most editors to censor strong suggestions for emigration which, they argued, implied coalescing with the American Colonization Society, and the notion of free blacks' inferiority.

Colonization as Viewed by White Abolitionists in the Black Press

As early as 1827, white abolitionists and pro-colonizationists were expressing divergent opinions on what was to become one of the most controversial issues facing antebellum America. Notwithstanding the fact that many of these differences were indirect responses to economic as well as moral assumptions, their exposure in the black press provided free blacks with an insight into political debates on issues which directly influenced their community.

In 1827, *Freedom's Journal* published a series of articles by John H. Kennedy and Thomas Clarkson on colonization. Differing in their estimation of colonizing free blacks in Africa, both argued their views over a period of two months in the journal. Clarkson, a well-known white abolitionist, was extremely emphatic about colonization as he explained:

> No geographical boundaries, no lines separating state from state, no exclusive legislative enactment can permanently arrest that moral influence which has emancipated the slaves of Pennsylvania and New York, and which will free those of the Carolinas and Georgia.[105]

Using pseudonyms such as "The Investigator," "A Subscriber," or the more revealing initials of "J.H.K.," "J.C.," or "R.S.," numerous abolitionists serving as a conduit of white America's fear about slavery simultaneously expressed a combination of emotions ranging from conciliatory empathy to paternalistic benevolence. Interestingly enough, attitudes by white abolitionists more often than not masked the effects of class interest and racial conflict among white Americans. Furthermore, the specter of having to compete for jobs with a skilled, low paid, socially subordinate ex-slave populace became an unwanted possibility for many job-seeking white Americans and emigrating Europeans. In other words, the one great obstacle to any abolishment of slavery was an antipathy of non-slaveholding whites toward blacks as competitors in the economic spheres of society. This provided a major stimulus for a rapid separation of the races on every social and political level. Similarly, being an abolitionist did not necessarily imply any biracial agreement on the issue of antislavery. Instead, many whites argued the issue from a racial-class perspective. Such whites premised their abolitionism on the condition that the newly freed slave would be deported along with the already-existing free black populace.

While many antislavery advocates, including Henry Clay (supporter of a colonization plan in the early 1800s), Francis P. Blair (author of the Republican colonization plan in the 1850s), James Madison and Thomas Jefferson, all shared the assumptions of their slave-owning class regarding race, they too attacked slavery primarily because of its effects on southern white labor.[106] A congressman from the "free" state of Ohio, also agreeing with the belief that free blacks constituted a social "nuisance," stated:

> A free White man could live where there are Negroes, and maintain his freedom; but no White non-slaveholder can live where slave laws, customs, and habits pertain and retain his rights.

For the white worker, newly arrived European immigrant, or farmer, slavery was a beneficial institution when it could provide an economic advantage similar to that of the profit-making slaveholder, or when it presented to society a class which could permanently be looked down upon. Addressing this issue, a leading antislavery paper, *The National Era*, stated to southern whites that: "We are not opposed to the extension of either class of our population, provided it be FREE, but to the existence of slavery and migration of SLAVES."

Yet more often than not, regardless of abolitionist moralizing, antislavery sentiments made little distinction between free blacks and slaves, in that any close association would be unwanted. Lyman Trumbull clearly voiced this opinion when he stated: "I want to have nothing to do, either with the Free Negro, or the Slave Negro."[108]

Throughout the free states, especially in the New England region, the conflict over slavery, free soil, and abolitionism is dramatically expressed when one examines the sectional differences between urban and rural populations. Generally, the smaller rural areas "with their small towns and independent farmers were not only centers of literacy, religion and economic progress," but of radical abolitionism. However, the urban centers, with their commercial ties to the South and their increasing numbers of immigrants, tended towards conservatism and class-racial stratification.[109] Nevertheless, beliefs of abolitionists such as Garrison and Owen Lovejoy were also influential as they attempted to reform the evils they saw in society, and foster a view of the world in which compromise with sin was itself a sin.[110]

With this perspective in mind, the pleas of white abolitionists appear as moral concerns which existed in deference to the needed growth of free blacks' political or economic power. Their sense that slavery was a moral transgression which prohibited the benefits of Christian society was evident:

> It is seen by the great body of the inhabitants of the Free States, that under all ordinary circumstances, their (Freemen's) progress in rational pursuits and social life, is equal to that of the Whites, of the SAME CLASS. Many individuals among them, are nobly trampling upon the disadvantages of color; the inveterate prejudice of their White neighbors, and rising them from the depths of degradation and misery, to an honorable station in society, claiming that respect due to moral conduct and integrity of mind; These are beacons directing their brethren to follow them, and the call is not unheeded; Thousands, stimulated by example, are aspiring after character, propriety and distinction, conscious of their ability to attain them.[111]

Attempting to extricate the American Colonization Society (ACS) from the more blatant racist propaganda of some antislavery elements, John Kennedy (who was once an assistant to Ralph Gurley, the Society's correspondence secretary in 1825), claimed that any enlightened advocate of the Society must first:

> Regret, that some have dwelt so much upon the necessity of ridding [the] community of PEST and NUISANCES! He will only defend the object of the society as such. He can only maintain that the motives are good, of the MASS of those composing it. He will merely claim that allowances must be made for the prejudice of the White man, as well as for those of the colored man. He will contend that a good cause ought not to be injured in our estimation nor the motive of his friends impeached, because that INDIVIDUALS befriend it on selfish principles.... For my own part, I am pretty well convinced that the motives of the institution

are pure; and this if I mistake not, is a point conceded by most of those essays on the subject, which have appeared in the "journal."[112]

Kennedy's appeal attempted to present a more functionalist view of the United States. He viewed free blacks' functioning in a manner which, while benefiting the society as a whole, did not aid their self-development beyond the level of "hewer of wood and drawers of water." Observing that, if a society such as the ACS is organized and composed of different classes of persons who, in turn, patronize it for a variety of noble reasons, it should not be attacked or condemned, as:

> It has contributed neither to the formation, nor to the continuance of the disabilities under which the colored man labours; But since these actually exist, it provides a remedy suited to the exigency. It deals with men as THEY ARE, and not as they OUGHT TO BE. It provides for the colored man an asylum, where this noxious influence cannot reach him; Its offers are addressed to the interest and to the intellect of those who are at perfect liberty to accept them, or to refuse them.[113]

Secondly, Kennedy asserts that one must be aware of "the happy influence exerted on slavery" by the society, in that:

> No great research is necessary to ascertain how colonies (Liberia, Sierra Leone) of civilized emigrants must interfere with this traffic. Even the natives, wrapped as they are in Egyptian darkness, were competent to this discovery.

Consequently, he argued that two beneficial developments would occur once progress (colonization or emigration) was made in this direction:

> 1. In its *moral* capacity ... it will be as a "city set on a hill." It will be imitated and emulated. The adjoining tribes will avail themselves of the advantages it proffers to them, and the colony will occupy every opening presented for the propagation of its blessings.
> 2. In its *commercial* capacity, it will serve as a place of *depot* for those articles that are now obtained in exchange for slaves.[114]

However, not all colonizationists were as subtle in their desire to colonize the African, a point Frederick Douglass emphasized by printing white colonizationist views in his paper for the benefit of his readers. For instance, when the *Daily News* printed a letter containing the views of Latrobe, a major advocate of colonization and the president of the Maryland Colonization Society in 1851, Douglass prefaced

Latrobe's opinions by noting that, "His policy is just of that accommodating *Laissez faire* character most despised by the really Free people."[115]

Answering correspondence from the noted French essayist and social critic Victor Hugo concerning America's slavery, Latrobe listed six propositions which he felt confronted the abolitionist position squarely:

> 1. That the two races of Whites and Blacks in the United States must forever remain separate and distinct....
> 2. That the necessary consequence of this state of things, as illustrated by the present, and in accordance with all history, must be that the weaker of the two races must, directly or indirectly, be oppressed — the extent of the oppression being in proportion to the occasion of collisions between the two in competition for employment.
> 3. There must be a colonization, to be carried on like all other previous colonizations, which may be facilitated by aid in the commencement, but which must ultimately be a self-paying colonization, the emigrants paying their own expenses.
> 4. That these circumstances, growing mainly out of the vast increase of our White population, by native birth and foreign immigration, are accumulating beyond all control, and will ultimately leave the free colored man no alternative but emigration.
> 5. That Africa is the place for which he is destined and that the colonies planted there — now the Republic of Liberia — are to be his ultimate home: That in Africa alone can he escape the White man's power, while the latter will be dependent on him for the missionary and commercial agencies here referred to.
> 6. That while the present means for emigration may be supplied by individuals or other aid, yet the commerce which is rapidly growing up between Africa and this country will in a brief time — looking to the ends to be obtained — furnish facilities for the same emigration from America to Africa that is now taking place between Europe and this continent — an emigration which would soon relieve the United States from its entire Free colored population and towards which, where the Irishman or German has one motive, the Free Black man has ten.[116]

Thomas Clarkson, from a more social-psychological perspective, took the opposite point of view. Insinuating that any pro-colonizationist perspective, regardless of its moral or commercial rationales, would only aid the cause of slavery, he posited the view that:

> It requires but a limited portion of foresight to see, that if pushed to the extent contemplated, it [colonization] will bring about a state of things in reference to the future happiness of the African race in this country of a melancholy description: The anticipation of which is sufficient to arouse

the most insensible to a sense of approaching danger, and the necessity of endeavoring to avert it.

The danger he perceived was not only camouflaged within the structure of society itself, but caused by the ignorance of whites about the effects of slavery on the enslaved race:

> I think we may properly recognize in our colored population two classes. One, the Free Blacks, residing principally in the Atlantic states, north of the Potomac; and the other, the Southern. That the colonizing system is intended to benefit the latter class, is not asserted by the society at the present time. It appears to have abandoned this ground so obviously and glaringly untenable, although it has been stated, and with plausibility too, that the absence of the Free Blacks with their vices and evil propensities, in the southern states, would produce a great degree of contentment and submission among the slaves, whose constant intercourse with the class to be removed, renders municipal regulations necessary, which frequently operate with severity greater than was intended, and this of consequence must be the case.

In this regard, he then asserted that,

> Remove the Free, the cause of those regulations, and the amount of misery on the part of slaves will be lessened! Reasoning and argument of this nature will do very well, to apply to those who do not think for themselves.... Weak indeed must be that cause requiring such arguments to support it; miserable in the extreme must be that measure, when its advocates are obliged to come forward and say that the deeper the abyss of slavery and misery a class of men are involved in, is their happiness prompted.[117]

Disregarding this process as futile and dangerous to the cause of abolition, Clarkson asked:

> If the removal of all the intelligent, industrious, enterprising, educated Free Blacks will not tend to sink the remainder still deeper in slavery, degradation and distress; for by it, will the removal of that great moral influence also take place, which providence in his wisdom has put in operation, to rend the chains of individual slavery, in our favored country, as well as throughout the world.[118]

One of the most prolific defenders of the ACS scheme was Henry Clay. As one of the society's founding members, Clay was not only its major advocate, but a strategist who structured a plan of action for the termination of slavery and the eventual deportation of blacks to Africa.

Though Clay did discuss alternative plans for deportation with abolitionists from as far away as England, his essential overriding concern was with the immediate future, or as he put it:

> I am aware that there are respectable persons who believe that slavery is a blessing, that the institution ought to exist in every well organized society, and that it is even favorable to the preservation of liberty.... I would, however, remark, that if slavery be fraught with these alleged benefits, the principle on which it is maintained, would require that one portion of the White race should be reduced to bondage to serve another portion of the same race, when Black subjects of slavery could not be obtained, and that in Africa, where they may entertain as great a preference for their color as we do for ours, they would be justified in reducing the White race to slavery in order to secure the blessing which that state is said to diffuse.[119]

In an 1849 letter, originally written for a white newspaper and reprinted by the *The North Star*, Clay explained that the emancipating of slaves could not, nor should not be a rapid process, but one slow enough to insure the orderly functioning of society. Secondly, his assertion was that the success of emancipation is indispensably connected with the immediate removal of those slaves emancipated. And finally, that the cost of this project should be "defrayed by a fund to be raised from the labor of each freed slave."[120]

Arguing from a racial perspective and assuming the stance of a self-proclaimed missionary, Clay continued:

> If indeed, we possess this intellectual superiority, profoundly, grateful and thankful to him who has bestowed it, we ought to fulfill all the duties and obligations which it imposes, and these would require us not to subjugate or deal unjustly by our fellowmen, who are less blessed than we are, but to instruct, to improve, and to englighten them.

However, many abolitionists disagreed with Clay's basic premise and expressed criticism about the influence of racial prejudice on political and economic decisions. They argued that Clay's position overlooked the "valuable" labor pool which would be lost if slaves and free blacks were deported. An abolitionist from England, who signed his articles with the letters "J.C.," explained that the development of settlements along the western coast of Africa was one thing, but to attempt the forceful removal of slaves, through whatever method, to Africa, was "visionary" and indicative of a societal thinking that has "yielded to the prejudices and erroneous views of the slaveholders."[121]

He continued by suggesting that if the slaveholders of Virginia could be induced to view the subject objectively, they would conclude that the economics of farming contradicted the policy of colonization, in that:

> As slaves increase upon the land, their value will necessarily diminish, but this is no less to their owner, who is also the owner of the land which is more than increased in proportion to the diminished value of the slaves. If land is plentiful, and labourers scarce, land will have little value. The price of labour, and the price of slaves, where that state exists, will be high.
> If labourers become plentiful, the price of labor or slaves will diminish, until they are not worth holding in a state of slavery at all; But if the market price of the produce remains the same, it will be merely a transfer of value from the slaves to the land. This would be the case, even if no greater inducements were held out to quicken the exertions of the labourer; but when he is converted into a Freeman, he will be induced to be so much more industrious, as not only to increase his own comforts, but also the profits of his former master [who] now becomes his landlord.[122]

Carrying his point further, the writer insisted that both a positive and evil omen for society would be derived from colonization, in that the natural increase of free blacks would, in time, compete with, "and in the end would destroy slavery itself." However, any attempt at colonizing would affect slavery in a manner which would be suggestive of its continuance.[123]

Another anonymous abolitionist using the initials "J.D." stated that not only would colonization increase the value of the slave, but that when the ACS became directly involved with the purchasing of slaves from traders for the benefit "of their miserable colony," credence would be given to the notion of blacks as articles for trade. Secondly, he claimed that the question of blame for the initiating of the slave trade must rest with the northern states, as "the south never engaged in the slave trade; it was northern capital and northern ships alone that carried on that business."[124] While the implications of this charge confronted slavery and its suggested cure—colonization—simply as a southern problem, it ignored the relationship between the political framework, economic development, and Christian morality as national ideological appeals attempting to justify a notion of racial elevation, *not parity for free blacks*.

Viewing themselves and the society around them as the criteria, white abolitionists found it natural if not crucial to remind free blacks in their own journals of this point:

> The advocates of the colony at Liberia are endeavoring to acquire support, by representing in the first place, the total unfitness of our Free coloured people to rise from their present ignorant condition and debasement in this country.

And that in a conniving manner and against the best interest of free blacks,

> This society, cold and heathen in its doctrine; destructive of the best interest of a whole people in its practice; is with unhallowed hands endeavoring to arrest their progress from slavery, to freedom, and from misery to happiness, by the removal of the virtuous, intelligent, exemplary Free Blacks; leaving the mire of brutality and vice, without advice, or a brother to protect them.[125]

By the 1850s, white abolitionist input in the black press was limited to a few individuals, as black editors became more critical of whites' paternalistic views. Though white abolitionists such as Garrison edited their own journals, thereby finding ample space for expression, others, such as Gerrit Smith and Lewis Tappan, were often at the mercy of an increasingly militant black press. Periodically, however, letters "from despondent emigrationist to White abolitionist" found their way into *The Colored American, The North Star,* or *Frederick Douglass' Paper,* expressing sorrow at the living conditions and social practices of the indigenous African population. Comments such as "the climate, soil, and economy here forbid that anything of importance shall be accomplished [in Liberia], at least for some time to come," were eagerly publicized by white abolitionists. In conjunction with this perspective, abolitionists were further underscoring what freemen conventions were demanding of the larger society—a society which protected their right for intellectual and political development, free from the debasement, degradation and crippling white American paternalism.

The Black Press as a Forum for Leadership

With the advent of the black press in 1827, a new socio-political element began to push its way into the American political arena. Forged by the social structure of an antebellum slave society which generally regarded them as interlopers, free blacks, assuming roles as "race leaders," turned to the press to express their views. Evaluating their effectiveness in utilizing this medium around the issue of emigration and colonization is critical, as is an assessment of the black community's capability to respond to such an issue.

While the issues of colonization and emigration were important enough to cause the concern of slaveholders and abolitionists throughout the country, the problem for black leadership was equally perplexing as editors toiled to transmit a set of well-defined messages to a targeted audience. Motivating the politically outcast free black into active participation on the issue presumed at the least the existence of a sizable readership whose reciprocal relationship with the press was assured. This, as we shall see, was questionable. Secondly, an examination of the literacy levels of free blacks raises questions as to this press's readership and its effectiveness as a disseminator of information and social values. It can be said that for this press, perceptions of social education and class values had as much to do with the transmission of information as did free blacks' physical ability to obtain an issue of the black newspaper.

For example, an examination of antebellum census data, with all its inadequacies, suggests that the level of illiteracy among free blacks limited the dissemination of direct information by the press (see Table 8, pp. 222-223). Statistics on school attendance were first collected in the 1840 census. However, school attendance data collected by this census have serious limitations and are not comparable with data derived from the 1890 and subsequent censuses. This is supported by the criteria used in an earlier 1870 census of respondents over twenty-one years of age who were asked by surveyors two questions: "Do you have the ability to read?" and "Do you have the ability to write?" From this, illiteracy was subsequently defined as the inability to write, "regardless of ability to read." Thus, when one considers that by 1860, out of a total black population of 4,442,000, a little more than 10 percent (or 488,000) were classified as "Freemen," and of that number, there were 230,000 living in the northern and western "Free States" with an illiteracy rate of 41.3 percent, questions arise as to the social impact of the free black press as a forum on colonization or emigration, *and* its editors' selectivity in audience and articles published.[126]

In fact, most antebellum black newspapers were not written for slave population consumption, but for free blacks who, living largely in northern states, identified with the philosophy of upward mobility and social equality.[127]

With the black press as a tangible example of social, if not political elevation, articles on the illiteracy of the common laborer were being published by editors advocating racial uplift through individual achievement.

That the antebellum black press was successful in providing a forum for political thought and was effective in presenting the issue of emigration to *literate* blacks, is attested to by the numerous conventions, speeches, debates and discussions which were reported on. However, in a cynical manner Cornish alludes to this by claiming:

> We were written about, preached to, and prayed for, as Negroes, Africans and Blacks, all of which have been stereotyped, as terms of reproach, and on that account, if no other, are unacceptable.[128]

Demonstrating a recognition and subtle acceptance of their differentness, many spokesmen were projected into positions of leadership by asserting that the elevation of the race was "inadvertently" accomplished, through the process of enslavement. By positing the immorality of slavery, and the involvement of Africans in this trade, they were able to rationalize a need to "stand by" their enslaved brethren while condemning African culture as being ill-equipped to resist the onslaught of "a more advanced European civilization." Attributing enslavement to cultural weakness and "heathenism," editors were quite satisfied to conclude that their political situation, regardless of its faults, was an advancement for the race. This dispossessing of one's past and its defects, while identifying with the present, provided an effective rationale for many free blacks to dissociate themselves from colonization and emigration.

The latter years of the antebellum period were distinguished by centralization of activity and purpose within the black press. Encouraged by the increasing desire by free blacks to express dissatisfaction, editors began to publish lengthy rhetorical articles ranging in content from colonization to the abolishment of slavery. How these controversies were interpreted by literate and illiterate blacks is important in judging the effectiveness of persuasive appeals in the press. Despite the fact that the black press was representative of specific class interest, the transformation of beliefs and practices from a socially articulate, educated elite, to its illiterate brethren, could not have occurred without the effective utilization of a viable social infrastructure. Therefore, it is important to recognize the existence of reciprocal relationships between the black press and its readers. We have already seen that only a limited number of blacks were literate enough to read these journals, not to mention reply to them. Furthermore, the material used and submitted for publication by subscribers was subject to the class interest of its editors, which was the development and continual reinforcement of a conservative ideology clearly establishing Christian morality and anti-emigration as editorial themes. The resulting concentration on internal goals — morality, individual development and assimilation — signaled a movement away from activism and one more towards intimate associations, self-containment and the cultivation of esoteric principles.[129]

When influential "spokemen for the race," "responsible leaders," and "men of social worth" accepted accommodation as an appropriate social attribute, they were also speaking for a respect for authority, social elevation and a "correspondence in outlook" with their own. With few exceptions, journals such as the *Colored American* and *Frederick Douglass' Paper* rejected the concept of the press as being the marketplace for the circulation of ideas, but rather viewed it as a forum for the expression of moral concepts. Conformity to Christian "truths" was to be the precondition for public expression. Enlightenment, elevation and social responsibility were to be the foundations of a black press based on class interest.[130]

Editors took it upon themselves to express viewpoints for the "inarticulate" mass, and in doing so attempted to galvanize the two free and slave classes into racial consensus. A self-image of leadership was validated by editors who viewed the dissemination of selected and often biased information as their sacred duty. As the editor of *The Weekly Anglo-African* stated: "We shall direct the attention of the masses to industry, to perseverence [sic], to economy, to self-reliance, to the obtainment of substantial footing in the land of our birth."[131]

Though one might suspect that the diffusion of information in urban centers would be significantly higher than in rural areas, the heterogeneity of antebellum cities must be considered. One cannot assume that this "heterogeneous" structure implies the lessening of racial, ethnic or class cleavages. Yet, consideration should be given to the deeply imbedded interpersonal relationships on the community level and their importance in the processing and transmitting of opinions on emigration. Opinions presented and argued at church meetings, conventions, and other assemblies were often occasions for vehement exposure of social injustice. As one might expect, these gatherings were usually held in church buildings, which afforded the incumbent pastor, church leader or community spokesman an opportunity to express himself fully in opposition to a variety of oppressive social conditions, and their perceptions on colonization or emigration.[132]

Therefore, thought should first be given to information processes — multi-step flow, information diffusion, rumor transmission — and the role they played in socializing blacks to the values and beliefs of an upwardly mobile class within the black community. Moreover, a subordinated class of free blacks, with its limited educational level and reliance upon face-to-face communication, was insufficient in number to retard the gradualist, accommodationist philosophy which stressed the familiar nineteenth-century homilies of education, moral rectitude and economic sufficiency. In fact, these conditions may have enhanced rather than retarded the process of anti-emigration.[133]

Secondly, the existence of the black press, and its insistence on the social elevation of free blacks, strengthened notions of community, as word-of-mouth communication (the pulpit for example), strengthened the legitimacy of the newspaper to act as a mouthpiece for the race. Similarly, dominant economic interests and the disseminating of ideological beliefs utilized an infrastructure which relied primarily on interpretative communicability. While evidence for this premise is scattered, its consistent appearance cannot be overlooked. When examining Henry Bibb's Canadian paper, *Voice of the Fugitive*, the perception one receives is of a journal intent on bringing free blacks to support financially and philosophically the plight of fugitives. Consequently, in an article titled "Colonization or Slavery," the plea was made:

> Our enslaved brethren, not to submit to, or accept of either [colonization or slavery], but to run away from the tyrant who holds them, and settle themselves in Canada, where all men are protected in the enjoyment of freedom by the laws of Great Britian.[134]

In another issue, a similar appeal was made:

> Colored men of the United States and Canada—we call especially on you in view of the subject, what position will ye take? If the subject commends itself to your minds favorably, will ye not support it? "Why stand ye here all the day?" There is no permanent stopping place in the United States upon which the hunted fugitive can stand—three million and a half of our own brethren are in chains, the slave holders of the South with the American Colonization Society are striving to prevent us from settling in Canada, on the one hand, and to induce the Free People of Color, to Africa on the other....[135]

Though impassioned pleas by editors were geared towards reaching every black in America, slave or free, neither their papers' circulation nor the numbers of subscribers suggested the feasibility of this. What was possible and evident in the style of many articles, was the expectation that the content of many papers would be orally transmitted to others throughout the society. How else could a journal, nearly 2,000 miles away, suggest revolt to slaves who were forbidden to read? Clearly, information or, as in this case, appeals, were not limited by the expository nature of the newspaper. Herein lies the basis for the "nuisance" characterization which slaveholders were so quick to label free blacks with, as the dangerous prospect of increased interaction between free blacks and slaves enhanced the possibility of a higher level of information diffusion among slaves. Secondly, the development of an infrastructure supported by social networks promised a greater degree of political agitation by both the slave and his "quasi-free" brethren.

While the above information processes suggest that the black press was able to reinforce concepts of social elevation, leadership and antiemigration, most free blacks' inability to receive fairly current issues of black newspapers led to a limited, *slective perception* and rumor transmission via word-of-mouth interaction. This played a crucial role in the opinion-making process of free blacks and their subsequent assessment of leadership. In the same view, Samuel Cornish's eagerness to publicly announce his right to edit out material from *The Colored American* that he considered to be "Heresy ... death to all our prospects," was not unique.[136]

While illiteracy for free blacks was approximately 43 percent in 1850, and virtually 100 percent among slaves, recent studies on word-of-mouth communication suggest that information is received by peasant groups through such a network. It is also suggested that a 100 percent illiteracy rate for slaves is highly suspect. "In general, the word-of-mouth network is the newspaper of the peasant." It is not that the upper classes do not receive word-of-mouth information; in fact they may receive it more frequently than the lower classes, but it is relatively less important. Consequently, the lower-class free black, being in less contact with communications media, put more emphasis on oral communication as a source of information.[137] In this regard, one can now assess the importance of "cultural modernization" in urbanized areas, and its relationship to a populace's identification with "characteristics indicative of modernity, skill or sophistication."[138]

Communication theory on information diffusion suggests that if successful socialization is to occur, critical attention should be given to:

> The amount and speed of the diffusion of items of information, to such factors as geographic distance from the point of origin of the message, time elapsed since the original infusion of the message into a commodity, size of the community ... [and] the degree of clustering with which the message was originally released, and appeals used.[139]

In this regard, an increasing ability by the black press to utilize the social infrastructure of free blacks becomes evident when we observe

Emigration vs. Assimilation

the role of the annual free black conventions from 1831 to 1835, and their subsequent growth into state and national conventions in the 1840s and 1850s.

By the 1830s the existence of conductors, or influential persons who would *successfully direct* a flow of information, was important in revealing a structure of hierarchical networks and power relationships for reciprocal social communication. As a result of this, the significance of the issue for society can be ascertained.

The 1848 Colored National Convention in Cleveland, Ohio, underlined the existence of these conductors of information, when a cross-section of delegates responded to Delany's call for the convention in *The North Star*. There were "Printers, Carpenters, Blacksmiths, Shoemakers, Engineers, Dentists, Gunsmiths, Masons, Clergymen, Barbers, Hairdressers, Coopers, Livery Stable Keepers, Bath House Keepers, and Grocers."[140] Though Delany's original call for the convention was published on July 28, some five weeks before the scheduled date of September 6, 1848, sixty to seventy delegates appeared from nine states. Within two days, due to its obvious influence, *The North Star* was proclaimed by the convention as sufficient for fulfiilling the purposes of a national press.

Realizing the conomic importance of using the convention to its utmost, the convention's Business Committee charged:

> Colored ministers and other persons throughout the Northern States to collect, or cause to be collected, accurate statistics of the condition of our people, during the coming year in the various stations and circuits in which they may find themselves located.[141]

Desiring to demonstrate their "total social authority," and to "actively organize so as to command and win the consent of the subordinated classes,"[142] the delegates further resolved to account for:

> The numbers of colored persons in the localities where they may be stationed; their general moral and social condition; and especially how many farmers and mechanics, how many are merchants or storekeepers, how many are teachers, lawyers, doctors, ministers, and editors; How many are known to take and pay for newspapers; How many literary, debating and other societies, for moral, mental and social improvement; and that said ministers be, and hereby are, respectfully requested to forward all such information to a committee of one, who shall be appointed for this purpose, and that the said committee of one be requested to make out a synopsis of such information and to report the same to the next Colored National Convention.[143]

With the establishing of the black press as an important element in the development and elevation of free blacks as a class, the diffusion of information was set in motion as copies of *The North Star* circulated among friends, associations, reading clubs, barber shops and the church.

For the nonliterate free black, the opinions and arguments expressed in the papers such as *The Colored American* and *The North Star* were received largely by word-of-mouth conductors and, as a result, were exposed to the misinterpretations and embellishments usually associated with this process. However, commensurate with this was the propagating of the concept of individual growth and social equality by the elite via the press. Grievances were now to be interpreted within the liberal guidelines of liberty and equality, in behalf of a growing American bourgeois society. Education and wealth were assumed to be the prerequisite for leadership. Furthermore, it was hoped that with the endorsement of *The North Star* as a "credible" source of information, Resolutions Four and Five of the 1848 National Convention, proclaiming "the occupation of domestics and servants among our people is degrading to us as a class," and the recommendation that "as far as in their power lies, to give their children especially a business education," would be continually propagated in this journal, as well as others.[144]

Spokesmen continually framed social concerns with the question: "What must men do to adjust to the divine will or the forces of nature?" Finding it politically more tenable to emphasize what ought to be done for social elevation, free blacks' critical examination of the problems of powerlessness and alienation among the lower strata of free blacks was ignored. By not scrutinizing social problems from an ethnocentric perspective, the importance of race was left to the individual reader's awareness. Even when pressured by increased fugitive slave acts and the threat of re-enslavement, editors demanded justice and equal protection under laws they assumed were relevant to their survival. As one writer, described only as "T", explained:

> We are of the opinion that we can get along with all the provisions made by our government, and think them just what we want on that score and nothing more. We want our rights as men, and shall never cease agitation until we attain them. When our political rights are acquired, the social will take care of themselves.[145]

It can be assumed that while the function of the black press was to create a feeling of political consensus among free blacks, it also focused public attention upon the printed word as an expression of power. But the influence of a variety of individuals among free blacks was critical in the oral diffusion of ideas and concepts. Circuit preachers such as John Chavis developed an important nexus between the press and the public. Advocating Christian morality and American nationalism, they penetrated the urban slum areas and rural sectors of the free and border states with their gospel of Christian-American nationalism. Similarly, editors like Samuel Cornish, Frederick Douglass, David Ruggles and Phillip Bell travelled, throughout their careers, from state to state asserting the values of social elevation, Christian morality and anti-emigration. For them the role of the press was supreme in that:

> We shall endeavor by a continuous correspondence from nearly every city and town in the country, to connect and keep astir our whole people, thus bringing them together weekly, to compare notes and learn of each other's prosperity.[146]

Information use and its processing by free blacks were heavily affected by a class-oriented press, whose editors sought to influence attitudes and opinions on emigration by manipulating and selectively controlling what was published. Consistent with Festinger's 1954 study on consensus formation, which suggests that lacking sufficient information, one tends to identify with the opinions of those who are closest to relevant information, the quasi-free reality of free blacks as opposed to the total dehumanization of the slave fostered their general acceptance of the notion of upward mobility and the basic truths of the American Constitution.[147]

The black newspapers were a critical factor in socializing free blacks towards the concept of assimilation and the propagation of "American" ideas. Social-psychological appeals by an elite strata of free blacks further enhanced the influence of assimilationist appeals, while causal inferences assailing emigration dominated the limited range of information sources available to the common free black. In this regard, literacy was a significant factor in the development of anti-emigration appeals, as the manner and saliency of available information were affected by the complexity and bias of the transmitting agent. Further, a reliance upon information conductors tended to add a sense of cohesiveness to the free black populace, as "trusted" interpreters of an event or printed information became viable sources of the world, or, reality.

Historical research into nineteenth-century America has indicated that very little evidence exists which suggests people first became literate so as to rise socially, but rather, people who had risen socially tended to become literate.[148] This contradicted a basic cornerstone of free black assimilationist philosophy, which asserted that social-political attainment is acquired first via formal education as opposed to personal attainment via manual labor. Only in this manner, it was argued, could progressive evolution of the race occur.[149]

For many emigrationists, the above meant obtaining the most literate, business-oriented free black for colonization, yet for the assimilationist editor, it meant publishing not only a weekly newspaper, but articles, pamphlets and books. Consequently, emigrationist and assimilationist newspaper editors, preachers, orators, and educators published a variety of pamphlets outside the restrictions of a journal.

Dorothy Porter, in her introductory remarks to *Negro Protest Pamphlets*, suggests that free black intellectuals, especially preachers, benefited from this alternative literary form. Its slender format was "no incumberance to their desires to reach beyond their immediate congregations to all those unnumbered blacks who were thought to be able to read. Clearly, the pamphlet writers realized that the words of ministers were a sure way of reaching and swaying not only their fellow blacks, but such sympathetic whites as might listen to the cause which they advocated."[150] As a result, throughout the period from 1827 to 1861, free black writers produced many pamphlets and books (see Appendix D, pp. 211-212).

The effectiveness of this literary form and the importance of its message in comparison to the more traditional, nonexpository format (appeal), is difficult to assess, yet several points should be noted.

As mentioned earlier, appeals in the press by editors such as Delany, Holly, Douglass and Shadd emphasizing the importance of selectivity in choosing emigrants were geared primarily towards a select readership, whose literacy was taken for granted. However, sufficient evidence exists from studies conducted on migrants to Canada from 1850 to 1870 which suggests that many of these migrants came from urban areas, and though illiterate, brought skills and advantages obviously obtained from the economic milieu of the city. From this, one might conclude that with the additional attainment of literacy, an elimination of social hindrances would occur, encouraging a process of upward social mobility. Though this seems plausible, strong indications suggest the reverse, in that education, or one's level of literacy was not significant enough to diminish the dominating and ascriptive conditions of nineteenth-century society. Practices which were supported by a rigid, stratified social structure placed far more importance on class backgrounds and ethnic mixture than educational achievement.[151]

However, in the Canadian cities of Hamilton and Kingston, and in the province of Canada West, literacy played a significant role in blacks' emigration northward. For example, in Hamilton, 48 percent of black adults were illiterate in 1861 (a similar rate existed for London and Kingston), but in 1850, eleven years earlier, the rate was 43 percent, some five points lower. This is reflective of the increasing "fugitive Slave" characteristics of the migrants in this area of Canada.[152]

As unreliable as statistics might have been during this period, several factors are indicated, in that there is an admittance that 57 percent of the black population in Canada West's three major cities in 1850 were literate. And while delineating free blacks from fugitive ex-slaves was difficult by 1861, we do know that the fugitive slave acts of 1850 sent many *free blacks* in a panic northward to Canada. Though literacy may not be the major factor accounting for this mobility, as suggested, its importance in the process of information use for or against emigration stands firm, as the emigrants' literacy level provided easy access to information, if not social prediction. Interestingly enough, literacy levels of fugitive blacks during this period (1850–60) exceeded that of free blacks in America who chose not to emigrate.[153]

Secondly, the threat of losing one's freedom and property, along with the vigorous debates which ensued throughout the press on free blacks' rights, suggests that one stratum of free blacks was better prepared to make decisions as to its future than another. In this instance, while word-of-mouth information on Canadian emigration was important for the fugitive slave and lower strata of free blacks, literacy and the concomitant social relationships implied by it provided educated free blacks and those imbued with the beliefs of eventual justice, a greater mobility to effect such a move to Canada. Thus, the importance of class position with free blacks' social structure on this issue of Canadian emigration is significant as it enhanced the process of selective emigration. Consequently, with treaties, pamphlets, and published debates replete with notions of class leadership, the black press became an "adjunct of action, a way of encompassing situations." However, even among these emigrants, their growth as an educated, business-oriented stratum in Canada simply established a battlefield for their bourgeois interests; interests which were often in conflict with those of the emigrating lower strata of ex-slaves and fugitives.

While literacy for free blacks was one of many entrance fees to a world otherwise beyond their control, it was a world which was presented in a systematic manner — one which clearly preferred one set of interests over another.[154]

III. The Black Press Examines Two Settler Movements: Liberia and Haiti

> *If, then we can carve out a separate existence here, either under the American flag, or over it, be it so. But if we cannot, then migration is our only policy, and sacred duty. Indeed were we fully alive to our true interests and the destiny of our race, migration would have been the preference of our past, not the* Dernier Resort *of today. Standing in the light of history, especially the history of our continent—conversant as the better educated among us are with the influences that have molded American society and its institutions, and continue to dominate its policy toward our race—our abject clinging to the skirts of a people who seek to cast us off, illustrated at once our degradation and the emasculating power of slavery.*
>
> The Weekly Anglo-African,
> New York, May 11, 1861

Liberia and the Colonization Movement

In the fall of 1819, the American Colonization Society, in conjunction with numerous slaveholding interests and the federal government, decided to finance the colonization of Liberia. While the process itself was not actualized until 1821, the ensuing controversy continued throughout the antebellum period. The major issue to be debated was Liberia's fitness as a haven for free blacks and emancipated slaves.

While a majority of black editors resisted positive identification with Liberia, opinions, criticisms and arguments on its existence ran the spectrum from acceptance of Liberia as a missionary outpost, to its rejection as a physical abyss. However, while those articles favoring Liberian growth and political independence were privately produced in the form of pamphlets, treatises and books, newspaper editors Frederick Douglass, Samuel Cornish, Mary Shadd and Martin Delany rejected any forceful deportation of free blacks from the United States. Terming Liberia "the colonization graveyard," one writer likened the conditions and suffering of Liberian colonists to the effects of "colonization-banishment-murder."[1] In addition to these characterizations of Liberia, the black press systematically reprinted selections from white newspapers of procolonization material such as Henry Clay's letter to the *Lexington Observer and Reporter*. These were clear attempts to demonstrate for readers the racist basis of the argument for colonization. Other more substantive (yet often subtly implanted) aspects of Liberian colonization were also identified and discussed for the readers' edification.

Major among these questions was inquiry into the feasibility of sending free blacks to Liberia at the cost of the state. Douglass' reprinting of Henry Clay's 1849 position on this question in *The North Star* exposes the image of a slaveholder and statesman, preoccupied by the prospect of seeing his country engulfed by a rapidly increasing slave and free black class; a preoccupation which was simultaneously overshadowed by a desire to profit financially in the removal of this "problem" from society. Clay's subsequent statement therefore masks the aims of class and racial interest as he asserts:

> A vast majority of the people of the United States, I believe, regret the introduction of slavery into the colonies, lament that a single slave treads our soil, deplores the necessity of the continuance of slavery in any of the states, regard the institutions as a great evil to both races, and would rejoice in the adaptation of any safe, just and practicable plan for the removal of all slaves among us.[2]

Using his home state of Kentucky as a model for possible nationwide application, Clay explained that as far back as 1799, the legislative body of Kentucky attempted to emancipate as many slaves as possible. However, as no established colony would receive them, their problem increased to its present state and now:

> ...by the successful establishment of flourishing colonies on the Western coast of Africa, the difficulty has been obviated. And I confess that, without indulging in any undue feelings of superstition, it does seem to me that it may have been among the dispensations of providence, to permit the wrongs under which Africa has suffered, to be inflicted, that her children might be returned to their original home civilized, and imbued with the benign spirit of Christianity, and prepared ultimately to redeem that great continent from barbarism and idolatry.[3]

Connecting emancipation with colonization in West Africa and, specifically, Liberia, Clay suggested that a date be fixed (1855 or 1860) whereupon all Africans in America born after that date, "should be free at the age of twenty-five, but be liable afterwards to be hired out, under the authority of the state." He further envisoned that:

> Until the commencement of the system which I am endeavoring to sketch, I think all the legal rights of the proprietors of slaves, in their fullest extent, ought to remain unimpaired and unrestricted. Consequently, they would have the right to sell, devise or remove them from the state, and, in the latter case, without their offspring being entitled to the benefit of emancipation, for which the system provides.... It will have been seen that the plan I have suggested proposes the annual transportation of all prescribed age, to the colony which may be selected [Liberia] for their destination, and that this process of transportation is to be continued until the separation of the two races is complete.[4]

While Clay ascertained that in Kentucky, during the preceding year, an increase of some 3,000 to 4,000 occurred, he speculated that if his plan were to be adopted, some "five thousand" could be transported the very first year of his plan, thereby lowering the number of slaves. Alluding to the practicality of annually deporting 5,000 persons, not including slaves, from Kentucky, he reminded his readers that America annually received from Europe more than 250,000 persons, "at a cost for the passage of about $10 per head." Further, he asserted that "if there were a certainty of the annual transportation of not less than 5,000 persons to Africa, it would create a demand for transports, resulting in the development of free competition."[5] This, he assumed, would lower the cost, one which "has been stated upon good authority to be at present $50 per head, including the passage and six months' outfit after the arrival of the emigrant in Africa." Concluding that the cost was almost irrelevant due to the hiring out of the "liberated slave" for a term of three years at "an estimated $50 or $150 for 3 years," Clay asserted that:

> Manifest blessings ... would flow from the diminished value of slave labor (i.e., the increased value of European immigrant labor) and from the humanity and benevolence of private individuals prompting a liberation of their slaves and their transportation, a general disposition would exist to accelerate and complete the work of colonization.[6]

Attempting to articulate the importance of white nationalism as a cornerstone of racial enfranchisement and economic hegemony in the labor market, Clay's advocacy for Liberian emigration camouflaged his underlying capitalistic thrust for white labor. Appealing to notions of racial solidarity, he asserted (as if talking specifically to the entrepreneurial segment of society):

> ...we shall acquire the advantage of the dilligence, the fidelity, and the consistency of Free Labor, instead of the carelessness, the infidelity, and the unsteadiness of slave labor, and elevate the social conditions of the White laborer, augment the value of our lands, improving the agriculture of the state, attract capital from abroad to all the pursuits of commerce, manufacture, and agriculture.... [7]

Clay's thesis was not to be dismissed, as it did advocate the elimination of slavery. Yet, it sought to deport the very same people whom it had previously enslaved! From this perspective, Liberia assumed the character of a colony, existing under the benevolent exploitation of a secure and economically expanding slaveholding society. Within this historical context, the differences between *colonization* and *emigration* became more definitive as the former came to imply direct motivation and control by external political and economic forces. The latter suggested a more inner and ethnocentric motivation with national sovereignty as a legitimized goal. Though this is not to suggest that the economic rationales or political philosophies of the resulting hierarchies would not converge within the same political framework, it asks the question, How does the projection of cultural affinity in a public forum such as the press affect social opinion in a multi-racial society? While much of the black press attempted to address this problem, white propagandists such as Clay not only attacked free blacks' feeble social-economic structure with threatened expulsion, but suggested that any voluntary departure from the United States would be in compliance with the wishes of slaveholders and most white Americans. In this respect, the very existence of Liberia raised questions for many free blacks as to its purpose.

Needless to say, letters expressing an opposite point of view were common in most black newspapers. In a letter signed "A man of Colour," the author asserted that such a proposal "cannot but be warmly patronized by slaveholders." But to then believe that free blacks in the South would accept such a plan ignored the fact that in some states, such as South Carolina, once slaves gained their freedom, the severest restrictions were placed upon them, forcing them to depart and prohibiting any return to that state. The writer further claims that at a meeting held in Philadelphia, attended by 3,000 persons, once the topic of Liberian colonization was approached, "there was not one who was in favor of leaving this country, but they were all opposed to colonization in any foreign country whatever."[8]

Cornish, in his *Rights of All*, vigorously attacked Clay's proposal, claiming that:

> However successful and prosperous the colony at Liberia may be, it will never reduce the coloured population of this country. Send 20 thousand annually to the colony, and yet this population will increase from 40 to 50 thousand yearly in the United States, and shall this vast body of our neighbors and our household be forgotten in our zeal for the interest of a small colony? That the interest of the Christian public, in behalf of the Liberian colony, is evident to every enlightened man of colour, is evident to every unprejudiced White man, and it is not our duty to call back, or at least to call for a division of the public attention, the public effort, and the public prayers in behalf of our brethren in this country....[9]

Advocates for West African colonization liked to assert that with the establishing of a strong Liberian colony would come the benefit of a terminated slave trade. The likelihood that such an occurrence would eradicate the slave trade was quickly tested, when as early as 1837 articles appeared in *The Colored American* on this issue. While this particular paper was opposed to colonization in West Africa, letters published by its editor periodically exposed more than the general criticism aimed at the colony. For example, in a reprint of a letter from *The Liberian Herald*, a writer dismisses the argument that the slave trade was terminating due to the presence of Liberia. He claims instead that, "This trade has been gradually acquiring strength for the last four years," and that "its ravages have been more fearful, and the vessels engaged in it more numerous, than at any former period of the colony's history."[10] Charging that any claim to the colony's power to reduce or eliminate the slave trade at this time is fallacious, he asserts that if anything, "Liberia is a great accommodation to the slavers in procuring supplies, and that the colonists are themselves engaging in the traffic." To buttress his claims, he refers to a letter from a Dr. Goheen, a Methodist missionary in Liberia, who inquired when an American vessel would be sent to suppress the slave trade along the Liberian coast:

> The community here is too young and weak to put down the evil, and being so, for want of sufficient aid, is obliged to regard with seeming indifference the numerous Baltimore clippers, and other vessels that are frequently seen on our borders, and known to be slave ships. Any indignities offered to the slaver and his vessels, would be revenged upon our colonial traders, perhaps to the total destruction of all the trading schooners, which would at once entirely destroy the trafficking carried on by our small craft—cut off the communication (by sea) with the seaboard

settlements, and thus stop one of the principle resources of wealth to the colony.[11]

A year and a half later, in June 1840, *The Colored American* ran a front page account of a battle between emigrant settlers and "natives," titled "Letter from Liberia." The author, George Brown, describes in vivid terms what might be described as a settlers' war for domination over the indigenous population:

> "War is come! War is come!" Brother Sion Harris got out of bed immediately and went out in town. But he returned in about one minute and told me to be out of bed and load the guns, for war is at hand. I immediately arose, slipped on my clothes, and was on my knees to ask God to help us. By the time the enemy were within musket shot of the mission houses, Brother Harris went down and gave them the first shot and was answered by 10 or 12 muskets from the enemy, while I was loading muskets in the chamber.... Tom's people sallied down toward the lower gate, and gave a few shots, at which time one of his men received a slug through his bowels, and immediately came into my chamber with his intestines in his hands.
> And notwithstanding Tom and his men retreated under the lee of the mission house, yet they turned as it were, the left wing of the enemy, who soon fell into the main body, directly back of the mission house. And in less than one minute, they were running up and down the picket fence, about three rods from the house, as thick as bees around a hive....[12]

When comparing the above accounts of Liberia with an earlier description in the now defunct *Freedom's Journal*, which claimed that "the colony has passed its weakly infancy, and its smiles in the future will effect more than its cries," one wonders at the accuracy of descriptive accounts about the colony.[13] One such account, by a white contributor to *Freedom's Journal* describing himself as "plough Boy," gave a description of emigrants readying themselves to leave for Liberia. Keeping in mind that this article was not originally written for a black publication, but rather to project the "noble" character of free blacks as settlers in the "White press," its reprinting in the *Journal* was laden with social implications.

While images of intrigue and anxiety must have swept through the minds of readers as they read accounts of numerous departures to Africa, this reaction was tempered by the attitude of the black press, which viewed any form of colonization and emigration outside America as destructive to the task of commercial and religious uplift in a country which many perceived as their native land. For liberal whites, a more cathartic analysis was available, in that any removal of blacks either by colonization or emigration would release them from the social-psychological pale of slavery. But more significantly, it would reduce the fear of competing economically, socially and politically with a race which was generally despised. Thus, "plough Boy" states:

> Having occasion to go down to *Rocketts* this morning for the purpose of seeing a friend about to depart in the steamboat Norfolk, I was unexpectedly a witness to one of the most interesting scenes you can imagine. About seventy or eighty colored people (chiefly from this place) of both sexes, and all ages nearly, have been induced by the favorable accounts received from *Liberia*, to go and seek a new destiny in the land of their forefathers. They have been led to take this step, principally by the letter from time to time received from their former associate *Lott Cary*, who was among the first emigrants from Virginia to Africa. This history of this man is singular, and highly interesting, but I have not time now to give it in detail. Suffice it to say that he was born a slave, lived many years in Richmond, at length purchased his freedom, and having learned how to read and write, embraced with decision, among the foremost, the offer of the colonization society to attempt a settlement for our free coloured population, on the coast of Africa. Being gifted with strong powers of the mind, accustomed to laborious exertions, and deeply impressed of the late lamented Mr. Ashmun; and since the decease of that individual, appears to have had the principal charge of the colony. He has written very frequently to his former friends and associates here, and they have at last made up their minds to go and join him. They had taken their passage on board the two steamboats for Norfolk, in order to embark there for Africa, and at the moment of my reaching *Rocketts* (the port of Richmond) they were all in bustle and movement, embracing and bidding farewell and farewell, to the numerous friends and acquaintances they were about to leave behind. The number of these was surprising. They completely covered and thronged the wharves and there were altogether nearly two thousand of them. The scene of *parting* was truly affecting, and would require a better pen at description than mine, to do it justice. Sighs and sobs, and loud laments, were heard by all, and tears in abundance were shed — but still very many of their countenance seemed lighted up with hope, and annotated by the confidence of bettering their condition.[14]

Idealistic imagery of free blacks as settlers contrasted with numerous accounts describing emigrants in less than flattering terms. For example, Cornish and Wright insisted that any successful establishment of a colony had to be based on "Christian" ideals. Similarly, such a colony had to formulate policies which sanction and maintain principles of dominance over a populace judged to be heathenistic. They argued that once this judgement was made, a relationship of incompatibility existed, one which could only be maintained by the settlers' assumptions of superiority. Once done, it was "unavoidable" for its proponents to establish an "upper caste."[15]

What concerned these writers was "the character of the colonists, in reference to their qualification for redeeming the continent of Africa from the voices and pollutions of idolatry and heathenism." Who, they asked, would be qualified to "know that the structure of heathen society is to be reformed and purified—not crushed, as it inevitably must be, whenever a Christian class in society is set up in the same country."[16]

Turning to the supporters of the ACS and their comments on colonists sent to Liberia, the writers noted that even the head agent for the society, Governor Ashmun, writing to the Board of Managers, stated:

> In the proportion of 6 out of 10, the emigrants might be expected to be illiterate.... I must renew the painful inference that the emigrants to this country will bring with them no established moral habits.

The Reverend Jones, a native from the South, who from time to time was a missionary among the slaves, also commented on the Liberian colonists: "Generally speaking, they appear to us to be without God, and without hope, a nation of heathens in our very midst."

Not to be outdone, the vice president of the Virginia Colonization Society remarked, "A horde of miserable people; The objects of universal suspicion, subsisting by plunder...."

A brief description of the colonists by Virginia politician John Randolph called them "depositories of stolen goods and promoters of mischief." The influential corresponding secretary of the ACS, the Reverend R.R. Gurley, asserted they are "notoriously ignorant, degraded, and miserable, mentally diseased—scarcely reached in their debasement by the heavenly light."

As a final example of what many white colonizationists perceived as the character of colonists, Henry Clay's comments stand as stark evidence: "...contaminated themselves, they extend their vices to all around them, to the slave and to the White."[17]

Assuring their readers that an unholy alliance existed between the whole and its parts—the ACS and the colonists—black editors vigorously suggested to free blacks that their racial commitment could not be strengthened by aligning themselves with a colonization scheme; that any insistent claim for "individual elevation" and racial advancement must also renounce the schemes of slaveholders. In turn, they asked of white colonizationists:

> Why, Sirs, do you look for an impression on the colony dissimilar from the lineaments of the nation that makes it? Why for offspring wholly unlike the parent? Is it, that, *cause* has ceased to produce effect? Or, that men are beginning to gather thorns from grapes and figs from thistles?[18]

Accounts of living conditions in Liberia were also not very complimentary, and they usually portrayed the adversity associated with any underdeveloped agricultural society. For northern free blacks, with their increasingly urban social focus, descriptions of thatched houses and muddy floors were too reminiscent of plantation life and its association with economic and social deprivation. In a manner suggestive of Marx's observation that "the conditions of human perceptions alter with the conditions of man's material existence," free blacks increasingly viewed the urban environment as preferable for social elevation than the rural farming districts of North America.[19]

Efforts by editors to change this perception seemingly fell on deaf ears as free blacks clashed with European immigrants over jobs in cities all along the eastern coast, from Boston to Norfolk. Of no lesser importance were the resulting notions of urban superiority over rural life, which by the end of the antebellum period had sown the attitudes of social separation between urban and rural, north from south. Consequently, Liberia's denunciation in the press was also a denial of class, if not racial, superiority in that colonizers were often viewed as being duped by the ACS.

In a series of articles on Liberia reprinted from the *New York Tribune* by *Frederick Douglass' Paper*, "A.W." portrays Liberia as being "heartbending and almost incredible." Himself an emigrant, "A.W." claimed that while everyone complained about conditions in Liberia, the lack of opportunity to leave the country and report to the "outside" world the misrepresentation about Liberia was bound to occur. He characterized the colony as the "last refuge of the oppressed coloured man, and a country that could as easily have been subjected by the whites, if they had no other, and were, thus compelled to make the same sacrifice of thousands of lives."[26]

Major among his complaints was what he considered to be the insensitivity and poor training among physicians. Explaining that while "no class of men are more needed in this country than thoroughly educated and skillful physicians," life was cheap, and that often "the neglect of duty is partly owning to the want of competition and an independent supervision by some agent or commissioner who is too honest and brave to be influenced in favor of wrong, by kind treatment, good wine, or splendid dinners."[21]

Warming up to his topic, "A.W." continues:

> I will not harrow up your minds by any accounts of fearful mortality caused by the want of medical attention and the comforts of life among poor emigrants. Suffice it to say, that of two hundred of the emigrants of

the Banshee (which arrived at the time we did) sent up the St. Paul's river, one third have died, and our agents, citizens, and physicians are all in controversy about it, in two party papers, published in this city, called the *Herald* and the *Sentinel*....

I have spent one whole day investigating the case of the Morgan Dix, which sailed from Baltimore, Nov. 1851, and arrived at Bassa with one hundred and fifty-one, all well. (see African report for Dec. 1851 and April 1852). They were then supplied with means—with a sawmill and agricultural implements. But where are they now? Could the grave disgorge those old gun-boxes into which their corpses were buried, it would disclose a horrid tale of the neglect of the physicians' agent or society [ACS];—or exhibit the murderous work of sending fresh emigrants to people new districts of country that resemble no place so much as golgoths. Read and understand, that of these *one hundred and fifty-one emigrants there are but nine survivors*. Others maintain that there are fourteen. Grant that there are fourteen survivors. I challenge the colonization society and their agents here and in America to prove that there are more. And all this is the result of sending men to the most unhealthy part of this country, and packing them into old, rickety, thatched houses, in which, the emigrants tell me, they had to hold umbrellas to keep them from the pelting rain. Besides, they have but one physician for Bassa and Simon which I think are one hundred and fifty miles apart, and I have too much evidence to not believe that some of the emigrants actually starve and die for want of food and medical care. —But let me speak softly. I well-nigh forgot that I must buy my goods and provisions in New York, Boston and Baltimore for my store, and after talking so loudly, I may be troubled to find an agent to discount my drafts, and forward goods in colonization vessels. Besides, I may be persecuted by a pack of hungry pork-eaters in Liberia.[22]

In a letter to the *Weekly Anglo-African*, a writer complained about the "meanness" and "coldblooded treatment" extended to Liberia by the American government in the area of economics. Asserting that Liberia's relations with America were becoming increasingly strained due to an unequal, nonreciprocal trade agreement, he cites one case in particular:

Mr. E.J. Roy, a man of color, emigrated a few years ago, from Ohio to Liberia, and by enterprise, industry, and much perseverence [sic], became a successful merchant there. Well, Mr. Roy, not willing to confine his mercantile operations to one or two continents, arrived the other day at our ports in his own brig, Eusidia N. Roy, a first sailor of over 300 tons, carrying Liberian register and colors, and with a cargo of African produce valued at $30,000. On this cargo, Mr. Roy was compelled to pay duty and a tonnage duty of 80¢ per ton upon his vessel. Why was this? Simply because he was a colored man, hailing from a colored government....

But says our American government, there is no reciprocity treaty between us and Liberia. And why not? Simply because we Americans

> refuse to form one with them, and force our goods upon the Liberian people on the same terms as other governments, who have formed just and equitable treaties; taking care, at the same time, to impose the heaviest possible duties that the absence of a treaty will allow. The American government has never paid the first cent to Liberia in the way of tonnage duties since she has been a colony.
>
> If we could with as little expense, manufacture a few hundred more Black merchants, like Mr. Roy, having them arrive at port every day or so, freighted with African produce, Uncle Sam might derive quite a handsome reserve—one sufficient certainly to grease the wheels of not only that part of the political machinery in the New York Custom House, but even in WASHINGTON.[23]

And with a slap at the press, who obviously had an interest in line with their financial backers, the writer concludes:

> The press that have at all ventured to mention the subject, have with characteristic meanness, spoken not one word of the injustice of the act, but with reference only to the probable pecuniary losses likely to ensue if such a course be insisted on by our government. Verily, we are a magnanimous people—a model for the rest of the world![24]

Throughout the antebellum history of the black press, antipathy to Liberian colonization did not hinder some free blacks from recognizing the economic possibilities in successful colonization, those not totally dominated by imperialistic jurisdiction, if that were possible. One such observer, writing under the pseudonym of "Viator," was quick to envision these advantages which are a major necessity for successful development. As an example of this he noted that the settlers' general ignorance about which season to emigrate proved to be a major liability, as seasonally inclement weather made the construction of homes and shelters difficult.[25]

Frederick Douglass argued that colonization, as promoted by the ACS in 1849, was geared to divert the attention of free blacks from the political and economic deterioration of slavery, and the growing effects of the antislavery movement. Douglass, in his paper, explained that:

> For two hundred and twenty eight years has the colored man toiled over the soil of America, under a burning sun and a driver's lash—plowing, planting, reaping, that White men might roll in ease, their hands unhardened by labor, and their brows unmoistened by the waters of menial toil; and now that the moral sense of mankind is beginning to revolt at this system of foul treachery and cruel wrong, and is demanding its overthrow, the mean and cowardly oppressor is mediating plans to expel the colored man entirely from the country. Shame upon the guilty wretches that dare propose, and all that countenance such a proposition.

> We live here—have loved here, have a right to live here, and mean to live here.[26]

It can be stated that in no significant manner did the black press advocate emigration to Liberia during the antebellum period. Efforts by Russwurm, as editor of *Freedom's Journal*, and years later by Thomas Hamilton's *The Weekly Anglo-African*, were limited in the former's case by the editor's departure to Liberia and, in the latter case, by a shifting of political emphasis as a result of the Civil War. When the issue of colonization did appear in the press, it was vigorously rejected as a viable path for individual or group elevation, except in cases where missions were clearly stated as the intended goal. Even in these instances, free blacks such as Alexander Crummell maintained an ideological position which was aimed at minimizing the validity of the indigenous population's attributes in deference to Christian expectations.

With the exception of a few, upper-strata free blacks found it hard to identify with a non-Western culture which they concluded possessed all the attributes of powerlessness. This they expressed with increased fervor in the press, as they sanctioned the prevailing social norms which declared the use of power as necessary to maintain freedom and respect. Conversely, it was believed that the denial of power was subjugation. Consequently, for many free blacks, even symbolic identification with power or authority—that is, the maintaining of upper class/racial mannerisms, was sufficient. As a result, identification with colonization as proposed by Clay and others was intolerable, and therefore, interpreted as a step backwards, towards possible assimilation with a "primitive" society and people, or, as *The Colored American* defined it, "a very GREAT hoax, got up by colonizationists for effect, a last shift to delude some, and thereby save a *sinking ship*."[27] Such a suggestion, it was concluded, was meant to imply free blacks' inferiority and inability to compete successfully in an open society with white America. By rejecting such a premise, free blacks were attempting to confront their status of inferiority.

In essence, the free blacks' desire for American acceptance and their subsequent rejection were not total expressions or desires for assimilation, but rather exertions of a trapped nationalism; a nationalism which America periodically rejected throughout the postrevolutionary years, but called upon during the Civil War. Therefore, one is not surprised by an 1849 Douglass editorial on colonization, where he asserts:

We are of the opinion that the Free Colored people generally mean to live in America, and not in Africa; and to appropriate a large sum for our removal would merely be a waste of the public money. We do not mean to go to Liberia. Our minds are made up to live here if we can, or die here if we must; so every attempt to remove us, will be, as it ought to be, labor lost. Here we are in bondage on these shores; it is idle to think of inducing any considerable number of the Free colored people to quit this for a foreign land.[28]

Nor are we surprised by an emigrationist who responded to the proposal of Haitian emigration in 1860 with concerns about nationalism by asserting:

...to him who desire the elevation of our people, as such, this then, is the question. How can we make ourselves a distinct people and a homogeneous nation? ... We hold that all measures for our advancement as a race, must contemplate the preservation of our identity, and the ennoblement of our hue. We consider it one of the worst features of our exceptional social position, that we are come to look upon our color as a badge of degradation, and are anxious to remove it.... In the overshadowing presence and constantly increasing bulk of the White population, there is no prospect for us, but subordination and absorption. The idea of retaining our present social attitude, in the hope of ameliorating its conditions, involves not the elevation, but the extinction of the most enlightened portion of our race. Surely this is not the result which any true lover of his race, who desires to wipe off the stigma which civilization has attached to the word NEGRO, wishes to attain? Our perfect development and consequent preparation for the work we have to do, requires our separation from the influences which draw us apart and cause us in our prurient desire for recognition as Americans, to lose sight of our duty to ourselves.[29]

Emigration Movement to Haiti

The emigrants' preparation for the social-political role of "settler" was a much discussed and debated issue among editors and contributors of the black press. Though experience of free blacks as settlers dating back to 1824 undoubtedly left an impression on many as to the hardships involved in such a venture, not to mention the cost in lives, others appeared ready to take the risk. One major critic of emigration, specifically Haitian, was a Glasgow-educated free black, Dr. James McCune Smith. Throughout this period, Smith considered it his duty to attack emigration and its leading supporters, such as J.T. Holly and H.H. Garnet. Describing Haitian emigration in the mid-1820s as a failure for the 2,000 to 4,000 free black emigrants, Smith maintained that responsible, influential spokesmen for the race should not have to be reminded that, "your duty to our people is to tell them to aim higher. ... In advising them to go to Haiti, you direct them to sink lower."[30]

Asking "to be excused from emigration either to Abbeokuto [Nigeria] or Haiti," Smith, in a rhetorical style reminiscent of earlier anti-colonizationist protestations, reminded the reader that, regardless of how tiring the argument may be, one is still bound by past pledges. Thus, Smith argued, the unfulfilled pledge to free the slaves or elevate free blacks symbolized a commitment to "labor in this land and for this land," until all is accomplished.[31]

Attempting to demonstrate the futility of emigration as opposed to the hourly advance towards the struggle for "affranchisement," Smith asks of emigrationist H.H. Garnet:

> Look at the advancement in wealth, intelligence and esteem that our people have made in the last ten years. In one of the eastern states [Massachusetts] we have advanced from step to step until we stand on equal citizenship. In Philadelphia, there is a school taught exclusively by colored teachers, in which youth pursue studies as far and with greater thoroughness than was taught in college from which you and I were excluded on account of our complexion. In New York City, in that very neighborhood through which we often fought our way to school and from school, an IRISH CONSTITUENCY have erected on the old site a splendid new school-house for colored children.... Do you ever go into Wall Street? Have you noticed quite a number of colored youth, neatly dressed, hurrying from bank to bank with vast sums of money in their hands? Do you not know as well as I, that it only requires dash and pluck for these young men to rise higher and higher?

Convinced the the African-American was wanted and needed in America, he repudiates Garnet's position by avowing:

> No, my dear sir, the Free Blacks of the United States are wanted in the United States. The people of Maryland said so the other day when they voted that they should not be reduced to slavery. Even the people of Charleston, South Carolina, say they cannot spare them as Free men, even to be converted into slaves. And our people want to stay, and will stay at home: we are in for the fight and will fight it out here. Shake yourself free from these migrating phantasms, and join us with your might and main. You belong to us, and we want your whole soul....[32]

One week later, Garnet answered Smith's comments with a retort replete with class innuendos, which placed the issue of emigration within a social framework laden with class conflict:

What are you doing for the young people of New York, and for those of the whole country? You are not an inch in advance of the emigrationist in this matter. You saw us struggling last winter in this city to establish a reading room for our sons, and you, and your whole tribe refused to contribute a cent to keep it open, and when it failed, your standing army laughed.... You anti-emigrationists seem to desire to see the hundreds of colored men and women who have good trades to stay here and be the druges and menials of White men, who will not employ or work with them ... and you anti-emigrationist, Dr. Smith, are no better in this respect, than your hard-hearted White brethren. You likewise, "Do not employ niggers." You pass by the black Tailor, Mantus-maker, Milliner, and Shoemaker, and Carpenter, and employ White people who curse you to your teeth. Why, your own party will not even employ a Black doctor as a general thing. A few weeks ago, an Irish gentleman showed me a beautiful mansion on the thriving sixth avenue, which to your credit, belongs to you. I looked upon it, and felt proud of the success of my early friend.... I looked in vain to discover a dark face at work. There was not one.... By the side of your property, another equally imposing [structure] was going up, owned by the Rev. James M Gloucester, and I saw there also an entire absence of the practical application of your professed principles. Mr. Gloucester is the largest Real Estate and house owner in the state of New York among the Colored People. But who builds and repairs these buildings? I mean the property of Dr. Smith and the Rev. Mr. Gloucester. Tell me, do you even go so far as to hire your house to Black people? There is one colored tradesman whom you patronize, that is the Black "Barber," for no one else will shave you![33]

While the *Anglo-African's* editor, Thomas Hamilton, published the most extensive articles, pro and con, on emigration, its format was basically neutral; a cross-section of opinions was generally published. However, as an increased number of articles on this issue were submitted to the journal, a shifting of ideological priority began to take place. This was dramatically noticeable during the editorship of George Lawrence from March to August 1861, as articles and notices pertaining to emigration were published. This was indeed a significant change from earlier newspapers, whose announced anti-emigrationist attitudes limited rather than enhanced a free flow of ideas on the issue.

For example, with a new editorial policy, articles pertaining to the names of emigration agents for Haiti were periodically printed in the weekly issues of *The Anglo-African* from at least the beginning of 1861. With the publishing of agents' names, the issue of Haitian emigration received a sense of legitimacy and recognition beyond that of any one individual's approval or disapproval. Yet, as was to be expected, such open propagandizement established a format for critics. For instance, in an advertisement on Haitian emigration, signed by James Redpath, a white abolitionist and emigrationist friend of John Brown wrote:

> By virtue of instruction from the government of Haiti, I have made the following appointments for the purpose of carrying out the project of emigration of the present administration of the republic [Haiti].

The article announced that Garnet would be the "resident" agent for New York, J.T. Holly would act as a traveling agent for New Jersey and Pennsylvania, and John Brown, Jr., would represent Canada. Other agents were listed as representing the states of Michigan, Indiana, Ohio, District of Columbia, Boston and the seaboard slave states. Criticism coming from many sources was not long in developing, as leading free black spokesmen questioned the wisdom of such tactics in the press. For example, Delany's letter from Chatham, Canada West, to Holly in New Haven, Connecticut, explained:

> I have nothing to say against Haitian emigration, except that I am surprised that in the face of the intelligent BLACK MEN who favor it, two of whom have been to that country and one to Jamaica (yourself, Mr. Harris, and Mr. Garnet), the government would appoint OVER THEM, to encourage Black emigration, a White man, thereby acknowledging Negro inferiority, and the charges recently made against them by Dr. J. McCune Smith, that according to their estimation, "next to God is the White man...."
>
> Neither do I regard or believe Mr. Redpath, the Haitian government agent, nor any other White man, competent to judge and decide upon the destiny of the colored people or the fitness of any place for the betterment of their condition, any more than I should a Frenchman to direct the destiny of an Englishman. If they have not now — if we with our claim and boasted equality have not yet reached the point of competency to judge and decide for ourselves, what, when, and where is the best for us to do or go, but must needs have White men to act for us, then indeed are we wholly unfit to fill the places they claim for us and should be under White masters.[34]

By 1861, proclamations referring to the guidelines to be used in emigrant selection were also being publicized. For example, "circular No. 1," subtitled, "Blacks, men of color, and Indians in the United and the British North American Province," proclaimed:

> Friends, I am [Redpath] authorized and instructed by the government of the republic [Haiti] to offer a home, and a free homestead in Haiti.
>
> Such of you as are unable to pay for your passage will be provided with the means of defraying it.
>
> Two classes of emigrants are invited — laborers and farmers. None of either class, or any class will be furnished with passports who cannot produce before sailing proof of good character for industry and integrity....[35]

Though Delany was critical of Redpath, he was not overly despondent about Haitian emigration nor of its possible detraction from his own emigration efforts in Nigeria, the Niger Valley Exploring Party. Advising Holly about the dangers of a movement being "precipitous—not sufficiently matured," he suggested that, as with Africa, what was needed was not a notion of a promised land with a spontaneous mass exodus of blacks from America. Moreover, he asserted, "the country needs no laborers, they're everywhere abounding, industriously employed in various occupations." But rather, "A select and intelligent people to guide and direct the industry, and promote civilization by the establishment of higher social organizations and the legitimate development of our inexhaustible commerce, which promises not only certain wealth to us, but all the rest of the world.... In this we desire not to shed their (the southern monsters') blood, but make them shed their tears."[36]

The opposite of this position was alluded to a few months earlier by H.H. Garnet who, in *The Weekly Anglo-African,* stated that for Haiti, a larger population was critical, "as any reluctance to do so" would leave her national economy in a weak state, inciting western subversion, if not outright invasion. While Garnet claimed that Haiti's potential capability for maintaining a population of 10,000,000 was not only possible but a necessity, with regard to Africa, the case was different:

> She does not need population, for that she has in abundance. *She needs but a few to direct the labor*, the elements of which are on her soil and to call them forth into systematic, productive, and economical activity. It is the power of the Colored Men of America to supply the wants of both countries, and thus give the death blow to slavery, and bless our scattered race throughout the world.

Making a concluding appeal to his major protagonist, Garnet explains to McCune Smith that:

> These are my views in brief, and I trust no one will trouble himself further about the probability of a change in views. Both of these grand and stupendous schemes have entered so deeply into my heart and thought that they have become a part of my existence, and hence, while I live, there can be no change in my principles and opinions on this subject.[37]

On this same issue of Haitian emigration, Holly, also a major proponent of "selective" exodus to Haiti, expressed the view that "Emigration is not only a necessity for the political enfranchisement of the colored people of the United States; but they are the only people in a proper position to contribute to the national regeneration of Haiti."[38]

Pertinent to this point was his rejection of "a nationality" based simply on geography. Only by positing the need for a strong national character, Holly argued, could the sinews of strength be developed which would confront and overcome the demands of a nineteenth-century slaveholding America. Indicating annoyance at those who viewed emigration as simply an escape, a movement devoid of nationalistic goals which would lead to the same failures as earlier emigrants, Holly demanded:

> We do not simply want a Negro nationality, but we want a strong, powerful, enlightened and progressive Negro nationality, equal to the demands of the nineteenth century, and capable of commanding the respect of all the nations of the earth.

Using Africa as an example of "simply Negro nationalities," Holly explains that Africa contains many such social-political entities:

> Almost every town can boast a King and a royal court. But the question now pressing upon us for solution is not to add to the number already existing; but to give to some one of them that grand national development which we have indicated. Then, around which of the many centers of Negro nationalities already existing shall the genius and power of our race be concentrated, in order to accomplish this result? Shall it be Foulah, Jaloff, Dehomey, Liberia, or Haiti? Thus, then, it will be directed to Hayti or Africa, the question narrows itself down to the work of removing the *disabilities of existing Negro nationalities.*[39]

The centralization of power in the hands of free blacks intent upon establishing a foundation for nationalistic development outside America, coupled with their challenging of nineteenth-century European-American political power in the Western hemisphere, were major ideological assumptions presumed by Holly as necessary for the establishing of a viable nationality. In this view he was not alone, as a writer using the pseudonym "volunteer" asserted:

> Listen! We want our rights! No one is going to give them to us, so perforce we must take them. In order to do this, we must have a strong nationality somewhere—respected, feared. We require a government that can not only catch slave dealers and slave holders, but *will* hang them so that they shall be to the Black, what England has been to the White races, the hope of progress and the guarantee of permanent civilization. Look at her position; she is at the center of a circle in whose plane lie Cuba, Central America, and the southern slave states. From that center let but the

first of Freedom radiate until it shall enkindle, in the whole of the vast area, the sacred flame of liberty upon the altar of every Black man's heart, and you affect at once the abolition of slavery and the regeneration of our race.

Let us prepare, then, to aid Hayti in the coming struggle, with our sympathies, our fortunes, and our lives. Contribute arms and hands to bear them.[40]

The black press was utilized as a medium for opinion, a means by which ideas, once published, became a part of the public domain as well as a basis for social motivation. While public articulation of one's position on critical issues provided a framework from which consensus formation might occur, on the issue of emigration the reverse was closer to the truth. Expressed disagreements in the press were more a reflection of ideological conflicts among black leaders than among a majority of the free black populace. What is more, the elitist bent of many spokesmen, pro and con, black and white, on the issue of emigration often circumvented any question pertaining to the economic-political needs of the totally disenfranchised and uneducated black populace, regardless of rhetorical appeals to the contrary.

For example, James Redpath, head agent for the Haitian emigrant movement, continually faced criticism not only because he was white, but as one black Presbyterian minister put it, he "is a comparative stranger to us, and we to him." Annoyed at the presumptuous attitude of black leaders and the power incorporated by Redpath's position, the minister explained:

> He comes among us, establishing his headquarters in Boston, and proceeds to parcel out our country into large districts, assigning one to each of his own appointed agents; as if to say to us NOLENS VOLENS, "you have got to submit to our administration."
>
> All this done under a foreign seal, with that flourish of the pen and air of authority peculiar to second and third rate White men who happen to find themselves invested with power in our matters. But patriotism, sound philosophy, and theological fidelity show it to be a great blunder in colored ministers to accept of these appointments under the circumstances, and at this time. You can no more serve the people under two governments than you can serve two masters.[41]

Expounding upon the rights of "Anglo-Africans" to explore, settle and develop independently of white approval or suggestion, he further argued that racism which entrapped the African was supported by a system of wealth, refinement and intellectualism structured to demonstrate the African's inferiority. Citing the influx of European emigrants to the United States as an example, he asserted:

> If a poor White foreigner hoping to better his condition, leaves his native land and comes to our shores, the act is called emigration; but if a Black man actuated by the same motives leaves this country for another, it is called expatriation. He may go, however, to California, or distant Australia, or to any other portion of the globe, so long as he follows in the wake and is under the control of White men; but let him attempt to set up for himself, and he is soon warned with tearful eyes to beware of expatriation.[42]

By the latter part of the 1850s, clear indications began to appear that at least one black newspaper, *The Anglo-African*, was prepared to publish more substantive articles on emigration, with a major emphasis on Haiti. By 1861, articles describing the living conditions, average volume of imports and exports, along with the most suitable cash products available, found their way into the pages of this newspaper. The distribution of this information not only indicated an assurance that the press was able to deal with controversial issues from a more liberal perspective, but also tended to add a level of legitimacy to the idea of Haitian emigration.

For instance, in the first issue of *The Anglo-African*, after its change in editors in March 1861, a policy statement on emigration by the paper proclaimed that while the paper had not previously expressed any opinion "editorially on the question of emigration to Haiti ... it has permitted the utmost latitude of debate, it has preserved a rather ominous silence as to the merits of the controversy." The editorial continued to proceed directly to the issue at hand, attempting to fasten the cords of racial responsibility by stating:

> We are not in favor of an indiscriminate emigration anywhere—to Canada, the Far West, Africa, Central America, or Haiti. Those of us who are content with our present condition and prospects, who feel that HERE we can work the most efficiently for the anti-slavery cause, will not and ought not to emigrate anywhere, for to leave what we believe to be our post of duty would be criminal and cowardly. But neither do we hold, on the other hand, that it is our duty BECAUSE we are colored men, to remain in the United States; and we have no sympathy with the theory occasionally advanced that to leave this country is in all cases a desertion of our brethren in bonds. It is the majority of the Whites alone, not the colored men or abolitionist in any degree, who are guilty of slavery in the United States, and on that majority, therefore, devolves the responsibility of the crime, and on them will the penalty for continuing the iniquity be inflicted.[43]

Propagating the rhetoric of individualism and free choice, the editor then asserts:

> Let everyone, then, be fully persuaded in his own mind whether to remain or emigrate. Let no man act without first counting the cost. Let him calmly investigate his chances for a decent future here; and, if they do not appear to him favorable, let him, both for his own sake and his children's, investigate what other countries offer him.... Should anyone, having determined to emigrate ask our advice in seeking a location, we should recommend him, without hesitation, to select the dominions of the queen of the Antilles as his future home. Hayti possesses various advantages over every other field that has opened for exiles of our race from the United States.[44]

Interestingly enough, the use of the word "exiles," instead of "settlers," suggests a point of view on the part of the editor which implies not only banishment from America, but the forceful displacement or dislocation of one people by another, regardless of the obstacles entailed. Consequently, the suggestion that America be rejected in its entirety, or that its basic political and social framework be denounced as impractical, was circumvented, if not ignored, by most antebellum free blacks, regardless of their opinions on emigration. By contrast, to be "exiled" afforded the emigrant the opportunity to leave America, without necessarily absolving himself of western orientation or cultural beliefs. Thus, for Holly, Garnet and, to an increasing degree, Frederick Douglass, *The Anglo-African*'s decision to opt for Haitian emigration ("exile") was significant, for it lent a form of "public" approval to a position which was otherwise relegated to "radical" spokesmen.

Defending his position while expounding on the benefits of Haitian emigration, the editor, George Lawrence, explained:

> To Hayti, we can go in less time than it requires to travel from New York to Minnesota, and the facilities for returning are equally easy. It is inhabited by men exclusively of our race, who are there demonstrating our capacity for self-government. Those who ostracize us here, themselves are pariahs there. It is a country of unsurpassing fertility, unquestionably the most fertile island in the New World. It is capable of supporting ten millions of inhabitants; it has the best harbors, richest mines, most valuable forests in the West Indies. It is a natural paradise, requiring only intelligent labor to develop its exhaustless resources. It has a government enlightened, liberal, and generous ... whose grand ambition is to create a colored England in America. Yet let no man think that paradise itself would be an EDEN WITHOUT LABOR. It would be madness to go to Hayti with the idea of suddenly becoming rich in idleness. Not many of us should go there, for sometime at least, unless he intends to cultivate the soil, to such emigrants, if they settle together in communities, the future holds fortunes in stores.[45]

While the desire to recreate the cultural attributes of a colonizing European power in the Caribbean—a "colored England in the Americas"—was amusing to many, *The Anglo-African* sought to minimize dissension in the press based upon personality differences. Here it was argued:

> ...the controversy which has been waged in the columns of this journal has been in a great degree irrelevant, and we shall most firmly put an end to the offensive personalities which have distinguished it. We shall not permit any trifling arguing for the mere sake of victory, or allow any dishonest garbling of the statements of others; no attacks on gentlemen of irreproachable character because they are opposed to it. Writers, therefore, will take notice to confine themselves to the question, which is not whether Mr. Garnet is this or that; or whether Mr. Holly is the one thing; or whether John Crown Jr. and James Redpath are not as devoted friends of our race as Dr. Smith or Dr. Delany, or Dr. Pennington; But simply, as Mr. Holly expressed it, this; "will you accept the invitation extended to you by the Haytian government?"
>
> Let our correspondents take the negative or affirmative as they please; But if they prefer to denounce their opponents instead, they must excuse us if we refuse to print their letters. It may be fun for them, but it is death for us.[46]

One such edition of *The Weekly Anglo-African* provided a detailed description of the traveling arrangements for Haitian emigrants, complete with a weekly Navy Ration schedule for each day of the week (see Table 9, p. 224). Besides considerations of food, there was an attempt to overcome the unpreparedness of previous waves of emigrants to Haiti and Liberia by establishing financial arrangements which would displace the burden of the initial cost for the trip. For example, Redpath (surely to the annoyance of protagonists such as McCune Smith), speaking on behalf of the Haitian Bureau of Emigration, announced:

> I have come to the resolution to have the ship provide provisions for all the emigrants, and to include the expense of board in the sum to be specified in the contract. That is to say, passengers will either pay $18 for an emigrant passage, their board being found and cooked for them, or sign a contract to pay that sum after one, two, or three years, as they prefer with the important exception, also, that those who may remain more than three years, and decide not to accept of the government grant of lands, will never be required to repay any amount whatever.[47]

Statements such as these did not ingratiate Redpath or the *Anglo*'s editor, George Lawrence, to black leadership, who viewed them as insensitive, tactless and disrespectful to their already precarious positions as "race leaders." On the same page, a listing of the *Laws on Emigration* for those of African or Indian descent specified in four articles the legal structure which emigrants were expected to adhere to. In addition, there was a civil code which provided for "those who possess the required qualifications to become Haytians, in order to enable them with facility to enter the immediate enjoyment of the right attached to naturalization."[48] In a similar article, Haiti's criteria for accepting emigrants was specified in a seven-point proposal stating:

> 1. The government will also find remunerative work for those of you whose means will not permit you to begin immediately an independent cultivation.
> 2. Emigrants are invited to settle in communities....
> 3. The same protection and civil rights that the laws give to Haytians are solemnly guaranteed to the emigrant.
> 4. The fullest religious liberty will be secured to them, they will never be called upon to support the Roman Catholic Church.
> 5. No military service will be demanded of them, excepting that they shall form military companies and drill themselves once a month.
> 6. All the necessary personal effects, machinery and agricultural instruments introduced by the emigrants shall be entered free of duty.
> 7. The emigrants shall be at liberty to leave the country at any moment they please; but those whose passage shall be paid by government, if they wish to return before the expiration of the three years, will be required to stand the money expended on their account. A contract, fixing the amount, will be made with each emigrant before leaving the continent.[49]

Efforts to procure emigrants were even extended to the slave states, as an article in the same newspaper titled "Agents for the Confederate States" indicated that the emigrants from the cotton and Gulf states would be welcome, but that they "must make the best arrangements that they can for a passage to Hayti . . . and the Republic will help them to defray the expenses thus incurred by repaying to each of them eighteen dollars, on the same terms as a passage is advanced to emigrants from the northern states and Canada."[50]

The final page in this edition was devoted to two articles which analyzed Haiti. The first was from a historical perspective, with a passage extolling the Haitian struggle for liberty and the need to protect oneself from the hypocrisies of white republicans. Written by Holly, this article emphasized the "dissemination of sound religious morality as the basis of public virtue, and the cultivation of literature, the Arts and Sciences, as the sources of national prosperity."[51] However, for the reader who wanted a sense of what the emigrant was experiencing, articles describing the various ships preparing to leave for Haiti were descriptive enough:

Emigration vs. Assimilation   **144**

> A large number of persons congregated Wednesday morning, the 2nd, to witness the departure of the Brig Janet Kidston, for Hayti with 61 emigrants. Notice had been given before starting, and about 11 o'clock, passengers and visitors assembled below deck....
> Most of the emigrants were from Philadelphia, where they had located themselves after having been driven from their homes in the south by the cursed enactments that sought to deprive them of that small moiety of freedom which had been before meted out (Fugitive Slave Acts, 1850 and the Dred Scott decision and enactment). Mr. John W. Williams was secured by Mr. James Redpath to bring on from Philadelphia all persons ready to go by this vessel. While there he succeeded in getting hold of two fugitives, and despite the effort of pursuers, who watched his every movement, one was safely forwarded to Canada, and the other is bounding o'er the billows towards Hayti's friendly shores. Most of the emigrants seemed in good spirits and to be quite intelligent; a number of them speak French and a few, three different languages. While preparations were being made for starting, the "Flying Eagle," bound for Port au Prince, Hayti, passed by having on board eleven passengers. She was heartily cheered, her passengers returned them with a will.[52]

For the potential antebellum emigrant, such articles were rare, even within the pages of *The Anglo-African*. As the editor explained in clarifying his paper's position on emigration, "We would add, further, that only a limited space can be given to the discussion of the question."[53] However, national events did affect free blacks' awareness on emigration, as did the encouragement by the Haitian government for emigrants via newspaper advertisements. It was an increased sense of powerlessness by a power-oriented segment of free blacks which led them to perceive the benefits of identifying with a national structure outside of America. The possibility of economic independence, without the restrictive bonds of racial classification, seemed not only possible but, for an increasing number of free blacks, the only positive step away from political and social ambiguity. While the general movement continually stalled on the question of "saving the heathen," and lifting a godless Africa, Haitian emigrationists were able to argue in the press the value of settling in a country which already possessed not only political independence, but a Christian foundation. Yet antagonists continually warned of an earlier failure in 1824, and that failure would occur again as long as language differences, climatic conditions and cultural backgrounds existed between the emigrant and the Haitian. But more importantly, assimilationists feared a growing "commercial" drain if the settlers were successful.

To this extent, *The Anglo-African*'s attempts to present a more positive image of Haitian emigration concluded that:

Our hope must be in ourselves—in the energy and vigor, the ability and courage we claim to possess, and for all of which we shall have a full one. We must throw off the yoke of policy, of subserviency, of submission, mark out a line of conduct, and pursue it carefully to the end. "It is the fear of death alone which makes oppression possible," and it behooves us to act in that spirit.[54]

While the black press was increasingly becoming a vehicle of information, a platform of ideas for the articulate, it was also the stage for bitter, vindictive infighting on the issue of emigration among educated free blacks. Also, their readership among free blacks was severely limited and often discouraged by abolitionist whites. Yet for those who could and did receive the intended messages, what emerged was a reflection of conflict not only between black and white abolitionists and antislavery advocates, but interfactional disputes based on differences in class and caste perceptions. Efforts towards an effective Haitian emigration policy provided prime examples of this conflict.

Projections of nationalism in Haiti had not fully penetrated the ideological conclaves of free black society by 1861. When the issue was addressed in the press, it was invariably discussed within a rhetorical context limited by ideological constraints of upper-strata blacks. As a battleground for ideological debate on Haitian emigration throughout the first few months of 1861, *The Anglo-African* provides an insight into the minds of black leadership and their problem in discerning the nature of the political situation before them. By March 1861, Holly, Garnet, Delany, Smith, Redpath, and a host of writers using various pseudonyms attacked and counterattacked each other's positions with zest. Never was the antebellum black press so divided. Never was this press so passionate in its appeals for one opinion over another.

For example, the Reverend S.V. Berry found it necessary to write:

> We have men among us whose views are respected, men of enlightened intellect, of large views and Liberal minds. Such are Douglass, and Garnet, and Dr. James McCune Smith. These men have spoken—they are qualified to speak and their opinions are entitled to respect. The first two have declared their fullest approval of the whole scheme, while the last bases his disapproval only on a contingency. The failure twenty-seven years ago, [a previous effort to emigrate to Haiti] has nothing more to do with the success of the present, than to guard us against the causes which produced that failure—it may therefore be regarded as the prestige of future success. It is to be hoped that the conduct of the colored people of the United States with references to the Haytian movement will be marked throughout with that unanimity and wisdom, and good sense which it deserves. We have long wearied ourselves with vain efforts to do

something, which in the end has amounted to nothing. Let us remember that our conduct in the matter of Haytian emigration, is watched by the whole civilized world, and therefore involves the character of our whole people.

This is not a matter for sarcasms and witticisms, nor are these times for men of wisdom to indulge such dispositions—the best efforts of our best powers are needed—the cowardly attacks of men, who have not the honesty nor the courage and manhood, to assume the responsibility of their own sentiments hardly deserves to be regarded; yet I desire to say to "A Presbyterian Minister," that my application for an appointment as agent for the promotion of the Haytian emigration, was to show my appreciation of the conduct of the Haytian people towards us, and to intimate my good wishes as well to those who shall feel disposed to go as those who choose to stay....[55]

On the same page, another writer who called himself "One of the people," with a strained patience which suggested an annoyance with petit-bourgeoisie vindictiveness, asked of H.H. Garnet:

We have watched your course with a great deal of anxiety—you have in previous years taught us to look at this courtry as our home, to feel that providence had for some inscrutable reason permitted us to be placed here ... with such feelings we have grown up, and this we have inculcated in our children.

I need not go through the arguments used to sustain these views, for you are better acquainted with them than I, for it was from yourself and S.R. Ward, that I heard the strongest reasoning on the subject. If there is now a change in your views, we would like to hear the reasons for it. We may not have our minds as open to the new truths as if they had not been previously biased, but still the vocation you follow has inured you to the utterance of unpalatable truths. Will you then give us through the columns of the "Anglo" a clear statement of your present views on the subject of emigration; I am sure the editor will be willing, for there are, so many persons seeking light on this subject, that his subscription list will be greatly increased by it—all I would ask is to avoid personalities. We do not care about Dr. Smith's, or Mr. Gloucester's private character, or how they build their houses or spend their money, that does not affect the subject of emigration at all. I have asked this method of getting your views before the public in preference to either an oral discussion or public meeting, because there are many persons out of New York, who could not attend a meeting, that are deeply interested in the subject, and we all know from experience how little light is usually thrown upon a subject by oral discussion.[56]

Playing a major role throughout this debate was Dr. Smith's abhorrence of emigration, Haitian or Liberian. Critical to his view was the belief that the dissimilarities in Haitian culture were too great to be overcome by a people already overwhelmed by the realities of the United States. Explaining this position in full, he asserted that:

I do not see reason to believe that the present experiment will be any more successful because:

1. While the Haitian government then gave emigrants six month's board and shelter [in 1824], NOW offers emigrants only eight day's board and lodging [see Redpath's guide to Haiti, p. 94].

2. Dissimilarity of language is the same now as in 1824. Our people do not understand French; the Haytians do not speak English. "A knowledge of the French language," says Mr. Redpath, "is absolutely essential to everyone who intends to reside in Hayti." He afterwards proves that a knowledge of Creole is equally necessary. How many of the emigrants whom you prayerfully dismissed to Hayti the other day knew anything of French?

3. Dissimilarity of manners and morals. Thirty years have made a vast difference in the manners and morals of the Free Colored people of the United States—especially in the now Free States, we are almost exclusively of the Protestant faith, and live and believe, as you know, in the marriage relation, and are accustomed to the proprieties, the joys, and the responsibilities that spring from them....

4. In your manifesto you say that Hayti needs population, and that you propose to remedy this by sending thither our colored population. The Bureau of Emigration is happily located, with this view, in Boston, where among the colored people in the year 1859, there were 326 deaths and only 183 births! How long would it take this class to populate Hayti or Hades? The true remedy for sparseness of population in Hayti is, that the Haytians should become so far Christians as to respect the marriage relations; and this, I take it, could be done by the preaching of one apostle sooner than by the landing of a few hundred emigrants, which will be the extent of your labors.

Your duty to the people is to tell them to aim higher. In advising them to go to Hayti, you direct them to sink lower....

We affirm by our lives and conduct that, if degraded, it is not by our innate inferiority, but by the active oppression of those who outnumber us. The Haytians have a proverb, universal among the masses, "apres Bon Jo-Blanc"—"Next to God is the White man." The Haytians, too, like the Liberians, further admit their inferiority by making it an article of their constitution that "No white man can become a Haytian (or Liberian) citizen...."

As the beloved pastor of a large and intelligent people in the center of a metropolis which appreciates your talents and acknowledges your genius, you have ample room and nerve enough for the marked abilities with which it has pleased God to empower you, without wasting your vigor in the vain attempt to people an island within the tropics.[57]

In this same issue, Holly was forced to defend his position on Haitian emigration from scathing assertions by Delany and Smith, that he had allowed himself to be subjugated by a white man, namely Redpath. Delany went even further, by asserting that all of this was accomplished with the knowledgeable support of a questionable Haitian political hierarchy. Holly's response, couched within an historical context, explained:

> Now my dear doctor [Delany], you and Dr. M'Cune Smith are both intelligent enough to know from the facts of Haytian history, and the spirit in which they have maintained their sovereign nationality for nearly sixty years, that it is all twaddle—the merest bosh and nonsense to suppose that, that government or people acts upon the principle, "next to God is the White man." You know if they acted upon this principle or acknowledged its force in any particular, they could not have maintained their self-respect for a moment. And without this, proverb is nothing more than an ironical curt phrase of the days of slavery, by which the crafty and knowing bondsman caricatured the haughty assumption of their cruel taskmasters. But the Negroes of Hayti never entertained such a sentiment in their breasts. They would abhor from their very souls to be suspicioned of the guild to subscribing to such an idea.... To be convinced of this, let the maligners and traducers of Hayti, read and ponder the immortal and ever glorious proclamation of the model man of Negro independence, Jean Jacques Dessalines, promulgated April 28, 1804.
>
> In the spirit of this proclamation, the Haytian government has ever been unfalteringly administered. Read that state paper, Doctor, and ponder it well until even your own Blackened cheeks shall blush for shame for insinuating what you have done, by repeating after Dr. Smith, a proverb by which the philosophic mind of James Redpath gathered up as one of the indices by which the mental idiosyncracies of the Haytian people might be studied.... How could you Doctor Delany, the recognized expounder of the doctrines of Negro nationality, join hands with the old opponent of our cause in this cold blooded assault on Hayti.
>
> If learned colored doctors in America, can only point their pens to villify and detract from the fair fame of Hayti, while White men like Wendell Phillips and James Redpath, are at the pains to exalt and glorify her noble deeds and heroic people, how can you wonder that the Haytian government should appoint one of such White men as its general agent and not one of such Negro doctors?
>
> But you ask, why Garnet, Harris or myself was not appointed. Let me answer first in respect to Mr. Garnet, as you have already indicated, he has lived in Jamica and not in Hayti. He has never made himself known to the Haytian people by one act prior to his present appointment, of any peculiar interest he had in them. Hence, it is mere folly to ask why he was not appointed.
>
> And almost the same may be said about Mr. Harris. He has visited the Dominican and not the Haytian portion of the island. He was unknown to the Haytian government until his recent appointment as agent, and never had expressed any public interest in the Haytian people until his letters, from Dominica, or more recently his work entitled, "A summer on the borders of the Caribbean Sea," were published. Hence, it is futile to ask why he was not appointed.
>
> Lastly, myself, which exhausts your vocabulary of preference to Mr. Redpath.... It is true that I have by voice and by pen, through good

report and through evil report, urged the claims of Hayti upon our people in the last six years, while you have during the same, veered around from a prospective residence in Central America, to an actual one in Canada, and finally brought up at the head of an exploring expedition in Central Africa. But notwithstanding all these bids I may have made for the general agency (and what Black man among us could have presented more?), let me tell why I escaped the appointment. I was not, as you well know, Doctor, sustained by the National Board of Black Emigrationists long enough in Hayti to terminate the negotiations I commenced. The promised outfit and expenses were not forthcoming, and the best part of the money expended came out of my own individual pocket. While the government was urgent that I should remain several months in the legislative assembly, I was compelled to leave for want to an immediate remittance which was promised and was not sent. Nevertheless, I pledged the honor of the Board to the government, that myself or another commissioner should be returned to finish the negotiations I had commenced....

I am thankful that I have had the opportunity to prove my devotion to the Haytian government, by serving in one of the humblest capacities in this emigration movement; and am thereby enabled to do all in my power to wish from my own personal reputation, any disgrace which may attach to me by my connection with the previous mission....

I might set forth the just reasons why Mr. Redpath should have been appointed, but before doing so, let me say in justice to the Haytian government, that this agency had been offered and accepted, as I understand, by the Rev. Consul Hanson, of England. But something prevented him from coming to enter upon its duties at the time appointed, and another had to be sought. It was then determined to appoint Rev. William P. Newman, of Canada, now in Port-au-Prince, but this gentleman having been fined by one of the courts of Hayti for defaming the character of a Haytian citizen named John Hepburn, formerly of Alexandria, and who has a brother in Canada, a member of the National Board elected at Chatham in 1858, the said Mr. Newman became irritated at the proper course of justice, and began to slander and villify the Haytian government. Of course the government was bound in self-respect to desist from appointing such a man. Having thus failed to obtain the services of competent and devoted colored men, the government was determined to do the next best thing by appointing a faithful and devoted WHITE man. A White man who has proved his undying devotion to the cause of our race, by his pedestrian tours, among the slaves of America and the peasants of Hayti, who subscribes to the glorious doctrine of Negro insurrection as Hayti has exemplified the same; who has trice visited that island moved by the noblest ethnological considerations—a White man in fire, who is willing to subordinate himself to the domination of the Negro, and become the servant of the Black government of Hayti, to promulgate its noble offers to our suffering race in the United States and the Canadas....

In such matters, it is not the color of the skin in the servant charged with great responsibilities, but his tried faithfulness to the cause of the race. I would execute a Black traitor as quick as a White one. I would set no premium on the color of either. Tried by this test, the Negro government of Hayti could not have found a more devoted, faithful, and competent servant in America to execute its desires in the cause of our race than James Redpath. To him therefore, belongs of right this appointment. I am sorry for the apathy and indifference of colored Americans to the historic greatness of Hayti, to be obliged to make this sad confession. It is true nevertheless.

It is unnecessary for me to reply to your charge that this movement is "too precipitous, not sufficiently matured," and that this is the commencement of my project for Haytian emigration. What I have said in respect to the history of the Cleveland Convention will show that I have been pursuing this idea for at least seven years gone by. A reference to the proceeding of a convention in Amherstburg, C.W., in 1853 will place me one year earlier still on the record in reference to Haytian emigration.

But Doctor, did you really mean to convey the idea that Blackmen should place Black men first in everything they do in respect to our race without any exceptions? If so, why did you not send your letter to which this is a reply to the "Anglo-African," or to "Fred. Douglass' Monthly" for publication first, instead of inserting it in that WHITE man's paper, the "Chatham Planet"—a paper whose editor, past or present, was one of the most bitter opponents of the Negro race in Canada?

Really, your inconsistency in this whole matter is so glaring and so unlike my old friend Dr. Delany, that I am almost tempted to believe that you are practicing upon me some Fetish Trick, learned perhaps from some savage tribe in the jungles of Central America.[58]

In a similar defense of his character, H.H. Garnet assails Delany's "consistency" with a counterchange:

You, too, my Dear Sir, have held me up before the public, and marked me, with your displeasure. The fault that you have charged me with is that I have accepted an appointment of agent of Haytian emigration from James Redpath, Esq., a WHITE MAN. For this you denounce me, and echo the slang of your friend, Dr. Smith. You are indignant at the acknowledgement of the leadership of a WHITE MAN. Now, sir, notwithstanding you are allopathic in your practice, nevertheless, I must give you a Homeopathic prescription. I see by the newspapers that in the convention held in 1848 at Chatham, C.W., one JOHN BROWN was appointed leader—commander in chief—of the Harper's Ferry invasion. There were several Black men there, able and brave; and yet John Brown was appointed leader. The unfortunate Stevens moved for the appointment, and one *Dr. Martin R. Delany seconded the motion*. Now, sir, tell me where I shall find your consistency, as John Brown was a *very* White man—his face and glorious hairs were all white. I am done with you on that point, Dr. Delany, you ought to have accepted of the office of surgeon under the great White leader, as a surgeon's place is in the *rear*, out of harm's way.

Now, turning his wrath upon a protagonist who would only describe himself as "The Colored Presbyterian Minister," Garnet charged:

> My dear Sir, if you dared to show your colores—if you had the courage to hang out your name—I would deal with you plainly; but as you manifest a becomeing modesty in concealing yourself, I will only give you a hint ... at one time you are crying out for equality, and at another you are denouncing it. A man is a man, White or Black, and my motto is, "tools to him that can use them best." We are all children of a common father—all brothers.... If you preach, I beseech you to practice. If you cannot practice what you preach, don't preach at all.

Finally, in defense of the Haitian emigration movement and Redpath's leadership, Garnet asserts:

> All of you have frequently dragged the name of this gentleman before the public, and have, with cause attempted to bring him into contempt. If you ask, "who is James Redpath?" I will tell you. He is a gentleman of great refinement, a scholar, a true philanthropist, an able journalist, and an excellent author, and has never written a line in favor of slavery. He is a practical abolitionist, and was a friend of John Brown; and when the old man was slain, he wrote his life, and scattered the book throughout the land, it is now flying among other nations; he stood by John Brown in the wars of Kansas, and blazed like a thunderbolt through the terrified ranks of the border ruffians of Missouri. If he and you (Dr. Delany, The Colored Minister, and Dr. James Smith) were measured to-day, gentlemen, by the rules of intellect, usefulness and true love to man, not one of you would reach to his knees. Such is the character and antecedents of the man whom you now attack in so ungenerous, so ungentlemanly a manner.
>
> I am a gentlemen, your humble servant, growing daily in the love of universal liberty and a Negro Nationality.[59]

The growing intensity of arguments, along with a rise in personal slanders, prompted at least one major spokesman on this issue to caution potential emigrants about confusing the issue with personalities: "I would ... suggest to all proposing to emigrate to look upon the cause in which they are engaged, and not upon men, who are but instruments in this matter."[60]

Interestingly enough, by March 1861, one month before the opening shot of the Civil War, the emigration level to Haiti was increasing, not only in human terms, but in produce being imported and exported to the United States. For example, in a letter submitted to *The Anglo-African*, J.P. Anthony of East Rock, New Haven, observed that "The whole number of vessels from Hayti to the Port of New York for three months is 24; seven of which were from the eastern part of the island." Carrying such items as sugar, mahogany wood, cotton, coffee, hides and salt, he estimated that:

> The average tonnage of each vessel may be estimated at 150 tons, making an aggregate of 3,600 tons, the value of which may safely be computed at from $8,500 to $9,000 per cargo, making a total of $216,000, saying nothing of the trade with Boston and Philadelphia.

Commenting on the significance of this trade, Anthony states:

> I have said 17 vessels were from the western part of the island (called Hayti) over which his excellency, president Geffrard presides as Chief ruler, he, together with the legislative body, have magnanimously invited and provided for the immigration of an industrial class of men and women of our race, to help develop the agricultural resources of that country. The question for Black men to decide today is, whether those vast plains and mountain slopes in Hayti shall be cultivated, or remain, as it were, a desert? It is not to be expected, that those whose physical organization has become contracted through city life and are unable to hold the plow-tail, will accept the invitation; Hence the Haytian government acted wisely when it extended the offer only to "Farmers and Laborers." I would say to all who are in for the fight (as they call it), stay and fight it out if you can.[61]

However, the call for a transplanted nationalism intensified the ideological confusion among free blacks, as article after article became increasingly imbued with liberal and often contradictory quasi-nationalistic rhetoric. Nor was much analysis made of the practical aspects of a call for Haytian and Liberian emigration. Emigrationists in fact asked for businessmen as opposed to frontier settlers ("Laborers and Farmers"). Though the Haitian government articulated in its advertisements a sensitivity to the importance of acquiring farmers and emigrants skilled in rural living, both Delany and Holly, as principal spokesmen for emigration, called for *economically self-sufficient individuals*—"select and intelligent" settlers, to Africa and Haiti! This, indeed, was self-defeating, as it clearly attempted to screen out one class of free black in preference for another.[62]

In addition, once the advocating of Christian religious principles in the press was correlated with emigration, many free blacks concluded that no particular advantage existed in returning to a "heathenistic" environment as emigrants. While the concept of African nationalism was continually attacked with negative images of Africa, "Americanization," many concluded, was at least a step towards "civilization."

Consistent misunderstanding and ignoring of hierarchical social relationships and dichotomies between rural and urban free blacks led many emigrationist editors to underestimate the importance of upward mobility as interpreted by free blacks within a slave society. As a result, free blacks minimized the importance of their own class/caste conflicts and focused instead on white racism as the central problem of the free black community. Emigrationists, instead of addressing themselves to the importance of economic processes to support any successful attempts at emigration, generally concerned themselves with narrowly defined rhetorical appeals aimed at specific class interests. Consequently, meager pleas for support in the press were geared to reach a small commercial and professional stratum of free blacks. In many instances, these appeals totally circumvented the laboring stratum of free blacks, while concentrating instead on organizations such as the white-dominated Africa Civilization Society of New York, England's African Aid Society, and the American Missionary Association. As a result, while the black press was viewed by emigrationists as a vehicle to galvanize support, their inability to actualize this was indicative of a faulty ideological analysis which called for providential nationalistic emigration, yet limited its application to a class of free blacks ill-suited to the task.

In this regard, subsequent positions taken by editors on the issue of Haiti and Liberia reflected one class's desire to reconstruct itself in its own image, its own ideal world, in its own time. Any intrusion of the illiterate, laboring populace into this world could only be tolerated through a process of caste/class purification, the subordination of African characteristics, and the development of political sovereignty via selective emigration.

It was left to Holly, possibly the most vocal advocate for emigration in the decade before the Civil War, to proclaim the aims for Haitian emigration. In his pamphlet "A Vindication of the Capacity of the Negro Race for Self Government and Civilized Progress," published in 1857, he not only presented an historical analysis of Haitian development, but what Haiti's revolutionary pact meant for blacks who questioned their own ability for self-government. Using paragraph subtitles such as "Reasons for Assuming Such a Task," "An Additional Reason for the Present Task," "The Hour of Destiny for the Blacks," and "Evidence of Civilized Progress: National Enterprise," Holly concluded:

> Here in this Black nationality of the New World, erected under such glorious auspices is the standpoint that must be occupied, and the level

that must be exerted, to regenerate and disenthrall the oppression and ignorance of the race, throughout the world. We must not overlook this practical vantage ground which Providence has raised up for us out of the depths of the sea, for any man-made and utopian scheme that is prematurely forced upon us, to send us across the ocean, to rummage the graves of our ancestors, in fruitless, and ill-directed efforts at the wrong end of human progress. Civilization and Christianity is passing from the East to the West; and its pristine splendor will only be rekindled in the ancient nations of the Old World, after it has belted the globe in its westward course, and revisited the Orient again. The Serpentine trial of civilization and Christianity, like the ancient philosophic symbol of eternity, must coil backward to its fountain head. God, therefore, in permitting the accursed slave traffic to transplant to many millions of the race, to the New World, and deducing therefrom such a Negro nationality as Hayti, indicates thereby that we have a work now to do here in the Western world, which in his own good time shall shed its orient beams upon the Fatherland of the race. Let us see to it, that we meet the exigency now imposed upon us, as nobly on our part at this time as the Haytians met theirs at the opening of the present century. And in seeking to perform this duty, it may well be a question with us, whether it is not our duty to go and identify our destiny with our historic brethren in that independent isle of the Caribbean Sea, carrying with us such of the arts, sciences and genius of modern civilization, as we may gain from this hardy and enterprising Anglo-American race, in order to add to Haytian advancement; rather than to indolently remain here, asking for political rights which, if granted a social proscription stronger than conventional legislation will even render negatory and of no avail for the manly elevation and general well-being of the race. If one powerful and civilized Negro sovereignty can be developed to the summit of national grandeur in the West Indies, where the keys to the commerce of both hemispheres can be held; this fact will solve all questions respecting the Negro, whether they be those of slavery, prejudice or proscriptions, and wheresoever on the face of the globe such questions shall present themselves for a satisfactory resolution.

A concentration and combination of the Negro race, of the Western Hemisphere in Hayti, can produce just such a national development. The duty to do so, is therefore incumbent upon them. And the responsibility of leading off in this gigantic enterprise Providence seems to have made our peculiar task by the eligibility of our situation in this country, as a point for gaining an easy access to that island. Then let us boldly enlist in this pathway of duty, while the watchwords that shall cheer and inspire us in our noble and glorious undertaking, shall be the soul-stirring anthem of GOD and HUMANITY.[63]

Any examination of influences of the black press upon ideas and actions of free blacks should first come to grips with the media's impact on its audience. Suppositions to the contrary ignore important elements for "cognition and communication that are bound up with the production of any world."[64] To the degree that the free black press was capable of acting as a conduit for aspirations and declarations within this context, many free blacks became enlightened to the social-political degradation of disenfranchisement. However, the antebellum press was not a monolithic social institution and, as such, did not exercise a total mandate within the black community, nor consensual influence, though its editors often claimed that such was the case. Editorial opinions not only challenged opposing viewpoints, but as shown in tables 8a and 8b, editors tended to change ideological positions with the passage of time. While the black press did establish a framework from which various spokesmen appealed, cajoled and sympathized on issues concerning the welfare of free blacks, a state of mind incongruous with reality (as some were to claim) did prevail, as the issues of emigration and colonization increased in importance.

Though a call for emigration as opposed to colonization was cause enough for most editors and their subscribers to express themselves vigorously in its opposition or approval, it was the emergence of an articulated stratum of free blacks, armed with strategies for mobilizing their class toward specific interests, which signaled the emergence of an historical crisis of significant proportions.

Secondly, the relationship between the press and the reader was an important part of the process of the dissemination of information. For example, the political disparity among free blacks on emigration was great, as social experiences and knowledge about the society at large differed from individual to individual as well as from stratum to stratum. In the past, attempts to generalize about response levels tended to be predicated upon individualized social experiences as opposed to group reaction. With this myopic view, editors rhetorically defined and then systematically attacked any deviation from what they considered to be the norm. Among those issues to receive special attention in this regard was that of the potential emigrant-settler. Furthermore, there was a presumption among anti-emigrationist editors that any worthwhile use of the press must unquestionably demand the inclusion of free blacks in the American society. While these stances opposed each other, they undoubtedly were both received by most white Americans as radically if not overtly threatening. Furthermore, expressions independent of white sanctions represented the unheard of "arrogance" of a subordinate race and class. In this regard, studies by Nisbett and Valins pertaining to causal inferences tend to suggest that an editor's self-interest (editorial prerogative) which attempts to channel the attributional processes of others, will generally be influenced by a desire to maintain self-respect while viewing others as subordinate, or as the case may be, less informed. Moreover, we learn that even those severely critical of emigration will find it expedient to blame or lower conflicting concepts if it will satisfy immediate needs.[65] Samuel Cornish's attitude about his "right as editor to distort" is a prime example of this.

As a framework for political dissent, or rather one in which argument was tolerated within the guidelines established by various editors, the struggle to influence and interpret emerging events was a primary motivational trait. Consequently, spokesmen and editors such as Delany, Holly and Mary Shadd possessed not only ideas, but the wherewithal to disseminate information, and they became influential leaders.

Characteristic of free blacks who considered themselves congnizant enough to articulate viewpoints in the black press was their concern with symbolic meaning. Thus, statements exclaiming: "To talk about prejudice against color is nonsense; but raise up sons learned and enterprising with offsets of 20 or 30 thousand dollars..." may have been exciting to read, yet it totally obfuscated the reality of most free blacks' social condition. Suggesting that simply a change in behavior was all that was needed to overcome the obstacles of antebellum America seriously misled free blacks into thinking that their condition was primarily related to the issue of education as opposed to complex processes of socialization. As a result, anti-emigrationists viewed racist attributional inferences as simply temporary aberrations of a superior society. However, this view was continually undermined by those same racist inferences.[66]

Thirdly, Martin Delany, in a published treatise concerning emigration, suggested that, "What is necessary to be done, in order to attain an equality, is to change the condition, and the person is at once changed." Of course the question of whether or not an editor, who is also an activist, is limited in his analysis of society due to his own social status becomes pivotal.

While the essence of objective reporting is to interpret reality in a truthful manner, reporting and editorializing fall within the scope of social interpretation and subjectivity. The contradictory nature of this process reveals the relative nature of truth. It is also noted that class conflict and self-interest among editors such as Holly, Delany, Shadd, Bibb and Cornish obscured rather than clarified the emigration controversy. Nevertheless, as advocates, their objectivity was not simply limited by a narrow ideological framework, but one which addressed itself first and foremost to development of class solidarity in the name of racial progress. Steeped in the values of Western social development, their newspapers and treatises interceded as filters or membranes which selected, transformed and modified beliefs which were judged to be dysfunctional. As a result, the black press was a catalyst for American values, a structural bridge reaching for social recognition as well as societal input. By the 1850s, socialization processes towards the development of the "African-American" had begun.

As a result, emigration, whether supported or denounced, was to a large extent a rhetorical battle among free blacks who saw themselves embodied with Western values and American tradition. Their duty, so they professed, was to fulfill an American mandate. Though much of this expression in the press was ideologically embedded in the structure of white America, a closer examination reveals the emergence of tangential cultural-political organizations which, in turn, suggests the existence of an infrastructure reflecting the differences in the distribution of substantive rights and power. Further scrutiny also suggests the existence of micro-structures which were connected to the much larger macro-structure of white America. Clearly free blacks' use of these micro-structural networks was an attempt to maximize political expression. However, the extent to which this structure could be used was curtailed as social action was converted into the less threatening realm of rhetorical appeals. Thus, the black press became a major agent in the containing, limiting and retarding of direct political action by free blacks, even to the extent of preventing them from developing a united response on the issue of emigration. Simply stated, the appearance of being involved in social action became the preoccupation of a social stratum indoctrinated in individualism rather than communalism, style rather than substance. The degree to which they were allowed to accommodate themselves within America validated the concept that "society is a framework of frames"; some dominate, while others are held accountable.[67]

IV. Evaluation of the Black Press

"Passion not spent but turned inward."

C.L.R. James. *The Black Jacobins*, p. 418.

"Do you suppose that I would go in the woods to live for the sake of freedom? No, indeed! If you wish to do so, go and do it. I am free enough here."

A Colored Lady of Intelligence from one of the "first families," in *The Condition, Emigration and Destiny of the Colored People of the United States*, Martin R. Delany, 1852

Its Influence on Emigration

As an issue of major significance, emigration threatened to further fragment an already divided society. In examining its impact, we are also concerned with the influence of the black press on collective behavior, for or against emigration. That is to say, efforts by the press to affect social change along lines which operate within the status quo as opposed to a more radical approach, which demands withdrawal or exodus from society. From a more empirical perspective, any examination of the effects of rhetoric on movements must concern itself not only with the historical aspects but the rhetorical component used to engender consensus.

While most free blacks never came in contact with a "returned" emigrant, they might have heard about someone preparing to leave for Haiti, Liberia or other places throughout Canada or the Caribbean. This being the case, news pertaining to living conditions or efforts at successful emigration was received either from persons who claimed to have knowledge of someone else, or by reading various accounts in the press. This inability to make direct first-hand assessment of emigrants' experiences relates to a dependency on second-hand information and interpretative accounts. If the account in itself was unique, then readers would tend to accept it as distinct, and viable, information. For example, in an earlier chapter we examined accounts of an armed conflict in Liberia between indigenous Africans and black settlers. These accounts were distinctive enough for readers to formulate a variety of causal inferences.[1]

One social observer has suggested that a second dimension of information processing, labelled consistency, also occurs when the events which provoke causal inferences continue over a period of time. In other words, continued descriptions of squalor or death by disease, fever, wild animals or "native" wars would provoke causal inferences of a negative type. Conversely, positive attributes relating to the community's growth through the enterprise and success of individuals would affect a more favorable attitude towards emigration.

This analysis is buttressed by the knowledge that the manipulative characteristics relevant to the withholding of important information, or its publishing in a slanted or garbled manner, can directly affect opinions made by an unsuspecting public. However, lacking distinctive and consistent information about an event, the creating of a consensus of thought is important, as individuals attempt to pool, collect or draw on the opinions of others.[2]

When examining the accounts of emigrants in Liberia and Haiti, as reported in papers such as Cornish's *The Colored American* or Bibb's *The Voice of the Fugitive*, we must keep in mind that for many free blacks, a tendency to discount or minimize the process of causal inference-making by emigrants themselves was bound to occur. While this may be expected, one must attempt to ascertain the influence of physical reality on a settler's interpretation of events. Struggling with a hostile environment, descriptions about their immediate environment should be expected to be vividly endowed with the problems of survival and the importance of social-psychological adaptiveness.

Lacking descriptions of physical trauma which were usually associated with settlers in Liberia, accounts about Haiti were comparatively mild, that is, of a stable society with well-established social institutions similar to those of American or European societies. As a result, press reports about Haiti tended to reflect a social reality more concerned with problems with language, food and business growth, than with "native" wars. Therefore, the impression was encouraged that Haiti was a society eagerly awaiting the appearance of free blacks as opposed to one filled with many inherent problems for emigrants. Thus, the medium itself, transferring information from one reality to another, was misleading, as many readers erred by assuming that the "projected" reality was factual, rather than one grounded in attempts at developing a social consensus.[3]

Consensus-making is again significant in the popular Republican abolitionist argument which exclaimed the physical reality of western life and its vast territories, as an impetus for progressive change, as opposed to the dehumanizing second-class status of eastern free blacks. While many free blacks did emigrate westward with this thought, the reality of day-to-day lifestyles in the "territories," with its increasingly European immigrant populace, tended to negate any such development. As one observer stated: "I want to have nothing to do either with the free Negro or the slave.... We wish to settle the territories with free white men." Similarly, one Simon Cameron of Pennsylvania stated that he also wished to keep blacks out of the territories because the white laborer "must be depressed wherever the Negro is his competitor in the field or the workshop."[4]

A critical examination of the black press on the issue of emigration does not support the thesis that the press was generally an effective spokesman for the emigrationist cause. However, emigration as an alternative to assimilationist formulations was controversial enough to stimulate a crisis. Similarly, acceptance by delegates at the Ohio 1848 National Convention on the concept of a national press (*The North Star* under Frederick Douglass' editorship), was significant as Douglass, a leading exponent of assimilation, could now address the issue from an "official" perspective. Still, this in no way suggests that any national press, regardless of the stature of its editor, could induce a level of homogeneity in viewpoints from the diverse segments of free black society.

For instance, while 41.3 percent of free blacks living in northern and western states were listed as illiterate in 1860, the remaining 58 percent were not representative of any specific class background. Nor were they all urbanized or socialized in the same manner. For example, Garnet's address to the slaves, first in 1843 at the Buffalo National Convention, and its reappearance as a pamphlet in 1848 demanding revolt by slaves, was not supported or "appreciated" by many free blacks such as Frederick Douglass. "Moreover, Douglass' encouragement of the use of education and propaganda had its influence in softening the effect of Garnet's militancy."[5] In fact, of the many social categories that antebellum free blacks labelled each other in the press, "moral suasionist" clearly implied not only an assimilationist political perspective, but one geared toward accommodation. Even more cogent in this regard is the rhetoric of the colored societies whose commonly used phrases such as "Live, and let live" and "Let *me* live first, and you afterwards," stand as testaments to the existing political framework.

Thus, we need not speculate on the thoughts of assimilationists when they announce:

> We rejoice that it is our lot to be the inhabitants of a country blest by nature, with a genial climate and fruitful soil, and where the liberty of speech and the press is protected by law. We rejoice that we are thrown into a revolution where the contest is not for landed territory, but for Freedom; the weapons not carnal, but spiritual.

Or in a more speculative nature on free blacks' inability to work in concert as emigrants, we read:

> Take a retrospect of the Colored people of Canada for the last thirty years. Their institutions—their divisions—their knots and "squads"—their White and Colored beggars.... The quarrels of these beggars.... The contentions about their land.... The caucuses, conventions, resolutions, and after all, the return of the pretended leaders of the people, "Like a dog to his vomit...."6

Examples such as the above, along with the more extensive data in Chapter I, suggest that the black press's audience was not a homogeneous body, but a varied one made up of interest groups which selectively chose bits of information which they considered relevant. Selecting information which seemed plausible to them, these interest groups utilized their belief system as screens, which, like Erving Goffman's structural membranes, filtered out what was considered to be unnecessary and accepted, with some modification, that which was useful for survival. It was these groups which, when confronted with issues of mutual concern, were able to call upon the press for an expression of unity, a "consensus."7

Herein lies a significant point about the diffusion of information on emigration as it was erroneous for emigrationists to conclude that the availability of Liberia or Haiti for settlers would, in itself, evoke a pro-emigrationist sentiment among free blacks. Neither was it correct to assume that emigration was beneficial, feasible, or even relevant to blacks' social survival. Furthermore, any decision to emigrate to Liberia, Haiti or even Canada would be critically affected by a population's ability to make causal inferences on the specific area or people they would be settling amongst. In journals where a consistent policy existed to reject any concept of emigration or colonization, such as *The Colored American*, descriptions of life in Liberia discouraged the process of recruiting settlers. Even more discouraging was the use of "eye witness" accounts of settlers battling "natives" for their lives in Liberia. Thus, the relevancy of an article to the reader depended on how representative its views were of its constituency.

A "discouraging Letter from Liberia," describing "harsh" living conditions in the colony, was anything but heartening to blacks seeking an alternative to America, yet this was exactly the kind of correspondence anti-emigrationist editors were eager to publish. Thus, we read:

> ...We cannot get any meat or bread here, at any price. There has not been any flour in Liberia for at least two months, and the only chance we have of getting a taste of meat, is once in a while when the natives bring in a deer from the bush. We have to live on rice alone nearly all the time, and you may know that that goes hard with me. I hope that the Liberia fever has got out of Mr. Scott, and that he will forever renounce the notion of coming here. If he had come here he would certainly have died. When he saw the suffering into which he had brought his family, he would certainly have grieved and grief coupled with fever inevitably produces death. Tell all the people you see not to come to torment before they die, for when they come here, they are coming to torment. More than half that come here die in a short time, and all that escape immediate death, suffer unspeakable misery all their lives. I live in a little town called Marshall, forty miles from Monrovia. We are surrounded with wild beasts of numerous kinds, elephants from four to twelve feet high. Tiger cats, wild dogs, deer, porcupines, monkeys, baboons and snakes from four to forty feet in length. The people are very willing to eat any of these animals and reptiles, because they cannot get anything else.[8]

If one argues that causal inferences about settlers' ability to adapt to a new land are heavily influenced on the direct information of an eyewitness who is representative of the settling population, then published accounts like the above must be taken seriously.[9]

Therefore, one might easily understand why convention delegates from Philadelphia's 1835 National Convention, in declaration of sentiment rejecting emigration, would exclaim:

> It is our fortune to live in an era where the moral power of this nation is waking up to the evils of slavery, and the cause of our oppressed brethren throughout this country.... Therefore, our only trust is in the agency of divine truth, and the spirit of American liberty; our cause is glorious and must finally triumph.[10]

By the 1850s emigrationists were suggesting variations about the entire issue, so that readers would clearly be able to see ideological differences between colonization and emigration. Articles employing a rhetorical strategy best described as "differential saliency" emphasized the necessity for editors to educate their readers in the geographical advantage of one area over another. Realizing that it was not a need for new rhetorical material that was primary, but a different emphasis on data already given, editors such as Delany, Garnet, and George Lawrence began, in the 1850s, to focus attention on the resolution of problems, rather than ignoring their existence. However, these issues were often obscured by a barrage of personal attacks and counterattacks which deferred the relevancy of the issue. Conflicts of this nature within the press tended to obscure and lessen the influence of emigrationists as they were often projected as deviant and dangerous to the well-being of free blacks and slaves. For instance, in a reply to Dr. McCune Smith's attack upon emigration and its major advocates, Delany and Holly, Garnet responded in *The Weekly Anglo-African*:

> Tell me, Doctor, what difference is there between your opinion of your own race and those of slaveholders and their apologists? Both you and they decry the abilities of Black men. They say that we cannot thrive unless we are in a state of slavery or in the immediate presence of it; That we must have White masters, and that we are not capable of self-government. Sir, your miserable argument arrays you on the enemy's side. In the name of my race, whom you indirectly slander, I pronounce the charge as false as the Koran. ... Now Sir, let me tell you, and all such traducers of my people as your letter represents you to be, I envy neither your head nor your heart. The man who willfully traduces his own injured brethren deserves to pass off the stage of life without even the form of regret and without arriving to the dignity of being hated. What other men have done, we can do also. If others have built cities and empire, and have arisen from a state of vassalage to the highest civilization, we can do the same.[11]

We must now examine the manipulative aspects of "publicized" political opinion operating under the rubric of political information. "Publicized" private opinion will often reveal information about corresponding viewpoints which were previously unknown to contending sides of disputes. Such revelations, once realized, will have a destabilizing effect, often causing a withdrawal by one or both parties from their stated positions. For example, any appearance of racially opposing groups (such as slaveholders and emigrationists) in agreement would negatively influence free blacks' opinions on colonization and emigration. Thus, for those blacks who were totally opposed to any separation scheme from America, a strategic windfall was in the making as article after article in *The Colored American* and *The North Star* was quick to associate the slaveholding interest of Henry Clay and members of the American Colonization Society with that of emigrationist efforts. Frederick Douglass' efforts to attack this "corresponding" of viewpoints is especially noted in his publishing of a letter in 1849 by Henry Clay to *The North Star*, and his subsequent analysis. Though Douglass was not sympathetic to colonization or emigration, his attempts at minimizing any confusion or influence created by Clay's letter were clearly meant to insure a calm, noncombative resistance to the wishes of slaveholding interests.

On the other hand, Senator Clay's perception of the threat an enlarged free black population posed for whites was considered by many whites as being rational, objective and logical. In any case, the social reality of Clay and that of Douglass left little room for negotiation, as Douglass underlined Clay's social practices, namely that slaveholding and trading were antithetical to the interests of free blacks who considered themselves to be Americans. Yet, in an accommodative manner suggestive of most assimilationist-oriented editors who were quick to assume the role of "race spokesmen," Douglass rationalized the necessity for a slow developmental process for the slaves' emancipation and blacks' assimilation into America. Exhorting free blacks to political acquiescence and gratitude that are "always strong in the oppressed," he championed an attitude which "would lead them to respect and have reverence (for) their former owners."[12] Douglass' rhetoric was replete with accommodative appeals. Needless to say, both Clay and Douglass left many questions unresolved in their attempt to change reality, yet more importantly, the simultaneous presentation of their views in *The North Star* did convey a framework for review, criticism and eventual rejection of emigration by free blacks.[13]

In a letter to *The North Star* (some of which appears on page 122), originally published in the white-owned *Lexington Observer and Reporter*, Clay posited the following:

> Hitherto, no such satisfactory plan [for the removal of slaves] has been presented — when on the occasion of the formation of our present constitution of Kentucky, in 1799, the question of the gradual emancipation of slavery in the state was agitated, its friends had to encounter a great obstacle, in the fact that there then existed no established colony to which they could be transported....
>
> After a full and deliberate consideration of the subject, it appears to me three principles should regulate the establishment of a system of gradual emancipation. *The first is* that it should be slow in its operation, cautious, and gradual, so as to occasion no convulsion, nor any rash nor sudden disturbance in the existing habits of society. *Second*, that, as an indispensable condition, the emancipated slaves should be removed from the state to some colony. And *thirdly*, that the expense of their transportation to such colony, including an outfit for 6 months after arrival, should be defrayed by a fund to be raised from the labor of each free slave.

Nothing could be more unwise than the immediate liberation of all the slaves in the state, comprehending both sexes and all ages. It would lead to the most frightful and fatal consequences. Any great change in the condition of society should be marked by extreme care and circumspection. The introduction of slavery into colonies, was an operation of many years' duration; and the work of their removal from the United States can only be effected after the lapse of a great length of time....

The colonization of the free blacks as they successively arrive from year to year at the age entitling them to Freedom, I consider a condition absolutely indispensable. Without it, I should be utterly opposed to any scheme of emancipation. One hundred and ninety odd thousand of Blacks, composing about one-fourth of the population of the state, with their descendants, could never live in peace, harmony and equality with the residue of the population. The color, passions and prejudices would forever prevent the two races from living together in a state of cordial union. Social, moral and political degradation would be the inevitable lot of the colored race. Even in the Free States (I use the terms Free and Slave States, not in any sense derogatory from one class, or implying any superiority in the other, but for the sake of brevity), that is their present condition. In some of those Free States, the penal legislation against the people of color is quite as severe, if not harsher, than it is in some of the slave states. As no where in the United States are amalgamation and equality between the two races possible, it is better that there should be a separation, and that the African descendants should be returned to the native land of their fathers.

Convinced that he had established a framework of joint interest by the emancipation of the slaves and their radical separation from whites, Clay continued:

Most of the evils, losses and misfortunes of human life, have some compensation or alleviation. The slaveholder is generally a landholder, and I am persuaded that he would find in the augmented productiveness of his lands some, if not full indemnity, for losses arising to him from emancipation and colonization. He should also liberally share in the general benefits accruing to the whole state from the extraction of slavery. These have been so often and so fully stated, that I will not, nor is it necessary to dwell upon them extensively. They may be summed up in a few words. We shall remove from among us the contaminating influence of a servile and degraded race of a different color ... Any wrongs which the descendants of Africa have suffered at our hands, and we should demonstrate the sincerity with which we pay indiscriminate homage to the great cause of the liberty of the human race.[14]

Commensurate with Clay's argument for forceful colonization and emigration was an ever-increasing population of free blacks, and Clay's perception of them as a social problem. By reprinting Clay's thesis in *The North Star*, Douglass was able to structure a rhetorical debate filled with urgency. The significance of this was not lost in Douglass' disavowing of colonization or emigration. Douglass was consciously transferring the issue from the realm of social action to that of modification by discourse. Douglass' response to Clay, therefore, provoked a situation which unwittingly involved Clay, a situation which, "handled" by Douglass, invited a reply. His subsequent influence in this rhetorical situation was premised upon an awareness that review by readers would not only be critical, but influential in the overall framework of public discussion.

Within this context, the skill of an editor to articulate convincingly his interpretation of reality was not only critical for information diffusion, but crucial in the creating of an acceptable version of "the truth." Furthermore, when this process is "handled" by an astute editor who also enjoys a level of public acclaim as did Douglass, the practical justification of rhetoric becomes analogous to that of scientific inquiry.[15]

Finally, Douglass' attacking of Clay's position in March 1849 underlines a highly ironic occurrence. By 1852, emigration plans by Delany would cite: "Nicaragua, in Central America, and New Grenada, The Northern part of South America, south of Nicaragua, as the most favorable points, at present, in every particular, for us to emigrate to."[16] This was also the scheme advocated by such white conservatives as Daniel Webster, Millard Fillmore and Francis Blair. In fact, Blair and his sons were such strong supporters of colonization that they proposed:

> The United States [would] arrange for the settlement of colonies of Negroes in Central America, either by the outright acquisition of land there or through the cooperation of the local government. [They hoped] that free transportation, free homesteads, and financial aid in establishing farms and businesses would make the colony attractive enough to induce a sizeable number of Free Blacks to settle there.[17]

More significantly, they argued, such a plan would reduce or eliminate the free black population so that "all within the limits of our union should be homogeneous in race and of our own blood," a condition which Blair assumed was "certainly the wish of every patriot."[18] Similarly, James Holly, in a letter to Frank Blair, Jr., that same year responded favorably to Blair's scheme, as did Martin Delany (contradicting the premise that once antagonists find themselves on the same consensus plane, a disassociation will occur). Moreover, while assuring Blair that it was free blacks' fear of being tainted by whites that kept a more open response from occurring to such a scheme, both Holly and

Delany expressed confidence that some 200 families per year for a settlement in Central America could be secured, and that any development of this scheme should take into consideration those advancements already established by this potential settler class of blacks. Holly further posited that an intelligent investigation prior to colonization should occur, one which would carefully select the first emigrants and any succeeding settlement, thus assuring that after five years the American government would see the feasibility of this plan.[19]

As sentiment for free blacks' removal from America increased, whites such as Republican Senator Salmon P. Chase, a long-time promoter of equal suffrage for free blacks and drafter of a bill in 1849 to repeal Ohio's "Black Laws" which limited the rights of free blacks, admitted to his wife in a letter that regardless of his previous efforts to support free blacks' rights in Ohio, clearly most Ohioans desired "a homogeneous population." But it was an Iowa Republican speaking at a convention who summed up the feelings of a "consensus" of white Republicans when he stated: "I have my prejudice against them [blacks]. My prejudice is such as to lead me to desire that they shall not be left in this country.... I am therefore, a colonizationist!"[20]

Within this context, emigrationist appeals in 1852 by Delany, in his "Condition, Elevation, Emigration and Destiny of the Colored People of the United States," and Holly, in his "Vindication of the Capacity of the Negro Race for Self Government and Civilized Progress" in 1857, synthesized with some abolitionist Republicans who also desired blacks' emigration, though for different reasons. The similarities between these two positions, regardless of their diametrically opposed motivations, led Douglass to speak of a "sinister" relationship which would "blast the hopes, and cover with darkness of utter despair, the bruised hearts of enslaved millions."[21]

Perceiving procolonizationists and emigrationists, both blacks and whites, to be vulnerable to attack because of their "seemingly similar" goals, Douglass attacked Clay's position:

> In reviewing the letter before us [Clay's letter], we would be just and even generous to its long-offending author. He is a man, though a wicked man, and one who has done as much, probably, as any other person in this country to degrade and oppress the downtrodden and deeply injured people to whom we belong and with whom we are classed. Gifted with powers of speech and personal address to an extent attained by few, and excelled perhaps by none in this country, he has again brought out the tremendous influence which he wields, to blast the hopes, and cover with the darkness of utter despair, the bruised hearts of enslaved millions. Wedded to that old atrocious persecutor of the colored inhabitants of this

land—The American Colonization Society—he has been held up by its agents as a model philanthropist and Christian, and his means for evil have increased accordingly.—Representing the religious sentiment of the nation, being a member of the church, he was pressed into the service of slavery and prejudice, the overwhelming force of our spurious theology. And yet, we would not treat him as one wholly bad, in whom there is no spark of goodness. On the contrary, we observe in him traits of character, evidences of feelings, which prove him to be a man of generosity far above the average class of slaveholders in this country. And this very circumstance makes him all the more dangerous and powerful for evil, for it serves, as the soft verdure of the field, to conceal the hideous folds of the viper ready to leap forth and destroy the unsuspecting.... One word further about colonization. We hold it to be downright impudence of Mr. Clay, or anyone else, to propose the removal of any member of the human family to any quarter of the habitable globe, and the very climax of injustice and tyranny for any class of persons to force such removal upon another class. How dare Henry Clay or any one else undertake to decide where an equal brother man shall live. He has just as much right to murder the slaves where they are free. The wrong in the one case only differs in extent, not in quality. Humble as we are, degraded, imbruted and enslaved as we have been, if Henry Clay or anyone else should propose to remove us, he should have his insolence rebuked, and if he should force us, it would be force against force. If we could speak to the colored people of Kentucky, we would entreat them to stand by their homes and firesides—To prefer DEATH in Kentucky rather than be driven to Liberia or elsewhere. But we think there is very little if any probability that this alternative will be presented. The colored people of Kentucky are too useful as laborers, and the sagacious landowners are too much disposed to consult their own interest, even to urge the colored laborer to leave the state.—Extinguish slavery, and the very elements upon which colonization has a name to live in the south, is destroyed. No one would ever have thought of colonizing the Free Blacks of the south, but that the presence of the Free spread discontent among the slave population. But how will colonization exist, when the foundations upon which it rests shall cease to exist? The one will go down with the other.[22]

Trying to allay fears whites might have about blacks' emancipation and entry into the competitive mainstream of America society, Douglass suggested that these important realms of national power would not be subverted by free black development. Rather, they would to a large extent exist outside the immediate range of blacks' interest or influence. In this regard, his appeasement policy was to project blacks as nonthreatening to white America, and reject colonization and emigration as viable political alternatives. This not only antagonized antislavery whites who favored emigration and colonization for the sake of white labor, but also proslavery elements who viewed any exodus of free blacks, voluntary or not, as the eliminating of a "social nuisance." Therefore, Douglass' insistence on free blacks' participation within America rested upon the assumption that the modifying of a major social constraint—racism—reduced the need for colonization or emigration. With this in mind, Douglass proposed to Clay:

> In our judgment there is not the slightest reason to apprehend unhappy difference between the White people of Kentucky and the Free slaves. It is not to be supposed that the slave will bound up to the full stature of a Freeman, the moment his fetters fall from his limbs, nor that he will swell up into a very high estimate of his own dignity all at once. No! The transaction from slavery to Freedom will be long and slow even after the slave is legally emancipated. A sense of gratitude, always strong in the oppressed, would lead them to respect and reverence their former owners; while the good sense of the latter would always enable them to cultivate this feeling by doing just what Henry Clay says they ought to do, "instructing, improving and enlightening them." It was long after we came to the North, where we ever thought ourselves on an equality with White persons. We long treated them (perhaps we do now) as our superiors. No one, not even a slaveholder, could exact more politeness than we were disposed to render every respectable White person with whom we had business. Judging from our own experience, then, we feel warranted in saying, that no danger need be apprehended from immediate emancipation, on that score. To suppose that the act of emancipation would at once change the passive slave into a proud and revengeful Freeman, is to suppose an absurdity gross and palpable. No, Mr. Clay; The change will be gradual enough. When the great point of emancipation shall have been gained, long and dark will be the years through which the freed bondsman will have to pass, ere he shall be fully clear of the badge of servitude, sunken deep into his mental constitution by the bondage of ages. No fear of haste, of inconsiderate action, need be entertained. Could all the powers of learning and religion be set in operation, to restore him to his natural manhood—still the process would necessarily be gradual. He is too low down to spring to the top at a leap. Emancipation would still have the journey from bondage to freedom before him. Hence, upon national as well as Christian principles, we may demand the immediate emancipation of every slave in the world.[23]

Douglass perceived the press as a new means for democratic expression, one which would bring the issue of political equality based on constitutional rights in focus with free blacks' arguments. He also sought to reduce white America's fear of the emergence of a powerful free black class.

While social imputation helps us to understand the structural aspects of rhetorical appeals, we must ask to what degree these rhetorical appeals led to counter-rhetorical appeals.

To the degree that free blacks enjoyed the rights of free expression in northern urban areas, the advent of a press was not only a benefit among those who were literate, but was also a persuasive force among those whose first knowledge of the surrounding society was received by word of mouth. The black press was a catalyst for determined and controlled social expression. This expression sought to engage the American nation in a dialogue principally concerned with the dynamics of and the dichotomy between individualism and equality. Furthermore, this dichotomy was reinforced by a press which focused upon the American West, while emigrationists looked eastward to Haiti or Africa. In addition, for many free blacks, the very existence of a black press was a refutation of the myth of blacks' ineptitude and dependency. It fostered a reassurance concerning their ability to shed an "unwanted" past while concentrating on day-to-day practicalities.

Emigration, as viewed by *assimilationist* elements in the press, was an escape for those incapable of fulfilling the expectations of an expanding, highly individualistic society. *The Colored American* asserted in an editorial:

> Some say, let the Colored People leave the country! We reply, NO BRETHREN, we would rather die a thousand deaths, in HONESTLY and LEGALLY contending for our rights IN THIS COUNTRY. We cannot act in this respect so IGNOBLY as our pilgrim fathers did. We will stay and seek the purification of the whole lump. With the character of the country we are identified, and with its character we intend to sink or swim. If the country sinks in disgrace, we will perish amidst its ruins — yet seeking its regeneration and salvation.[24]

Despite the increased legislative and physical pressure placed upon free blacks to withdraw from any area of political, economic or social endeavor, the anti-emigrationist, pro-assimilationist press clearly dominated this medium of expression. Thus, the philosophies of individual growth and universal betterment as professed by the wealthy sail-maker James Forten, and "Augustine," became frameworks for black social analysis. The latter part of the 1840s and early 1850s also saw the emergence of editors of the caliber of Van Rensselaer of *The Ram's Horn*, Thomas Hamilton and, later, George Lawrence of *The Weekly Anglo-African*, who began to view their role as spokesmen for the "oppressed class." Furthermore, this class now had its interests expressed either favorably or otherwise on a weekly basis. As a result, spokesmen and editors operated within a framework defined by a constituency who, while assuring the right of intellectual freedom, were limited in their ability to practice this freedom as efforts toward social involvement were circumscribed by a propensity for introspective analysis of American society. Editors such as Douglass and Delany, once invested with the power of unquestioned leadership, were by the

1850s forced to make concessions, clarifications and denials, as the demands and resulting social consciousness of various strata of blacks began to increase. As one delegate at the 1849 Ohio State Colored Convention put it: "I for one Sir, am willing, dearly as I love my native land ... to leave it, and go wherever I can be free," even as a colonizing agent.[25]

By the mid-1850s, Douglass, the most prominent editor of this period, still opposed emigration and was to be shaken only to the degree that by 1861 he could remind his readers of the impending dangers of European immigration, claiming:

> It seems to me that the slavery party will gain little by driving us out of this country, unless it drives us off the adjacent islands. It seems to me that it would be, after all, little advantage to slavery to have the intelligence and energy of the free colored people all concentrated in the Gulf of Mexico ... That this continent is not without significance ... Let him [the Colored Man] remember that a home, a country, a nationality, are all attainable this side of Liberia.[26]

However, on the eve of the Civil War, *Douglass' Monthly* printed a "Change of Heart" letter on emigration, written by H.O. Wagoner, himself once a forceful anti-emigrationist from Chicago. The importance and influence of Wagoner's recantation must be judged within the context of Douglass' growing identification with the emigrationist cause, as well as the increasing appearance of Haitian emigrationist literature in George Lawrence's paper, *The Anglo-African*. Wagoner concluded that:

> In view of the character and facts of the North, to whom we have so long looked for succor, would it not be well for some of us — many of us — to concentrate our efforts by going into the different countries occupied by our people, and carry with us all the civilization, education, arts and sciences which we have gained. When masses shall have developed their capabilities for self-government, then let us appeal directly and in a proper and respectful manner, to the slaveholders themselves, in behalf of the freedom of four millions of our brothers and sisters in bonds in the south. But should they disregard our appeals, then VOUS VERRONS.[27]

Though Douglass himself was to take a similar position after the beginning days of the Civil War, the process of motivating free blacks towards Haiti, Liberia or the Caribbean was terminated, and with it, the antebellum emigration movement. Any evaluation of the free black press on this issue must now ask to what extent, if any, was it successful?

In answering this question, close attention must be given to the general nature of the press as a tool for the expression of interest, closely identified with the ruling strata of free blacks. Directly stated, the championing of equal rights within American society reinforced the prospect that emigration to Africa or the Caribbean would not be served well by a press whose proposals to the public emphasized a de-Africanized colored American. The internalized drive of the settler found little expression in a press whose ideological framework denoted assimilation and negotiation. The following newspaper preambles bear this out:

The Colored American:
   This paper will contain, independent of a general summary of the news of the day and other interesting miscellaneous matter, a condensed portion weekly of the history of the *Colored Race* from the earliest ages. It will also contain biography and sketches of character of *those Africans and people of color*, who have distinguished themselves in ancient and modern times; But more particularly those of *our own country*.
The Aliened American:
   There are, in all the United States, but two newspapers conducted by Colored Americans, and those in New York State, while west of New York State reside the majority of the Colored Americans of the Free States. ...This paper speaks for them, first through its name – Aliened American. Born under the United States Constitution and entitled by it, to all the rights and immunities of other citizens, the State and National Governments have not only disfranchised, they have ostracized – have made them aliens – through their law, their public opinions and their community regulation, no matter how learned, how eloquent, or how well disposed we have been.
The American:
   We believe that whatever measures are used, or resorted to, having for its objects the removal of our active, free born Colored population out of these United States, ought, by all true Philanthropists, to be considered and treated as measures taken to perpetuate slavery, with its baneful effects, in this great Republic. The primary objects of the AMERICAN shall be, to convey useful and wholesome information to our colored brethren and at the same endeavor to stimulate them in the paths of education and virtue. Religion, Morality, and Temperance being the three greatest steps in civilization, shall always find a conspicuous place in our sheets. The constitution of these States shall be respected by us, whilst we shall unceasingly cry against Slavery in any manner, firmly believing there exists no such term in the Philanthropist's vocabulary, as Humane slaveholders. The sheets of such pithy Philanthropy as is set forth by the American Colonization Society and its emissaries. For before God we know of no other home for the native born man of color, than these United States. The true interest of our brethren shall be faithfully watched and zealously advocated. Under such impression and with these promises, we have deemed it expedient to call our friends and brethren to support us in our undertaking, resting perfectly satisfied that they are sensibly

convinced of the reality of establishing such a vehicle in this city. The first number of the AMERICAN will appear as soon as a sufficient number of subscribers are obtained to warrant the publishing.

The Weekly Advocate:

We need scarcely say, we are opposed to COLONIZATION. It matters not to us what features it may assume whether it present itself in the garb of philanthropy, or assumes the mild and benign countenance of Christianity, or comes with the selfish aspect of Politics; we will believe, assert, and maintain (So help us God) that we are opposed to the exclusion emigration and colonization of the People of Color of these United States. We hold ourselves ready; at all times to combat with opposite views, and defend these our principles to the last! In regard to TEMPERANCE, we go the whole in this good cause. But our motto is TEMPERANCE IN ALL THINGS. We shall advocate Universal Suffrage and Universal Education, and we shall oppose all Monopolies, which oppress the poor and laboring classes of society.

The Weekly Anglo-African:

In issuing *The Weekly Anglo-African*, we hope to supply a demand too long felt in this community. We need a Press—a press of our own. We need to know something else of ourselves through the press than the everyday statements made up to suit the feelings of the base or the interest of our opponents. We need something more than the general news or the mere gossip of the hour, such as is usually presented to us through the press, in general. Our CAUSE (for in this country we have a cause) demands our advocacy.[28]

In most black newspapers, mobilization appeals were towards the goal of American assimilation. For those blacks who did accept emigration as a viable alternative, Haiti and Central America were considered conditionally favorable. Furthermore, the press's influence on emigration was only significant to the degree its leading advocates could publish pamphlets and treatises. By the late 1850s numerous articles on emigration in papers such as *The Anglo-African, The Fugitive* and *The Pine and Palm* helped to keep the issue before the public's eye; however, these papers were shortlived and their effectiveness could not be compared to that of the anti-emigrationist papers. For example, *The Colored American* was published for over four years under the leadership of Phillip Bell, the Reverend Charles B. Ray, and the Reverend Samuel Cornish. Similarly, *The North Star*, which ran from 1847 to 1850, was edited by Frederick Douglass. The editors of these two journals were influential in the editorship of other papers. Their anti-emigrationist sentiments far exceeded the life span of any single paper they edited. Thus, Cornish's influence as an editor spanned from 1827 to 1840, beginning with *Freedom's Journal* in 1827 and followed by *The Rights of All* in 1829, *The Weekly Advocate* in 1837 and *The Colored American*, which ran from 1837 to 1839. These were critical years for the issue of emigration, years in which Cornish doggedly fought against any notion of colonization or emigration.

As for Douglass, his fame as a runaway slave in 1838 and a lecturer and agent for the Massachusetts Anti-Slavery Society from 1841 to 1847, put him in good stead for his founding of *The North Star* in 1847. However, this was just the first of three publications which would be credited to him. The others were *Frederick Douglass' Paper*, which ran from 1851 to 1855, and *Douglass' Monthly*, from 1858 to 1863.

Thus, the question of self-development was representative of a segment of a community who found "Americanization" and the accumulation of property as significant symbols of their own individual upward mobility. Their ability to continually propagate this interpretation of America for a period of some thirty-four years with very few lapses in between was significant in retarding the development of any large emigrationist movement.

A major point must be established about the distribution capabilities of the black press. An examination of the various newspapers published by the most prominent black editor and writer of antebellum America, Frederick Douglass, shows that from the inception of his first paper, *The North Star*, a fierce "intimate relationship between the editor and his publication" was maintained. Plagued by a discouraging number of cash subscriptions, the paper was supported by Douglass' lectures "in order to keep our heads above water." However, by May 1848, *The North Star* had less than thirty subscribers, and was being ignored by the most prominent abolitionist at that time, William Lloyd Garrison. Notwithstanding the fact that free blacks did not respond to the paper as Douglass would have liked, *The North Star* had five white subscribers for every free black subscriber. In fact, Douglass was to sarcastically remark about the situation of many free blacks' thinking whites should support the paper, while blacks "ought to have copies out of complement."[29] And in an even angrier frame of mind, he editoralized: "That a well conducted press in the hands of Colored Men, is essential to the progress and elevation of the Colored Man . . . [yet] they will read you as one merely seeking a living at public expense."[30]

Assimilationists were similarly restricted in their ability to motivate the free black community. Data also suggest that while 230,000 free blacks lived in the northern and western free states, about 136,000 were literate; yet one observer claimed that less than 20 percent of free blacks in the United States were active or sympathetic abolitionists![31] While this, in turn, does not imply any particular level of support for emigration, it does suggest apathy among blacks on this question.

By 1850, *The North Star*, seeking to pool its readership, was forced to seek subscribers as far away as Great Britain: Glasgow had 42 subscribers; Edinburgh, 14; Falkirk, 8; Belfast, 7; Dublin, 8; and a total of 18 in Derby, Liverpool and London. Yet the paper failed and was forced to be re-published under the name of *Frederick Douglass' Paper* in 1851. While this new publication was also plagued by financial woes, it was able to maintain some semblance of solvency by sponsoring a series of fund-raising activities, including antislavery bazaars where books, letters and poems by contemporary authors were sold under the title "Autographs for Freedom." While these "Belles-Lettres" helped to support Douglass' efforts, they failed to motivate free blacks to vigorously support his paper. This paper—as was also the case with Douglass' last antebellum effort, *Douglass' Monthly*— failed to capture more than a few of the available, literate free black population within the northern free states as subscribers.[32]

Douglass' despair was reflected in a statement made in 1853: "The American Colonization Society tells you to go to Liberia. Mr. Bibb tells you to go to Canada. Others tell you to go to school. We tell you to go to work."[33]

For a readership that was mostly white, Douglass' barbs at the free black populace served to convince a number of white Americans who were receptive to free blacks' demands that the perceptions of slaveholders and their sympathizers with regard to blacks were not limited to that slaveholding group alone.

However, in spite of these criticisms by Douglass and others as to the financial support received by the free black press from their community, black intellectual development was clearly demonstrated by an apparent quality of social analysis in numerous publications. For example, one writer, in examining the relationship of nationalism and free blacks' self perceptions, commented:

> Those of our brethren who are excitedly anxious to fund and endow a "Negro Nationality" in some part of the habitable globe, may possibly be relieved in mind by pursuing the following considerations. Some of us are so keen sighted that a hundred yards distant, and without seeing his face, we can tell a colored man by his walk. Others have such quick ears, without seeing him at all, we can tell a colored man by his voice, and especially by his laugh.
>
> Now, as able editors ought to be, we are as keen sighted and as sharp-eared as the rest; and our ears and eyes have discovered, in one of these United States, nothing short of a "colored state" which during seventy odd years, has successfully "passed for White," but cannot do so much longer.
>
> Our suspicions were aroused a winter or two ago when the representa-

tives of this state in Congress were characterized in the Washington correspondence of the "Tribune" as gentlemen distinguished by "Africanized oratory." That phrase sank deeply into our mind and brain. It did not lie idly, but it turned itself over, and germinated, and led us to keep a watch on the state aforesaid. By and by we discovered that the people live in shabby houses, but loved music and dancing: that they had an eye to art; That their voices had a sweet, musical quality that their young ladies were the veriest witches in the land; That their old men were rooty, and that they did not support their own newspapers. Still, these varied facts did not assume definite form until we further reflected that this state—doubtless shy, as colored people will be in the matter of entering White people's meetings, came very reluctantly into the union. Moreover, it has always been distinguished for "passing first rate resolutions" and then forgetting all about them.

But the crowning fact, which flashed the whole truth upon us like a burst of sunshine, did not occur until last week, when we read the proceedings of the legislature of the state, full of fire and zeal and patriotism, and carrying everything before them *until the hat was handed around for a million dollars.* Then—they behaved so that we incontinently exclaimed, *"Thunder! That's Colored People's meeting."*

Need we say what state this is? Certainly not, for everybody will recognize it [South Carolina]. Being matter of fact, we will give the figures of its progress in population since 1790.

Year	White % incr.	Free Colored % incr.	Slave % incr.
1800	40.00	76.84	36.46
1810	0.14	42.98	34.85
1820	10.85	49.89	31.62
1830	8.6	16.04	22.02
1840	0.47	4.48	3.68
1850	5.97	8.26	17.71
	75.03	198.49	145.82

Entire population in 1850: 274,568   8,960   384,984

Population of its largest city: 25,000   3,849   44,376

The Colored people in this state, and in its principal city, are as two to one White. They increase more rapidly than the Whites and have stamped in their impress upon the state so thoroughly that, in the event of secession, no earthly power can prevent them from becoming it absolutely, as they are now its virtual masters! And what better way is there to account for the desperate energy with which this state struggles to veer from its moorings, than to say that her feeble legislators are magnetized by the terrible energies of their Black superiors to do that act—secession—which will forever consecrate it to God and liberty![34]

For most free blacks the controversy over emigration was suspended with the first shots of the Civil War, leading to reconciliation between some opposing factions. For example, influential emigrationists such as Martin Delany became officers in the Union Army, while assimilationists like Frederick Douglass argued for blacks' greater participation in the armed conflict, by publishing recruiting appeals and posters. But for those blacks who wanted to, or did emigrate to Haiti or Liberia, the pages of *The Weekly Anglo-African* were enough. As late as April 1861 the paper advertised:

> A sailing vessel will leave New York City on May 17th for Hayti. Fifty-one emigrants are already engaged for this vessel. Any others intending to go, under the terms announced by the agents of the government of Hayti, are earnestly requested to give immediate notice to the Bureau.

Though emigrationist spokesmen would shift their efforts towards the North's war efforts, some 2,000 emigrants did travel to Haiti in 1861. However, it was later reported by Holly that two-thirds of them eventually returned dejected, as unpreparedness and complaints about the climate forced them to abandon this alternative to American racism.[36] In addition, elitist appeals to "selective categories" in the press based on financial background, literacy, Christianization and ability to speak French, did little to prepare the emigrant for success. Under these circumstances a betrayal of sorts occurred as emigrationist leaders did not prepare prospective settlers for the type of living conditions awaiting them in Haiti. This was bound to occur as long as the promise of an exciting adventure was placed far above the reality of the social implication of such a move.[37] Furthermore, the very same spokesmen who professed the necessity for emigration ironically retarded its development. It wasn't that this leadership was inarticulate or lacked significant access to the press. Their problem was an inability to counter assimilationist rhetoric with meaningful arguments conceptualizing the relationship between the everyday life of a settler and the pain incurred while developing political-economic sovereignty.

The Rejection of Emigration

Several factors, once publicized in the black press, mitigated against any significant number of free blacks' emigrating to Africa, Haiti or other areas during the antebellum period. There were several reasons for this. Primary was the inability of free blacks to establish a meaningful, well-organized structure which would secure their financial and physical well-being. Laden with the moral ironies of a Christian slaveholding society, blacks' social analysis generally viewed Christianity as a blessing, while condemning Christian slaveholders as hypocrites. However, a still more condemning attitude was maintained in respect to Africa as an un-Christianized continent. In this regard, colonization and emigration were tolerable, if the propagation of the gospel was the stated goal.

There was still a more politically intriguing viewpoint, one which saw emigrationists and settlers as auxiliary colonists for imperial expansion. From this perspective, "outward bound" free blacks, as suggested by Frank Blair, were "suitable emissaries of empire," which could be trusted to remember their benefactors, while laying the foundation for further American expansion in Africa.[38] Sensing that "The colonization scheme was set on foot and is yet maintained by slaveholders, with the view, as they have not been backward to declare, of perpetuating their system, undisturbed," Cornish and Wright in their article "The Colonization Scheme Considered" described the colonized mind and its undesirableness for free blacks. Commenting on a 1825 letter from Jehudi Ashmun, a colonial agent in Monrovia, Liberia, in which Ashmun pressed "upon the managers of the society [ACS] the importance of sending WHITE missionaries to Africa," rather than blacks like Lott Cary, they stated: "Every month's experience proves ... [that the natives] ARE CORRUPTED BY THE INFLUENCES OF BAD EXAMPLES, AND DERIVE NO BENEFIT FROM THE GOOD, that are set in the colony."[39] Supporting Ashmun's argument on the unsuitability of free blacks as colonists in Africa, Cornish and Wright quoted freely from Ashmun's complaints to the ACS in 1827:

> "It is not known to every one how little difference can be perceived in the measure of intellect possessed by an illiterate rustic from the United States and a sprightly native of the coast." — The fact certainly is, "that the advantage is oftenest, clearly on the side of the latter. — 'an unlimited' indulgence of appetite; and the labored excitement and unbounded and gratification of lust the most unbridled and beastly — are ingredients of the African character." Such is the common character of all; and it operates with all the power of an ever present example of the colonist, from the moment of their arrival in Africa. It must produce its effects. It has produced them, and without a powerful counteracting agency, it must, at no great distance of time, as surely leaven the whole mass, as human nature shall continue what it is. "Colonists thus suffer a double dis-advantage — are subjected to all that is contaminating in the character of the natives, at the same time that they have passed beyond the reach of corrective example of enlightened Christians.[40]

Interestingly enough, while drawing upon a variety of reasons why free blacks should resist Africanization, assimilationists throughout the antebellum period were also developing intellectual arguments which questioned the philosophical assumptions of white America, those asserting that blacks were undisciplined, childlike people who fitted well within John Locke's fundamental ideas of a propertied class and its need for political control and subservience.

A major aspect of this rejectionist argument was centered on a "practical response" needed for day-to-day living, which almost by definition excluded emigrationist appeals. This argument also suggested that free blacks should reject emigration outright, due to kinship ties and social commitments which had developed in America and were too difficult to either renounce or terminate. Such ties, they claimed, were bound to evoke apprehensions, if not renunciations, if any call to leave America was pursued, whether it was labelled colonization or emigration. As one writer explained:

> If we look minutely, we shall discover the demon of colonization busy at work—doing as she always has been, since its first organization, exciting oppression and prejudice upon an already injured but useful portion of the community. Some of the members of the convention even went so far as to say, that by drawing the cords tighter upon the Blacks, they would consequently be forced to look at Africa for a home, and thus fall in with the conservative measures of the colonization society! Such sentiments, such language should inspire every one of us to take a renewed stand to become united ... and with a like spirit to that which prompted Hamilcar, the Carthagenian general, to make his son, Hannibal swear, at the altar of his country, eternal hatred to the Romans—prompt each and every one of us to renew our opposition, and swear eternal hatred to the American Colonization Society.... In conclusion, I trust that, that spirit which prompted us in Philadelphia, to take a stand against the colonization society in 1817, at its outset, is glowing in us, and in the bosom of every colored man throughout the country, and that we will determine from this day, now, henceforth and forever, to sacrifice our lives and all we hold dear, before we will consent to emigrate to the burning shores of Africa.[41]

Throughout this antebellum period, both colonizationists and emigrationists found it extremely difficult to develop any collective resolve around this issue. While the vehicles for social expression were increasing, so were the restraining conditions inherent in them. Social ambiguity and political indecision were matched with feelings of collective apprehension that further restricted outward expression of self. American platitudes, such as upward mobility, education, Christianization and equality, were mimicked rather than mocked. While advocating a superiority of moral intent, they also assumed that sociopolitical progress was a result of an elite stratum's pursuance of justifiable economic and cultural goals. Emigration and colonization, they suggested, were the immoral twin sisters of slavery, and, as a result, the outgrowth of an allegiance to a former system of authority which in its final analysis must be destroyed.

Most editors were acutely aware that financial solvency of their newspaper depended on the political and social relevancy of its message to potential backers. As a result, much of this "elitist" interest for "journalistic truth" was coterminous with the concepts of assimilation and anti-emigration. That the efforts of assimilationists were not geared towards the destruction of America attests to their felt obligations to inform a journalistic leadership poised with a sense of duty and responsibility to liberate people intellectually, not physically, out of the land of their oppression. Consequently, anti-emigrationist editors such as Cornish argued that "the delivery" must not be a return to the "wilderness" of an ignoble past, in that: "we cannot act in this respect so ignobly as our Pilgrim fathers did.... We will stay and seek the purification of the whole lump."[42]

This was the rhetoric of a perceived consummation, a fulfillment in its initial stage. Accordingly, by rejecting emigration, this leadership affirmed their Americanism with the "rhetoric of a pro-movement," which clearly and decisively articulated "a rhetoric of assent and allegiance" to America.[43]

In similar fashion, when the minutes from an 1839 anti-colonizationist meeting in New York was published by *The Colored American*, delegates supported by McCune Smith resolved:

> That the first principle of Republican government is, "that all men are by nature free and equal," and that the American Colonization Society, by denying that the Colored Man can rise, in the Republic, to the full enjoyment of its institutions, denies the eternal principle of Freedom and Equality, and is anti-Republican in its principles and tendency....
> The men whom we never solicited thrust their advice upon us; When men whom we never injured, load us with malignant abuse; When cold, crafty and designing men, select us, the few and feeble, as the instruments by which they may strike a death blow at the vitals of the Republic, then we are called upon, by our duty to ourselves, to those very men, and to our country, by all that is holy in principle and noble in patriotism, to meet and lift our warning voice to our fellow citizens, so that if they listen the republic may be saved, and if they heed not, we may at least have the consolation of having warned them in season.[44]

The attempt by pro-assimilationists to communicate, petition and pray for a stronger commitment of the races to work together during the antebellum period had at its core two major strategies. First, there was a desire to get blacks to respond "obediently" to the precepts of a leadership class well indoctrinated in aspirations of upward mobility. Secondly, they sought this actualization, through the development of a counter-movement's "perfecting myth." That is to say, it was necessary that anti-emigrationists appear to be successful in their efforts "to achieve the incarnation, or embodiment, in the actualities of the material world," by the creating and visualization of "America's promise [of] "Heaven, paradise, the good society, utopia."[45]

Needless to say, in rejecting emigration, assimilationist editors were not remiss in their "duty" to remind their readership of the need to become pure Americans in material acquisition and in moral standing. Praising and exclaiming the virtues of American citizenship and Christian development, their explicit claim to be part of a superior political entity requiring total dedication to its precepts, minus slavery, were paramount. Within this context, emigration, colonization, and even Africa, were unacceptable visions for social or political elevation.

The second strategy, as explained earlier in Chapter II, was also critical, in that an editor's ability to transfer "assumed" social expectations of an elite stratum to the general free black populace was primary in retarding emigrationist appeals, regardless of the mounting intensification of anti-black restrictions and legislation throughout the 1850s.

Critical to the success of these strategies was the existence of a supportive public constituency. However, the defining or interpreting of social reality rested largely within the hands of those whose vested interest in society and their own development within a relatively secure structure was assured.

The propagation of assimilation as the most viable political alternative for social elevation was now in place. In this regard, admissions by Cornish that it was within his province to restrict the publishing of various articles which contradicted his position simply underlined the discrepancy between *The Colored American* and reality. In a similar fashion, editorial dictates of Frederick Douglass, Phillip Bell and David Ruggles strongly suggest that the conflict between what *was* published in their newspapers was often biased, if not in contradiction to reality. This must have been undoubtedly reflected in free blacks' evaluation of social and historical occurrences.[46]

In like fashion, the effects of such an editorial policy based upon pluralistic causal inferences camouflaged class conflict while reinforcing the incongruency between ideas, conduct and social experiences. As a result, it is concluded that the restraining of salient information about society by assimilationist editors crippled the ability of an unknowing public to make clear decisions, in line with their best interests. Therefore, it is not surprising to read emigrationist complaints, such as:

> The reader ought also to bear in mind, that objections are not unfrequently the offspring of partial knowledge. A little more light, and the frightful apparitions will appear to be familiar and harmless objects. Difficulties ought indeed to be pondered, and obstacles may be so numerous and insurmountable as to prove the project utterly chimerical; but we maintain that many real and apparent difficulties may be attendant on an enterprise highly prudent and benevolent.[47]

Nevertheless, assimilationist writers and editors dismissed such analysis as another example of whites trying to convince the "weak at heart" as to their total unfitness as a people to rise from "their present ignorant condition and debasement in this country."[48] Attempting to "convert" free blacks into social assets, they chided emigrationists' rhetoric for not:

> Patronizing and protecting those most worthy: Teaching them morality and religion, assisting and encouraging them in learning and pursuing the mechanic arts; extending their efforts to the lowest among them, and the slaves.[49]

The disseminating of social constructs on this order had a cogent effect upon free blacks, for it attacked the context of their day-to-day existence, while reinforcing the individual's sense of belonging geographically and possibly occupationally to America. Thus, in another article from Douglass' paper, one writer exclaims:

> The intelligent and gifted colored men are more wanted here than anywhere else, because here are so many befogged and prejudiced Whites whose vision needs to be corrected by examples near at hand, and because, also, here are so many of their colored brethren to be cheered, guided and elevated by their examples and counsel.[50]

The significance of this point rests largely upon the black assimilationist newspaper editors who reproduced and disseminated the ideology of individualism by selectively publishing the works of sympathetic writers, ministers and educators.[51] Furthermore, in rejecting emigration, assimilationist editors projected themselves and their publications into an ideological fight to "clarify" conflicting perceptions of America: The variances between liberty and equality; democracy and an enforced social hierarchy; human rights and property rights; and finally, social dispersion and cultural convergence. In addition, Douglass' publishing of resolutions from an 1854 anti-colonization and anti-Nebraska meeting accentuated what assimilationist editors saw as their role in focusing free blacks' attention on social justice and political integration.

Protesting the United States Senate's passing of the Nebraska bill, which allowed "485,000 square miles of territory, solemnly consecrated to freedom ... to the slave power, to satiate, for the time being, its merciless ferocity, its evergrasping cupidity," assimilationists resolved:

> That we are fully satisfied that the American Colonization Society is using every effort to excite prejudice against us, to prevent our elevation in the United States, and deserves not only our condemnation, but that of every true lover of liberty.
>
> That any Colored Man who can prove so recreant to the interest of his brethren, as to advocate their expatriation to Africa, or countenance the colonization society by word or action, deserves the execration of every one of our people throughout this country.
>
> That we reiterate the sentiments of our fathers expressed in 1817, viz; To oppose colonization at all times and in all places; and to promulgate to the world that we intend to remain in this, the land of our nativity.
>
> That the colonization of the colored people of the United States to Africa or elsewhere, should be wholly discountenanced by them because it is based on a denial of their equal manhood.
>
> That the Homestead Bill, as passed by the House of Representatives, is not only unchristian, but basely ungrateful, seeing that it deprives men of their rights on account of their color, when that color was not thought of as a hinderance to their suffering in two wars to maintain the rights of the American people.
>
> That our opposition to the Nebraska Bill is not based simply on the fact that it violates the Missouri Compromise of 1820, but grows out of our conviction that therefore no opportunity whatever ought to be given the people in any new territory to declare hereafter as property *Human Rights* who can never be made property.
>
> That whatever differences of opinion may be entertained on the right of new territories to legislate for themselves, we understand too well the policy of the south not to know that the Nebraska Bill contemplates the extension of slavery, and we therefore regard it as peculiarly affecting us, by our identification with the slaves of the South.
>
> That we are opposed to all compromises between Freedom and Slavery, believing that slavery has no rights, but is pregnant wtih wrongs; and therefore we stop not to consider whether the Nebraska Bill violates this

or that compromise, but seeing in it a foe to Freedom we stamp it as a document meriting the execration of every friend of man.

That the thanks of the colored citizens of Philadelphia be tendered to the Hon. Messrs; Seward, Chase, Sumner and Wade, of the Senate, and the Hon. Messr. Smith of N.Y. and Giddens of Ohio, of the House, for the able manner they defended our rights.[52]

Herein lies the political spectrum which motivated assimilationist editors to theoretically legitimize America as the political framework for free blacks. Neutrality, they argued, was no longer a question, as both social and political commitment were now defined by a necessity for material gain. While Africans in America were now generally defined by at least two newspaper editors as "Colored Americans," possibilities for upward mobility as "Americans" clashed with racial and class barriers, fostering a social duality which often presented conflicting descriptions of self by free blacks, as when we read:

Thus this society [ACS], cold and heathen in its doctrine; destructive of the best interests of a whole people in its practice; is with unhallowed hands endeavoring to arrest their [Free Blacks'] progress from slavery to freedom, and from misery to happiness, by the removal of the *virtuous, intelligent, exemplary* Free Blacks; leaving the more debased and miserable to wallow a few ages more in the mire of brutality and vice, without a friend to advise, or a brother to protect them; subject to the exercise of a mean and unjustifiable prejudice on the part of the Whites....

Here, then we have contradiction in terms, and which I assert no man of ordinary judgement and reflection can possibly reconcile; to *select men profoundly ignorant and debased, and send them to Africa to civilize and Christianize those equally so with themselves*, is revolting to common sense; and here let it be remembered that these are among the most plain and distinct avowals of the society.[53]

These conflicting sentiments were indicative of an unavoidable strain within the black press, in that any acceptance of emigration, assimilationists argued, suggested racial "gullability." Yet it was Douglass' warning of selective emigration, stripping free blacks of their most "intelligent populace" from the upper strata which clearly indicated the class nature of their fears. Concerns of this sort were rampant throughout the black press as editors attempted to legitimize the system as a whole, while condemning those aspects which ran counter to their perceived assimilationist interests. Objectivity and balance were often pulled in conflicting directions, as blacks' self-interest at one point projected the social institutions of America, yet at another point, opposed the institutional framework of slavery. The extremity of these factors often left free blacks exposed to the dangers of an ambiguous interpretation of their reality, especially when leaders such as Douglass would assert: "The best defense of Free American institutions is the heart of the American people themselves."[54] Thus, rhetorical appeals by editors like Douglass defined social involvement as the systemization of "legitimized" beliefs of social cohesion. Moreover, the restraining of blacks' social recognition as equals, intensified rather than diminished their demands for social entry. In fact, Douglass, in a terse disclaimer on emigration and overt racial politicalization, opined:

> I think the course to be pursued by the Colored Press is to say less about race and claims to race recognition, and more about the principles of justice, liberty and patriotism.[55]

Though one cannot assert that editors such as Douglass or Cornish disavowed *all* racial loyalties in deference to interests based on upward mobility, their interpretation of such loyalties seriously shaped their construction of reality as editors in two ways.

First, with the rejection of emigration and colonization came the establishment of a political platform based upon the concerns and beliefs of an elite segment of Americans, who envisioned individual growth as the prerequisite for social attainment. Any exclusionary process, it was rationalized, negated the possibility of an eventual pooling of blacks now living in slavery, into the American political structure. In a sense, black editors were acutely aware of a narrowing sociopolitical base if they were to ever emigrate to a society lacking an established commercial structure, such as Liberia. Conversely, they argued, if forced to Haiti, only the selected, entrepreneurial type should be allowed to emigrate, so as to eventually establish a basis for the eventual financial subjugation of the southern slave states' cotton industry.

Second, while the political goal of assimilationists was based primarily upon an idealized belief in the American Constitution, their severe questioning of its interpretation, implementation, constitutional process, and its effectiveness as an instrument for cultural and political "enlightenment" or "civilization" was pronounced.

Yet the reformist characteristics of anti-emigrationist rhetoric clashed with the more radical approach of its protagonists. With a free black population well indoctrinated, socialized and accepting of "American" beliefs, reformist rhetoric was more in keeping with the antebellum emphasis on individual development, than the rhetoric of emigrationists, whose appeals continually failed to equate social elevation with political sovereignty. Indeed, major attention must be given to the situational context of political rhetoric as it coalesces with the ongoing events of the day or differs in a manner which prohibits any galvanizing of political elements for social change. For example, not until the emergence of another exigency, re-enslavement as the result of the stringent Fugitive Slave Act of 1850, did black editors begin to entertain emigration as a viable alternative. Thus, it is observed that while the efforts by anti-emigrationist editors were not as radical as emigrationists', their demands for equal political involvement within America were viewed as a serious threat by white America. In a more dramatic manner, the insistence of assimilationists to participate equally within society was an attempt by free blacks to practice American nationalism. It demonstrated their acceptance of the philosophical notions of individual growth, social betterment and Christian enlightenment.

In their rejection of emigration, prominent editors such as Cornish, Douglass, Bell, and Ruggles continually expressed a reluctance to abandon the slave. Aware that the existence of 3,953,760 slaves in 1860, compared to 488,070 free blacks, represented a political threat of considerable proportion if utilized effectively, editors were acutely sensitive to any argument which suggested separation from this potential power base. Cornish, recognizing if not fearing the loss of such a base, argued:

> The discharge of duty also, renders our situation, in this country, even *desirable*. Much better that we suffer affliction with our Brethren than we flee our country, and "enjoy the pleasures of sin for a season." Let no man, therefore, endeavor to seduce any of us to forsake the land of our birth, and the graves of our fathers. For high and holy purposes we have determined to remain here.
> The few of us that have qualifications for, and the means of leaving the country, should act the part of *Base Traitors* were we to do so, and leave behind the millions of our Brethren, who are in bondage, and cannot go. We will never do it! God hath placed beneath a Colored skin a soul too noble to be guilty of such conduct. We have suffered sore affliction, and we know how to suffer still. Our tribulation has worked in us patience, and patience experience, and experience hope—such as maketh us not ashamed.
> We will never swerve from our purposes—universal emancipation and universal enfranchisement—should we die in the pursuit, we will die VIRTUOUS MARTYRS in a holy cause.[56]

Finally, attention must be directed towards attempts to trivialize emigrationist rhetoric. We know, for example, that social movements must work industriously to transmit their messages without having them trivialized, fragmented or rendered incoherent by counterarguments. In other words, emigrationists' radical philosophy, whose ideas conflicted not only with existing political frames but with day-to-day practicalities, made assimilationist efforts appear to be legitimate if not logical states for social elevation. Expounding upon the virtues of a Christian society, editors converted their papers into reformist publications as opposed to the more dangerous stance of political deviants. Though the suggestion that being a "free black" was in itself a "deviant" classification, editors of an assimilationist bent and the elite strata were generally convinced that the acquisition of individualized worth and industriousness would soon produce a change in social attitudes for the better. It was also their analysis that the rejection of emigration would provide a moral "signal" to abolitionists that the struggle for equality was ideologically connected with antislavery movements. The two issues, they argued, were inextricably connected. This development tended to polarize the more controversial writers of the day, while marginalizing their effectiveness.[58] Similarly, emigrationist editors in their attempt to place moderate free blacks in social frames which would reduce their effectiveness failed as their efforts were largely relegated only to treatises and pamphlets up until the late 1850s. On the other hand, Cornish and Douglass were able to publish anti-emigrationist journals from 1827 until late 1863. Their adroitness in rejecting emigration signified an ongoing dilemma which reached down into the social fiber of the Africans' struggle, first for survival, and then for recognition as individuals possessing all of the qualities attributed to humans. This internal struggle for external societal respect is a significant aspect of the free blacks' antebellum experience.

While the dominant social structure sought to keep the conflict over emigration a domestic issue, slaveholding interests were aware that a deeper challenge to the social order existed if assimilationists and emigrationists were to resolve their conflict. Given this fact, the reluctance of assimilationist editors to forgo the trappings of a well-mannered, well-ordered, status-oriented movement condemned any possibility of their integrating their efforts with those of a radical political movement, much to the pleasure of slaveholding interests.

Furthermore, pro-emigrationist articles in the liberal-minded *Weekly Anglo-African* could not offset or retard years of assimilationist rhetoric. Efforts by Delany in Africa and Holly in Haiti were trivialized as symbols of emotional rather than *pragmatic* events. Assimilationists had seemingly won the day, as Douglass' 1854 statement noted "The Colored Man can be improved or elevated here— or he can be improved and elevated nowhere." Yet on the very eve of the Civil War, Douglass was surprisingly pushed by events to assert:

> We are in favor of emigration as a Colored Man, just as we should be if we were an Englishman or an Irishman, living in England or Ireland. To you who have no foothold HERE, we should say, go THERE. But as we should not be in favor of saying to all the people of those countries, be off, so we are not in favor of saying to all, the Colored people here, move off. We are far from calling upon any part of our people to emigrate, for public reasons, such as inability to live among White people, or for the charms of a "COLORED NATIONALITY." The things for which men should emigrate, are food, clothing, property, education, manhood and material prosperity, and he who has these things where he is, had better stay where he is, and exert the power which they give him to overcome whatever of social or political oppression which may surround him.[59]

Straddling the ideological chasm of "A Colored Nationality" and the "promises" of American absorption, Douglass personified the duality which black editors projected and fostered in their publications. By denying free blacks the right to emigrate, or develop a progressive identification with their history, cultural nationalism was denigrated as a step *away* from social elevation and national assimilation. Moreover, an increasing hostility towards blacks by whites raised such a level of "incessant self-questioning and hesitation" that a nullifying, politically impotent, philosophical agenda was adopted by the few existing editors on the question of emigration. While this agenda did vary in its intensity, its general assimilationist position inquired of blacks: "What, after all, am I? Am I an American or am I a Negro? Can I be both? Or is it my duty to cease to be a Negro as soon as possible and be an American?"[60]

Annoyed at this indecisiveness in the black press and incensed at the constant baiting, mudslinging and status-motivated rhetoric, one writer, signing his name anonymously as "P," openly declared his feeling to Douglass by asserting:

> Now, Mr. Editor, a word more, and I am done. Since all profess to labor for the same end—the elevation of our people—why need we impugn each other's efforts. Argument may at length convince those in the wrong of their error, and convert those in the right, but contempt and ridicule, never.—Vinegar never catches flies, except those little tiny flies of wings too feeble for independent flight, that are always found hovering about, and resting upon that what looks bigger than themselves.[61]

Thus, a prolongation of belief steeped in the bitterness of social experience, finding expression in rhetorical constructs reflecting hope, fear and an indefatigable insistence on social respect, *could not* erase the oppressive reality of antebellum America from the pages of the black press. Being so, the ghostly aura of a movement lived on to inspire, and haunt, the next generation of reformers, while the most radical elements curdled into sectarian isolation. A movement's spirit and its single-issue programs were split apart, to the detriment of each other.[62]

Epilogue

Throughout antebellum America a myriad of class, caste, gender and racial dynamics underlined the relationship between an embryonic black press and that segment of the population which it claimed to represent. During this particular era, the pale of politics overshadowed but did not germinate from the free black communities of America. With this in mind, most free blacks considered the acquisition of power (economic and political influence) a possibility only at the sufferance of white America.

For a few who appeared successful, the hope of a future, as nebulous as it seemed, was measured by the most humble of attainments. Their battle, personalized by a day-to-day struggle for survival, was geared to find relief from the blinding, numbing reality of physical needs and the psychologically debilitating comprehension of their social-political irrelevancy for white America. Added to this were social exigencies which placed heavy emphasis on the individual's ability to cultivate a compliant attitude which disguised bitterness while seeking redress from the status of being a member of a pariah class. For a variety of "individualized" reasons this led many to agree that only by extirpating themselves from the mass of "Black folk" could they demonstrate an individuality, humility and dependability acceptable to the larger society.

At the nexus of this contradiction was the existence of naked, abusive, coercive power. This in fact formed the basis for all social relationships; power whose use and interpretation of society were not only disarming but sedutive in their ferocity, as shibboleths of the "noble western man" were transformed into the ideology of terror. Within this political atmosphere, the push for "assimilation" by free blacks was an attempted withdrawal from a condition of powerlessness. However, in a more succinct fashion it was a process, highlighted by expository challenges, aimed at established state power for the removal or modifying of social grievances. It carried with it the suggestion of an alternative direction for a reluctant society. For blacks it was the gathering of influence on the community level and the recognition of a need for authority figures on a national level.

Social response to this development was never consistent, even as individuals began to assess their chances to rise and did so in deference to the entire community. Some concluded that in individualized effort a level of respect otherwise denied would result. It did at a price, for power (the drive for domination, the ability to act and control consequences in antebellum America) required of the individual an obedience to the demands of racial/class hierarchy, social stratification and the emphatic condemnation of themselves as members of a pariah class. Furthermore, many free blacks concluded that, "if this was reality," then the drive for power was the only alternative, the only way to "set an example" for the race, via individual attainment. Thus, individual attainment became a double-edged sword in that while it was accepted as being synonymous with racial progress, it also implied isolation, restlessness, unfulfillment, and a search for freedom through autonomy; it was the creating of a terrible social anxiety within the individual as it was the establishment of a social enigma. From this, cursory assumptions formed that economic parity would somehow emerge between free blacks and a growing white labor class, minimizing the importance of racial/class contradictions in an expanding capitalistic process.[1] In other words, the concept of "racial uplift" as a communal process was replaced with notions of racial equality vis-à-vis individualized attainment. For free blacks, this of course challenged their awareness of social practice, namely, American platitudes on the "ideal" society.

Individualism in antebellum America was viewed as an indicator of character. It was what legitimized and separated the free black from the stigma of slavery. For the editor/publisher it also represented the needed growth of entrepreneurship which, it was hoped, would eventually be converted into increased newspaper sales and financial backing. Thus, it was argued the success of the individual would establish "the race" for most blacks, for this represented a breaking away from the "ordinariness of being simply black," a state of being which editors generally viewed as "shapeless, unremarkable, bland-in-a-word, an amorphous condition of life."[2]

Within this context, the black editor was a power broker articulating from a biased class perspective the exploitive relationships between the state and the individual. To an even greater extent, he was the personification of "power," (influence) within the free black community as he negotiated, bargained and defined reality with a flair which suggested privity, social sophistication and insight.

The problem of translating "American individualism" into a social lexicon acceptable to both a racist social structure and its oppressed race left few if any totally acceptable options for racial harmony, yet most editors viewed the following positions as possibilities:

> [To] pursue the concept of accommodation and assimilation thereby hoping to convince other Blacks that to assimilate into the United States would be the best policy for survival. Such a policy in a sense suggested that official tolerance of the American government should be sought on all levels of Free Black society, and that the enactment of a variety of strategies geared towards social entry and acceptance should commence.
> [To] attack the entire social structure as being a racist slave-owning society which Blacks must separate from, regardless of the economic and political ramifications. While this view came close to advocating an outright attempt towards successful rebellion with national sovereignty as a possible goal, it generally favored the development of separate settlements within America in a more accommodating manner. Its interesting twist was the advocating of settlements in Canada, the Caribbean and Africa with eventual nationhood as a possible political goal.

With few exceptions, the black press as the major vehicle for political discussion by blacks chose the former opinion while only "reporting" on the latter position's more militant viewpoint. Consequently, in a manner typical of a reformist press financially "bonded" to the economic rationale of society, most black antebellum newspapers chose not to disengage themselves from the American experience.

Interestingly enough, while touting the values deemed acceptable and necessary for social integration, this press played an increasingly influential role in the demystification of white political hegemony. Arguing that the eliminating of racial hegemony would reduce social conflicts, it was hoped that any resulting political involvement would then become a more pleasurable experience for the entire society. However, key to this "pleasurable" experience was blacks' acceptance of the dominant social-political "truths" of America and its valued perception of individualized power. Succinctly put, it was the internalized, imitative images of the dominant culture which had to be legitimized for all blacks. Consequently, subverting America was not an acceptable value for most black editors; demanding recognition was. Herein was the inner meaning of an earlier observation, in that, "We rejoice that we are thrown into revolution where the contest is not for landed territory, but for freedom; The weapons not carnal, but spiritual."[3] Moreover, the concept of "individualized growth" was not aimed at the total delineating of free blacks from their enslaved brethren, nor to undo Western Christian culture, but to sensitize free blacks to an eventual correction of their penalized condition within America.

Finally, with the exception of a few newspapers, journals and broadsheets, emigrationists such as Martin Delany, James Holly, and John Russwurm were characterized by assimilationists as irresponsible editors who were not totally appreciative of the enlightenment of Western civilization. Little favor was received in the black press for those advocating colonization or emigration, be they conspiratorial slave owners, white politicians such as Henry Clay or emigrationists. It was only with the emergence of militant postbellum editors who chose to view emigration with active curiosity, if not open approval, that we begin to see an attempt to relate terms such as nationalism and emigration with self-determination and nationhood.

While the confusion and indecision of this era retarded any dynamic push toward emigration or political sovereignty, the voices of the abused yet resilient African in North America maintained a bitterness which to this day defies any misinterpretation:

> Emigration may place a very important role in the solution of the question of our position in this country. Whatever may be the wishes of the thoughtful men of the race, the mass of our people in the south are growing fearfully restless under the wrongs and outrages to which they are subjected daily, and they will certainly attempt, in the near future to seek in emigration, or otherwise, that protection and immunity which the lying constitution of the United States denies, and has always denied them.
>
> anonymous, *The Globe*,
> New York, January 13, 1883

Chapter Notes

Introduction

1. Martin Dann, ed., *The Black Press*, New York: Capricorn Books, 1972, p. 12.
2. *The North Star*, April 27, 1849, p. 1.
3. Armstead Pride, *Registry and History of Negro Newspapers in the United States, 1827–1950*, Ph.D Thesis, Northwestern University.
4. Rashey B. Moten, *The Negro in Kansas*, Master's Thesis, University of Kansas, 1938, pp. 20–21.
5. *The Colored American*, February 16, 1839, p. 1.
6. *Freedom's Journal*, September 1827, November 2, 1827.
7. *The Rights of All*, June 12, 1829; *The Colored American*, April 15, 1836; Paolo Friere, *Pedagogy of the Oppressed*, New York (The Seabury Press, 1973), pp. 33–36.
8. *The Weekly Anglo-African*, July 23, 1859.

Chapter I

1. *The Weekly Advocate*, January 14, 1837, p. 2.
2. Edward S. Abby, *Journal of a Residence and Tour in the United States of North America* (3 vols., London, 1835), III, pp. 246–47.
3. Ira Berlin, *Slaves Without Masters: The Free Negro in the Antebellum South* (New York, 1976), p. 45.
4. Oliver Cox, *Caste, Class and Race* (New York, 1948), p. 291.
5. Berlin, p. 37.
6. Ibid.
7. Carter G. Woodson, *Free Negro Heads of Families in the United States in 1830* (Washington, D.C., 1925), Intro., p. vi.
8. Franklin Frazier, *The New Negro Family in the United States* (New York, 1945), p. 145.
9. Berlin, p. 178.
10. Ibid.
11. Donald Robinson, *Slavery in the Structure of American Politics, 1765–1820* (New York, 1979), pp. 122–30. Quotation in petition from Henrico County, 1784.
12. Benjamin Quarles, *The Negro in the American Revolution* (Durham, 1961), pp. 19–32.

13. Benjamin Quarles, *Black Abolitionist* (New York, 1969), p. 9.
14. David Cooper, *A Serious Address to the Rules of America, on the Inconsistency of Their Conduct Respecting Slavery.*
15. Walter Clark, ed., *The State Records of North Carolina, 1777-1790*, 10 vols. (AMS Press), reprint of 1895 edition.
16. Berlin, p. 22.
17. John Bassett, *Slavery in the State of North Carolina* (1899), pp. 40-42.
18. Ibid., pp. 41-42; Berlin, Appendix I, p. 396.
19. *Maryland Colonization Journal* (new series), p. 122.
20. *Third Census of the United States*, 1810, p. 82.
21. *Fifth Census of the United States*, 1830, pp. 105-06.
22. Frazier, p. 146.
23. *Laws of Louisiana*, 1816-1817, pp. 44-48.
24. *Seventh Census of the United States*, 1850, p. 473.
25. *New Orleans Semi-Weekly Creole*, November 5, 1854.
26. *Opelousas Patriot*, February 19, 1859.
27. Ibid., December 4, 1858.
28. *Baton Rouge Daily Gazette and Comet*, January 28, 1859.
29. Woodson, p. xv.
30. *The Colored American*, July 8, 1839, p.2.
31. *The Pacific Appeal*, August 23, 1862, p.1.
32. Cox, p. 304.
33. Grace King, *New Orleans, the Place and the People* (New York, 1915), pp. 334-46.
34. Marvin Meyers, *The Jacksonian Persuasion: Politics and Belief* (Stanford, 1957), pp. 123-25.
35. Noelle Bissert, *Education, Class, Language and Ideology* (London, 1979), pp. 7-13.
36. H.E. Sterkx, *The Free Negro in Antebellum Louisiana* (New Jersey, 1972), pp. 7-13.
37. Ibid., pp. 203-04.
38. David Dodge, "The Free Negroes in North Carolina," *Atlantic Monthly*, 57 (January 1886): 24.
39. Robert B. Toplin, "The Spector of Crisis: Slaveholder Reactions to Abolitionism in the United States and Brazil," *Civil War History*, 18 (June 1972): 136.
40. John Hope Franklin, *The Free Negro in North Carolina, 1790-1860* (New York, 1943), p. 136.
41. Frantz Fanon, *Towards the African Revolution* (New York, 1965), p. 40.
42. David B. Davis, *The Problem of Slavery in Western Culture* (New York, 1966), p. 309.
43. *The Colored American*, February 9 and 16, 1839; February 17, 1838.
44. Delaware State Archives, *Petitions, Slavery and the Negro*, 1832.
45. *Minutes of the Proceedings of the Convention for the Improvement of the Free People of Color*, 1830, pp. 10-11.
46. *The Colored American*, September 20, 1837, p.2.
47. Franklin Frazier, *The Negro Church in America* (New York, 1963), p. 82.
48. *The Colored American*, April 19, 1839, p. 2; April 15, 1837, p. 2; June 24, 1837, p. 3; October 28, 1837, p. 1.
49. Frazier, *The Negro Church*, pp. 17-34.
50. M.W. Fisher, "Lott Cary: The Colonizing Missionary," *Journal of Negro History*, 7 (October 1922): 381.

51. Samuel Cornish, *Rights of All*, August 7, 1829, p. 29.
52. Ibid.
53. Frederick Douglass, "The Present and Future of the Colored Race in America (June 1863)," in *Negro Social and Political Thought*, H. Brotz, ed. (New York, 1966), p. 268.
54. Quarles, *Black Abolitionist*, p. 49.
55. Woodson, "The Friend of Man (Utica, March 14, 1838)," p. 91; "Standards" (July 2, 1840); "Martin B. Duberman," in *Negro Orators* (Russell Press, 1925), p. 165.
56. Carol George, *Segregated Sabbaths: Richard Allen and the Emergence of Independent Black Churches, 1760-1840* (New York, 1973), p. 136.
57. Floyd Miller, *The Search for a Black Nationality* (Chicago, 1975), p. 7.
58. Rev. Issac Van Arsdale Brown, *Biography of the Rev. Robert Finley* (New York, 1969), p. 123.
59. Ibid.
60. *The Anglo-African Magazine*, 1:10, October 1858, p. 307.
61. *Genius of Universal Emancipation*, IV, November 1824, pp. 27-28.
62. *Journal of Proceedings of Bethel Church, 1822-1831*, p. 94.
63. *Address of the Board of Managers of the Haitian Emigration Society of Colored People, to Emigrants intending to sail to the Island of Hayti, in the Brig. DeWitt Clinton*, 1824, p. 7.
64. Miller, p. 78.
65. P.J. Straudenraus, "Table of Annual Receipts and Colonists Sent to Liberia by the American Colonization Society," Quoted in *The African Colonization Movement* (New York, 1961), Appendix.
66. George, pp. 140-151.
67. John Dowling, "Sketches of New York Baptists," in *Baptist Monthly Record*, IV (1949): 297; also see George, p. 145.
68. Daniel Coker, *Journal of Daniel Coker* (Baltimore, 1820), pp. 42-43.
69. *African Repository*, Vol. XI, p. 277.
70. "Education for Colonization: Attempts to Educate Free Blacks in the United States for Emigration to Africa, 1823-1833," *Journal of Negro History*, 43 (1974): 93.
71. *African Repository*, loc. cit.
72. *Freedom's Journal*, November 2, 1827.
73. *African Repository*, Vol. XI, p. 294.
74. Ibid., Vol. IV, p. 204.
75. George William, *History of the Negro Race in the United States from 1619-1880* (New York, 1968), p. 67.
76. Woodson, p. 261.
77. National Negro Convention of 1835, *Minutes of the Fifth Annual Convention of the Free People of Color in the United States*, held by Adjournments, in the Wesley Church, Philadelphia, 1 June inclusive to 1835. pp. 26-27.
78. Ibid.
79. Ibid.
80. *National Enquirer*, September 21, 1837.
81. *The Colored American*, August 26, 1837.
82. *National Negro Convention of 1835*, pp. 14-15.
83. *The Colored American*, March 15, 1838.
84. Ibid.
85. Ibid.
86. The North Star, February 16, 1849, p. 2; March 23, 1849, p. 2; April 13, 1849, p. 2.

87. *African Repository and Colonial Journal*, March 1825.
88. *New York Times*, March 3, 1853.
89. Ibid.
90. Urich B. Phillips, *American Negro Slavery*, (New York, 1928), pp. 420-421.
91. *Seventh Annual Report of the Baptist Board of Foreign Missions in the Latter Day Luminary*, Vol. 11, p. 317.
92. *The Rights of All*, August 14, 1829.
93. *Berlin*, p. 288.
94. Daniel Payne, *The Semi-Centenary and the Retrospective of the African Methodist Episcopal Church in the United States of America*, pp. 20-21.
95. Berlin, p. 284.
96. *Hazard's Register*, V (1830): 143.
97. W.E.B. DuBois, *Souls of Black Folk* (New York, 1969), p. 17.
98. George, p. 168.
99. *Anglo-African Magazine*, October 1859, p. 327.
100. Ibid.
101. Ibid.
102. Ibid.
103. *Freedom's Journal*, November 2, 1827.
104. Ibid.
105. *Rights of All*, New York, June 12, 1829.
106. Herbert Aptheker, *American Negro Slave Revolts* (New York, 1943), pp. 293-324.
107. Emile Durkheim, *The Elementary Forms of Religious Life: A Study in Religious Sociology* (London, 1915), p. 416.
108. Gossie Harold Hudson, "John Chavis, 1763-1838: A Social-Psychological Study," *Journal of Negro History* (Spring 1979).
109. *Freedom's Journal*, New York, November 2, 1827.
110. Durkheim, pp. 17-18.
111. Ibid., p. 427.
112. *The Colored American*, July 10, 1841.
113. Ibid.
114. Ibid., February 17, 1838; *Freedom's Journal*, December 5, 1828, p. 283.
115. Berlin, p. 276.
116. *New York Daily Tribune*, July 9-10, 1851.
117. Karl Mannheim, *Ideology and Utopia* (New York, 1936), p. 224.
118. *Sketches of the Higher Class of Society in Philadelphia* (1841), pp. 69-70.
119. Henry Tajfel, "The Roots of Prejudice: Cognitive Aspects," in *Psychology and Race*, Peter Watson, ed. (Chicago, 1973), pp. 76-94.
120. Richard Sennett, *The Fall of Public Man* (New York, 1977), pp. 38-39.
121. *The Colored American*, December 9, 1837.
122. James Wymms, *The Blackman: His Antecedents, His Genius, His Achievements* (1863).
123. *Sketches...*, pp. 16-17.
124. Ibid.
125. Ibid.
126. *The Colored American*, December 9, 1837.
127. *Sketches...*, p. 22.
128. William Douglass, *Annals of the First African Church in the United States of America* (Philadelphia, 1862).
129. Dorothy B. Porter, "The Organized Educational Activities of Negro

Literary Societies, 1828-1846," *Journal of Negro Education* (October 1936), pp. 555-76.
    130. *The Colored American*, March 11, 1837.
    131. *Sketches...*, p. 94.
    132. Ibid., p. 96.
    133. *The Anglo-African Magazine*, April 1859.
    134. *Sketches...*, pp. 97-100.
    135. Ibid., pp. 101-10.
    136. Porte, p. 566.
    137. I.N. Stokes, ed., *Iconography of Manhattan Island* (New York, 1918), v. 1438.
    138. *Address to Parents and Guardians of Children Belonging to the New York African Free School by the Trustees* (1818), p. 20.
    139. Woodson, ed. *The Mind of the Negro as Reflected in Letters Written During the Crisis of 1800-1860* (Greenwood, 1926), p. 278.
    140. Joshua Coffin, *An Account of Some of the Principal Slave Insurrections* (New York, 1860), p. 23.
    141. Woodson, *The Education of the Negro Prior to 1861* (New York, 1968), pp. 237-40.
    142. *The Colored American*, March 6, 1841.
    143. Ibid.
    144. Ibid.
    145. *The Weekly Anglo-African*, February 1861.
    146. Ibid., February 9, 1861.
    147. Ibid.
    148. Ibid., February 16, 1861.
    149. David Nickens, "Address to the People of Color" (in Chillicothe, July 20, 1832), *The Liberator*, August 11, 1832.
    150. Martin Delany, "The Political Destiny of the Colored Race," in *The Ideological Origins of Black Nationalism*, Sterling Stucky, ed. (Boston, 1972), p. 198.
    151. *The Colored American*, February 10, 1838, p. 19.
    152. "Sidney," *The Colored American*, March 13, 1841.
    153. Delany, p. 202.

Chapter II

    1. Michael D. Storms, "On Actors' and Observers' Points of View," *Journal of Personality and Social Psychology* (1973): 165-75.
    2. *The Weekly Anglo-African*, July 12, 1861, p. 2.
    3. Robert Cathcart, "New Approaches to the Study of Movements: Defining Movements Rhetorically," *Western Speech* (Spring 1972): 83-87.
    4. *The Weekly Anglo-African*, January 12, 1861, p. 2; *Voice of the Fugitive*, May 7, 1851; *Provincial Freeman*, March 25, 1854, p. 1.
    5. *The Anglo-African*, March 16, 1861, p. 2; Floyd Miller, *The Search for Black Nationality: Black Emigration and Colonization, 1787-1863* (Chicago, 1975), p. 251.
    6. *Frederick Douglass' Paper*, May 25, 1855, p. 3.
    7. Harold Kelly, "Causal Schemata and the Attribution Process," *Nebraska Symposium on Motivation* (1967): 192-238.
    8. Leonard Sweet, *Black Images of America, 1784-1870* (New York, 1976), p. 50.

9. Martin Dann, ed., *The Black Press, 1827-1890: The Question of National Identity* (New York, 1972), p. 17.
10. *The Colored American*, March 4, 1837.
11. Ibid.
12. Henry Highland Garnet, "The Past and Present Condition and Destiny of the Colored Race (1848)," in *Negro Social and Political Thought*, H. Brotz, ed. (New York, 1966).
13. *Rights of All*, New York, September 18, 1829.
14. Martin Delany, *The Condition, Elevation, Emigration, and Destiny of the Colored People of the United States (1852)* (New York, 1969).
15. Sweet, p. 71.
16. Wilson J. Moses, "Civilizing Missionary: A Study of Alexander Crummell," *The Journal of Negro History* (April 1975).
17. *Minutes of the Fifth Annual Convention for the Improvement of the Free People of Color*, 1835.
18. *The North Star*, February 18, 1848; Philip Foner, *Frederick Douglass*, pp. 98-99.
19. Henry L. Taylor, *The Afro-American in New York Life and History*, p. 78.
20. Howard Brotz, ed., "Frederick Douglass, An Address to the Colored People in the United States," in *Negro Social and Political Thought* (New York, 1966).
21. Sweet, p. 132.
22. Moses, pp. 236-37.
23. *Freedom's Journal*, November 2, 1827.
24. Ibid., March 16, 1827.
25. Ibid., November 2, 1827.
26. Ibid., March 28, 1829.
27. *The Colored American*, April 22, 1837, p. 2.
28. Ibid., February 10, 1838, p. 18.
29. *Voice of the Fugitive*, July 16, 1851, p. 1.
30. *The Colored American*, April 19, 1838, p. 2.
31. *The North Star*, March 2, 1849, p. 1.
32. *The Colored American*, August 21, 1841, p. 3.
33. Ibid.
34. Ibid., January 27, 1838, p. 11.
35. Ibid.
36. Ibid., October 28, 1837, p. 4; August 31, 1839, p. 3; May 16, 1840, p. 3; April 3, 1841, p. 3.
37. Ibid., May 3, 1838, p. 54.
38. Ibid., July 28, 1838, p. 90.
39. Ibid., November 16, 1839, p. 2.
40. Ibid., July 7, 1838, p. 78.
41. Ibid., March 4, 1837, p. 2.
42. Ibid., July 28, 1838, p. 4.
43. Ibid., July 13, 1838, p. 2; April 3, 1841, p. 3.
44. Delindus R. Brown, "Free Blacks' Rhetorical Impact on African Colonization: The Emergence of Rhetorical Evidence," *Journal of Black Studies* (March 1979): 251-65.
45. Cathcart, p. 87.
46. Anthony Giddens, *New Rules of Social Methods for Research* (New York, 1976), p. 110.
47. Brown, p. 262.

48. *Freedom's Journal*, July 6, 1827.
49. Ibid., August 31, 1827.
50. Ibid., May 18, 1827.
51. *Rights of All*, New York, September 18, 1829.
52. Samuel E. Cornish and Theodore S. Wright, *The Colonization Scheme Considered; Its Rejection by the Colored People* (Newark, 1840), p. 4.
53. Ibid.
54. *The Colored American*, March 2, 1838, p. 3; Howard Holman Bell, *A Survey of the Negro Convention Movement, 1830-1861* (New York; 1970), pp. 124-27.
55. Cornish and Wright, p. 6.
56. Ibid., p. 4.
57. Ibid., p. 14.
58. Ibid.
59. Ibid.
60. *The Colored American*, September 18, 1841, p. 2.
61. Ibid., p. 21.
62. Ibid., p. 22.
63. Ibid.
64. Ibid., p. 26.
65. Albert Memmi, *The Colonizer and the Colonized* (Boston, 1968), p. xxviii.
66. *Voice of the Fugitive*, February 26, 1851, p. 3.
67. Ibid., November 19, 1851, p. 1.
68. Ibid.
69. Ibid.
70. Ibid., September 24, 1851, pp. 2-3.
71. Ibid., May 7, 1851, p. 2.
72. *The Provincial Freeman*, March 25, 1854, p. 2.
73. Ibid.
74. Ibid., April 15, 1854, p. 3; May 20, 1854, p. 2.
75. Ibid., July 12, 1856, p. 50.
76. Ibid., January 31, 1857, p. 2.
77. Ibid.
78. "Dr. James McCune Smith to Gerrit Smith (28 July 1848)," in *Gerrit Smith Papers*.
79. "Garrison to his Wife (Oct. 20, 1847)," in Boston Public Library Collection.
80. *The North Star*, January 28, 1848, p. 2.
81. Ibid., September 14, 1849, p. 2.
82. Ibid., January 26, 1848, p. 2.
83. Ibid., September 14, 1849, p. 2.
84. Ibid., January 28, 1848, p. 1.
85. *Proceedings of the National Conventions of Colored People* (October 6-9, 1847), p. 18.
86. *Report of the Proceedings of the Colored National Convention*, Cleveland, Ohio (September 6, 1848), p. 16.
87. Ibid.
88. *Proceedings of the Colored National Convention*, Rochester, New York (July 6-8, 1853), p. 34.
89. Ibid., p. 35.
90. Ibid.
91. Ibid., pp. 35-36.
92. "African Civilization Society," *Douglass' Monthly*, February 1859.

93. Ibid.
94. *The Anglo-African Magazine*, August 1859, p. 241.
95. Ibid., p. 242.
96. Ibid.
97. Ibid.
98. Ibid., p. 84.
99. Ibid.
100. Ibid., p. 86.
101. Ibid., p. 95.
102. Ibid., p. 91.
103. Ibid., p. 96.
104. Ibid.
105. *Freedom's Journal*, September 21, 1827.
106. William E. Smith, *The Francis Preston Blair Family in Politics* (daCapo, 1933), p. 433.
107. Eric Foner, *Free Soil, Free Labor, Free Men: The Ideology of the Republican Party Before the Civil War* (New York, 1970), p. 107.
108. *The National Era*, May 3, 1849.
109. Foner, p. 107.
110. Ibid., p. 109.
111. *Freedom's Journal*, September 28, 1827, p. 3.
112. Ibid., September 21, 1827, p. 3.
113. Ibid.
114. Ibid.
115. *Frederick Douglass' Paper*, October 23, 1851.
116. Ibid.
117. *Freedom's Journal*, September 28, 1827, p. 1.
118. Ibid.
119. *The North Star*, March 23, 1849, p. 1.
120. Ibid.
121. *Freedom's Journal*, August 10, 1827, p. 86.
122. Ibid.
123. Ibid.
124. Ibid.
125. Ibid., November 16, 1827, p. 1.
126. *United States Bureau of Education, Circular of Information* (1884), Nos. 1-7.
127. Dann, p. 16.
128. *The Colored American*, March 4, 1847.
129. Ernest Manheim, *A Paper Presented at the Annual Meeting of the American Sociological Association* (1958).
130. Ibid.; Bernard Berelson, "Communication and Public Opinion," in *Public Opinion and Communication*, Berelson and Janowitz, eds. (Glencoe, 1950), p. 450.
131. *The Weekly Anglo-African*, July 23, 1859.
132. Dorothy Porter, ed., *Negro Protest Pamphlets* (New York, 1969), pp. iii-iv.
133. *New York Tribune*, August 6, 1967; Herbert Menzel, "Communication Through Institutions and Social Structures," *Speech Association of America* (1967), pp. 22-24.
134. *Voice of the Fugitive*, February 26, 1851, p. 3.
135. Ibid., May 7, 1851, p. 1.

136. *The Colored American*, March 2, 1839, p. 3.
137. David M. White and Lewis A. Dexter, eds., *People, Society and Mass Communication*, pp. 418-21.
138. Harvey Graff, *The Literacy Myth: Literacy and Social Structure in the 19th Century* (New York, 1979), p. 69.
139. Menzel, p. 24.
140. Foner, p. 113.
141. *Colored National Convention*, Cleveland, 1848, pp. 13-14.
142. Todd Gitlin, "News as Ideology and Contest Area: Toward a Theory of Hegemony, Crisis and Opposition," *Socialist Review* (November 1979): 11-51.
143. *Colored National Convention*, Cleveland, 1848, p. 14.
144. Ibid., p. 13.
145. *The Weekly Anglo-African*, August 20, 1859.
146. Ibid., July 25, 1859.
147. L. Festinger, "A Theory of Social Comparison Processes," *Human Relations* (1954): 117-140.
148. Silvia Scribner and Michael Cole, "The Psychology of Literacy," *New York Times Book Review*, December 13, 1981, p. 1.
149. Graff, p. 70.
150. Porter, p. 111.
151. Ibid., p. 69; *Provincial Freeman*, January 31, 1857, p. 1; Graff, p. 71; Holly, "Thoughts on Emigration," *The Anglo-African Magazine*, 1859, p. 241; "The Condition, Elevation, Emigration and Destiny...," in Brotz, ed., *Negro Social and Political Thought*, p. 37.
152. *United States Bureau of Education* (1870), pp. 478-79.
153. Ibid.; *The Provincial Freeman*, January 31, 1857.
154. Marie H. Nichols, "Rhetorical and Critical Theory," in *Rhetoric and Criticism*, M.H. Nichols, ed. (Louisiana, 1967), p. 83.

Chapter III

1. *The Colored American*, March 28, 1840, p. 1.
2. *The North Star*, March 23, 1849, p. 1.
3. Ibid.
4. Ibid.
5. Ibid.
6. Ibid.
7. Ibid.
8. *Freedom's Journal*, May 18, 1827.
9. *The Rights of All*, New York, June 12, 1829, p. 2.
10. *The Colored American*, December 22, 1838.
11. Ibid.
12. Ibid., June 13, 1840.
13. *Freedom's Journal*, May 18, 1827.
14. Ibid., February 7, 1829, p. 352.
15. Samuel Cornish and Theodore Wright, *The Colonization Scheme Considered: Its Rejection by the Colored People* (Newark, 1840), pp. 14-15.
16. Ibid.
17. Ibid., p. 17.
18. Ibid., p. 24.

19. Karl Marx, *The Communist Manifesto* (New York, 1883), p. 107.
20. *Frederick Douglass' Paper*, December 15, 1854, p. 1.
21. Ibid.
22. Ibid.
23. *The Weekly Anglo-African*, July 23, 1859.
24. Ibid.
25. *The Colored American*, December 29, 1839, p. 178.
26. *The North Star*, January 26, 1849.
27. *The Colored American*, April 24, 1841, p. 3.
28. Ibid.
29. *The Weekly Anglo-African*, May 11, 1861.
30. Ibid.
31. Ibid., January 5, 1861, p. 1.
32. Ibid.
33. Ibid., January 19, 1861, p. 2.
34. Ibid., February 2, 1861, p. 3.
35. Ibid., January 19, 1861, p. 3.
36. Ibid.
37. Ibid., December 22, 1860, p. 2.
38. *The Anglo-African Magazine*, August 1859, p. 242.
39. Ibid., November 1859, p. 3.
40. *The Weekly Anglo-African*, April 13, 1861.
41. Ibid., January 19, 1861, p. 3.
42. Ibid., February 1861, p. 2.
43. Ibid., March 16, 1861, p. 2.
44. Ibid.
45. Ibid.
46. Ibid.
47. Ibid., April 6, 1861, p. 4.
48. Ibid.
49. Ibid.
50. Ibid.
51. Ibid.
52. Ibid., January 12, 1861, p. 2.
53. Ibid., March 16, 1861, p. 2.
54. Ibid.
55. Ibid., February 1861, p. 1.
56. Ibid.
57. Ibid., January 12, 1861, p. 2.
58. Ibid., February 7, 1861, p. 1.
59. Ibid.
60. Ibid.
61. Ibid., January 19, 1861.
62. Floyd Miller, *The Search for Black Nationality: Black Emigration and Colonization, 1787-1863* (Chicago, 1975), p. 251.
63. Holly, "Thoughts on Emigration," *The Anglo-African Magazine*, 1859, pp. 168-70.
64. George Gonos, "Situation Versus Frame: The Interactionist and the Structuralist Analysis of Everyday Life," *American Sociological Review* (December 1977): 854-67.
65. Richard E. Nisbett and Stuart Valins, "Perceiving the Causes of One's Own Behavior," in *Attribution: Perceiving the Causes of Behavior*, E.E. Jones,

D.E. Kanouse, H.H. Kelly, R.E. Nisbett, S. Valins and B. Weiner, eds. (New Jersey, 1971), pp. 79-94.
66. *Rights of All*, New York, September 18, 1829.
67. Erving Goffman, *Gender Advertisements* (New York, 1976), pp. 10-23.

Chapter IV

1. Harold Kelly, "Attribution Theory in Social Psychology," *Nebraska Symposium on Motivation* (1967): 192-238.
2. Leon Festinger, "A Theory of Social Comparison Process," *Human Relations* (1954): 117-140.
3. Avi Gottlieb and William Ickes, "Attributional Strategies of Social Influence," in *New Directions of Attribution Research* (New York, 1976), Vol. 2, pp. 261-296.
4. Eric Foner, *Free Soil, Free Labor, Free Men: The Ideology of the Republican Party Before the Civil War* (New York, 1970), pp. 266-67.
5. Bell, *The Journal of Negro History* (October 4, 1957): 247-60.
6. *Sketches of the Higher Class of Colored Society in Philadelphia* (Philadelphia, 1841), p. 40; *Minutes of the Fifth Annual Convention for the Improvement of the Free People of Color,* --- (Philadelphia, 1835), p. 22; Alexander V. Murray, *Journal of Negro History* (1959): 132.
7. Erving Goffman, *Frame Analysis: An Essay on the Organization of Experience* (New York, 1974).
8. *Frederick Douglass' Paper*, March 30, 1855, p. 1.
9. Gary Wells and John Harvey, "Do People Use Consensus Information in Making Causal Attribution?" *Journal of Personality and Social Psychology* (May 1977): 279-93.
10. *Minutes of the Fifth Annual Convention*, 1835, p. 23.
11. *The Weekly Anglo-African*, January 26, 1861, p. 2.
12. *The North Star*, March 23, 1849, p. 2.
13. Lloyd Bitner, "The Rhetorical Situation," *Philosophy and Rhetoric* (1968): 5-6.
14. *The North Star*, March 23, 1849, p. 2.
15. Bitzer, pp. 1-14.
16. Martin Delany, *The Condition, Elevation, Emigration and Destiny of the Colored People of the United States* (1852), p. 87.
17. Foner, pp. 268-69.
18. Francis P. Blair to Gerrit Smith, in *Gerrit Smith Papers*, April 9, 1858.
19. Letter by J.T. Holly to Frank P. Blair, Jr. (January 30, 1858), in Howard Bell, *A Survey of the Negro Convention Movement, 1830-1861* (New York, 1970), Appendix, 34-37.
20. *Debates of the Iowa Constitutional Convention* (1857), p. 700.
21. *The North Star*, March 23, 1849, p. 2.
22. Ibid.
23. Ibid.
24. *The Colored American*, September 30, 1837.
25. Foner, p. 274; *State Convention of the Colored Citizens of Ohio*, Convened at Columbus, January 10-13, 1849.
26. *Douglass' Monthly*, January 1861, pp. 386-87.
27. Ibid., March 1861, p. 420.
28. *The Colored American*, November 10, 1838; *The Aliened American*, April

9, 1853; *The Liberator*, Boston, July 2, 1831; *The Weekly Advocate*, New York, January 7, 1837.

29. Benjamin Quarles, *Frederick Douglass*, p. 84; *Douglass to Delany*, January 12, 1848.

30. *The North Star*, April 27, 1849.

31. Ibid., October 20, 1848.

32. Quarles, *Frederick Douglass*, p. 94.

33. *Frederick Douglass' Paper*, in the *African Repository* (Washington, D.C.), XXXIX, 137 (May 1853).

34. *The Weekly Anglo-African*, November 24, 1860.

35. Ibid., April 23, 1860.

36. Letter of Bishop Holly to Alexander Crummell, in Floyd Miller, *The Search for Black Nationality* (Chicago, 1975), pp. 247-48.

37. Karl Mannheim, *Ideology and Utopia* (New York, 1936), p. 268.

38. Foner, p. 274.

39. Cornish and Wright, p. 19.

40. Ibid.

41. *The Colored American*, January 27, 1838.

42. Ibid., September 30, 1837.

43. Leland Griffin, "A Dramatistic Theory of the Rhetoric of Movements," in *Critical Response to Kenneth Burke*, William H. Ruechkert, ed. (Minneapolis, 1969), p. 468.

44. *The Colored American*, January 19, 1838, p. 1.

45. Griffin, p. 468.

46. Mannheim, p. 195.

47. *Freedom's Journal*, October 26, 1827, p. 1.

48. Ibid.

49. Ibid., November 16, 1827, p. 1.

50. *Frederick Douglass' Paper*, February 17, 1854, p. 1.

51. Todd Gitlin, "News as Ideology and Contested Area: Toward a Theory of Hegemony, Crisis and Opposition," *Socialist Review* (November-December 1979): 16.

52. *Frederick Douglass' Paper*, April 7, 1854, p. 4.

53. *Freedom's Journal*, November 16, 1827, p. 1.

54. Quarles, *Frederick Douglass*, p. 141.

55. Ibid., p. 80.

56. Ira Berlin, *Slaves Without Masters: The Free Negro in the Ante-Bellum South* (New York: 1976), Appendix 1, p. 396, 136; *The Colored American*, April 15, 1837.

57. Gitlin, p. 44.

58. Ibid.

59. *Douglass' Monthly*, May 1861.

60. W.E.B. DuBois, "The Conservation of Races," in *Negro Social and Political Thought*, Howard Brotz, ed. (New York, 1966) p. 488.

61. *Frederick Douglass' Paper*, January 4, 1855, p. 1.

62. Gitlin, p. 49.

Epilogue

1. Richard Sennett, *Authority*, New York, p. 118.
2. Ibid., p. 92.
3. Foner, 1970, pp. 266-267.

Appendices

A. Prominent African American Antebellum Editors in the United States and Canada from 1827 to 1861

Samuel E. Cornish (1795–1859) raised in rural Delaware, relocated in his twenties in Philadelphia where he received an education from a free black minister, John Gloucester of the African School. In 1819 he received a license to preach. By 1821 he moved to New York, where he became pastor of The First Colored Presbyterian Church (later the Shiloh Presbyterian Church). After viewing the problems free blacks were having in emigrating to Haiti, he became a strong anti-emigrationist/colonizationist spokesman. In 1827, Cornish became co-editor of the first African newspaper in the United States, *Freedom's Journal*. Resigning his position a few months later to John Russwurm, the paper's other editor, he became the paper's general agent. In 1829 he returned to publishing with *Rights of All*. Later, he was editor of *The Colored American* from 1837 to 1838, and stayed active with the paper until 1841.

John B. Russwurm (1799–1851) raised in Port Antonia, Jamaica, was one of the first Africans to graduate from Bowdoin College in 1826. His co-editorship with Cornish of *Freedom's Journal* was soon terminated, as a difference of opinion on the issue of colonization led Russwurm to convert the paper to a more liberal approach to the concept of emigration. His decision to emigrate to Liberia and terminate the paper did not stop his journalistic efforts. He established the *Liberian Herald* in Monrovia. From 1836 until his death, he was Governor of the Maryland Colony at Cape Palma, Liberia.

Phillip A. Bell (1807–1899) was editor of *The Weekly Advocate* for a period of one month in 1837, until Samuel Cornish assumed editorship and changed the name to *The Colored American*. Bell later moved to San Francisco where he edited the *Pacific Appeal* in 1857. During the postbellum era, Bell published *The Elevator* until it was taken over by *The Mirror of the Times*. In 1880 he was doorkeeper to the California Senate.

Peter H. Clark (1829–1895) was an anti-emigrationist and socialist who later became principal of Cincinnati's African High School. Clark also worked on

Frederick Douglass' Paper in Rochester, N.Y. In 1854 he published *The Herald of Freedom.*

William H. Day graduated from Oberlin College, Ohio, in 1849. An active supporter of the convention movements, he also published a newspaper in Detroit, Michigan, called *The Excelsior.* In 1853 he assumed the editorship of *The Aliened American* in Cleveland, Ohio. In the same year he was selected to be vice president of the National Negro Convention (a major supporter of his newspaper). By 1855 he was living in an all-African settlement at Buxton, Ontario. In 1871-72 he was co-editor of the Harrisburg, Pennsylvania, newspaper, *National Progress.* Later he accepted a post as clerk in the Pennsylvania State Department.

James W.C. Pennington (1809-1871) was a self-educated man. Pennington moved from Maryland to Brooklyn, N.Y., where he became a minister before moving to Hartford, Connecticut. Active in the abolitionist movement, he traveled to Europe and the West Indies and then returned to the United States where he became a pastor of Shiloh Presbyterian Colored Church. In 1841, he published a textbook of *The Origins and History of the Colored People.* In 1849, he published *The Fugitive Blacksmith.* This same year he was a delegate to the Peace Congress at Paris, attended the National Levee at the mansion of the foreign minister, De Tocqueville, and received a Doctor of Divinity degree from the University of Heidelberg. By 1859 he was pastor of the Second Colored Presbyterian Church, Newton, Long Island, and a correspondent to *The Weekly Anglo-African.* His death was reported as being hastened by excessive use of alcohol.

Charles B. Ray (1807-1886) served as co-editor of *The Colored American* in 1838. Ray's previous education was that of clergyman. Born and educated in Massachusetts, he attended Wesleyan Academy in Massachusetts and Wesleyan University in Connecticut. He served as pastor for twenty years as the Bethesda Congregational Church. In 1837 he became general agent for *The Colored American* under Phillip A. Bell. Assuming editorship in 1838, he took charge until 1812 as an anti-colonizationist.

Samuel R. Ward (1817-1864) was born a slave on a plantation in Maryland. He escaped from slavery and eventually settled in New York City, where he taught school and became a preacher. From 1837 to 1840, he was an agent for *The Colored American* in Newark, Pennsylvania, while also editing *The Farmer* and *The Northern Star.* By 1850 he was editing *The Impartial Citizen* in Boston, Massachusetts, and co-editing *The Aliened American.* The record is unclear as to whether he edited *The Aliened American* in Canada or the United States. He also authored *The Autobiography of a Fugitive Slave.* Ward evinced a strong and growing desire for emigration, which was fulfilled when he emigrated to Jamaica where he lived until his death.

Martin R. Delany (1812-1885), a native of Charleston, Virginia, developed into a forceful proponent of emigration, advocating sites in the Caribbean and West Africa for freemen settlers. An editor of *The Mystery* in 1843, Delany eventually became co-founder and co-editor, in 1847, of the influential journal *The North Star,* with Frederick Douglass, and authored a novel called *Blake; the Huts of America,* in 1859. His final work was titled *Principles of Ethnology,* published in 1879.

Frederick Douglass (1817–1895) functioned as editor of three major antebellum newspapers: *The North Star, Frederick Douglass' Paper* and *Douglass' Monthly*. Douglass' newspaper reflected the central issues of his time for many free blacks and whites. Symbolizing the idealized American trait of pulling oneself up by one's bootstraps, Douglass used his publications to berate those who suggested that emigration was the only path for freeman development. His publication *The North Star* at one time enjoyed the position of being named the "official" freemen newspaper.

William J. Whipper was editor of *The Northern Star*, a temperance newspaper, which was published monthly out of Albany, New York. As a supporter of the Moral Reform Society, Whipper was generally viewed as an advocate for passive resistance to slavery. By 1856 he was advocating emigration.

Louis H. Putnam acted as editor of *The Colored Man's Journal* from 1852 to 1861.

Bishop Jabez Campbell (1815–1891) was editor of *The Christian Recorder* (once named *The Herald*) in Philadelphia from 1856 to 1865.

Mifflin W. Gibbs (1823–1915) was born in Philadelphia, Pennsylvania. Gibbs traveled to San Francisco in 1849. Beginning as a bootblack, he later formed a partnership in the shoe business. In 1855, Gibbs founded *The Mirror of the Times*, California's first freeman newspaper, and published it until its merger with *The Pacific Appeal*. He eventually became a lawyer, then United States consul to Madagascar, prior to and through President Theodore Roosevelt's presidency.

B. Free Black Newspapers, 1827–1861

Freedom's Journal (1827–1829), New York City
Rights of All (May–September 1829), New York City
The Weekly Advocate (1837), New York City
The Colored American (1837–1841), New York City
Palladium of Liberty (1839–1842), Columbus, Oh.
The Elevator (1842–1844), Albany, New York
The People's Press (1843–?), New York City
The Mystery (1847–1848), Pittsburgh
Ram's Horn (1847–1848), New York City
The North Star (1847–?), Rochester, N.Y.
The Struggler (1830–1831), New York City
Demosthenian Shield (June 1841–?), Philadelphia
The Night Watchman (1842), Troy, N.Y.
The Northern Star and Freeman's Advocate (1842–1843), Albany, N.Y.
Genius of Freedom (1846–1847), New York City
The Clarion (1846–1847), Troy, N.Y.
The Christian Herald (1848–?), Pittsburgh
The Christian Recorder (1848–?), Philadelphia
Impartial Citizen (1848–1856), Syracuse, N.Y.
The Colored Man's Journal (1851–1861), New York City
Frederick Douglass' Paper (name changed from *The North Star*) (1851–1859), Rochester, N.Y.
Voice of the Fugitive (June 1851–1853), Sandwich, Canada
The Aliened American (c. 1853–?)
The Provincial Freemen (March 1853–1859), Toronto

Mirror of the Times (1855–?), San Francisco
Herald of Freedom (1855–?), Ohio
Douglass' Monthly (January 1859–June 1863), Rochester, N.Y.
The Anglo-African (July 23, 1859–1865), New York City

C. Free Black Literary Societies Listed by States and Cities, with Date of Formation*

Pennsylvania
Philadelphia:
  Demosthenian Institute, 1837
  Edgeworth Society, before 1837
  Female Literary Society, 1831
  Gilbert Lyceum, 1841
  Library Company of Colored Persons, 1833
  Minerva Literary Association, 1834
  Philadelphia Association for Moral and Mental Improvement of the People of Color, 1835
  Reading Room Society, 1828
  Rush Library and Debating Society, 1836
Pittsburgh:
  Theban Literary Society, 1831
  Young Men's Literary and Moral Reform Society of Pittsburgh and Vicinity, 1837

New York
New York City:
  Female Literary Society, before 1836
  Ladies Literary Society, 1834
  New York African Clarkson Society, 1829
  New York Garrison Literary Association, 1834
  New York Philomathean Society, 1830
  Phoenix Society, 1833
Albany:
  Literary Societies (two), before 1843
Buffalo:
  Debating Society, before 1837
  Young Ladies Literary Society, before 1837
Poughkeepsie:
  Literary Society, before 1837
Rochester:
  Debating Society, before 1843
  Ladies Literary and Dorcas Society, 1833
Schenectady:
  Debating Society, before 1843
Troy:
  Debating Society, before 1837
  Literary Society, before 1837
  Mental and Moral Improvement Society, before 1837

Massachusetts
Boston:
  Adelphic Union for the Promotion of Literature and Science, 1836
  Afric-American Female Intelligence Society, 1832
  Boston Philomathean Society, 1836
  Thompson Literary and Debating Society, before 1835
  Young Men's Literary Society, before 1845
New Bedford:
  Debating Society, before 1837

Connecticut
Hartford:
  Literary and Religious Institution, 1834

Rhode Island
Providence:
  Literary Society, 1833
  Debating Society, before 1837

New Jersey
Newark:
  Tyro and Literary Association, 1832

Maryland
Baltimore:
   Young Men's Mental Improvement Society for the Discussion of Moral and Philosophical Questions of all Kinds, before 1835

Washington, D.C.
Debating Society, before 1837
Literary Society, before 1837
Washington Sovential Society, 1834

Ohio
Cincinnati:
   Literary Society, before 1843
Columbus:
   Literary Society, before 1843

Michigan
Detroit:
   Young Men's Lyceum and Debating Society, before 1846

*Source: *Journal of Negro Education*, Vol. 5 (1936), pp. 557-558.

D. Books and Pamphlets Produced by Free Black Writers, 1827-1861

An Address: Delivered on the Celebration of the Abolition of Slavery in the State of New York. 5 July 1827, by Nathaniel Paul, Pastor of the First African Baptist Society in the City of Albany. 24 pages.

Address to the Fourth Annual Convention of the Free Black People of Color of the United States. Delivered at the opening of their session in the City of New York. June 2, 1834, by William Hamilton. 8 pages.

Treaties on the Intellectual Character and Civil and Political Condition of the Colored People of the United States; And the Prejudice Exercised Towards Them; With a Sermon on the Duty of the Church to Them. By Rev. H. Easton (a Colored Man), 1837. 54 pages.

Our Rights as Men. An Address, Delivered in Boston, Before the Legislative Committee on the Militia. 24 February 1853, by William J. Watkins (in behalf of sixty-five colored petitioners, praying for a charter to form an independent military company). Boston. 21 pages.

Walker's Appeal in Four Articles, by David Walker. (a)*An Address to the Slaves of the United States of America* (rejected by the National Convention, 1843), by Henry Highland Garnet, Troy, N.Y. April 15, 1848. 96 pages.

The Condition, Elevation, Emigration and Destiny of the Colored People of the United States, "Politically Considered," by Martin R. Delany, 1852.

A Vindication of the Capacity of the Negro Race for Self-Government and Civilized Progress. Dedicated to Rev. William C. Munroe, Rector of St. Matthew's Church. Detroit, Michigan, by James T. Holly, 1857.

Official Report of the Niger Valley Exploring Party, by Martin R. Delany, 1861. 75 pages.

Appendices

Clotel, on The President's Daughter: A narrative of Slave Life in the United States, by William Wells Brown, 1853. 245 pages.

The Origin and Objects of Ancient Freemasonry, its Introduction into the United States and Legitimacy among Colored Men: A Treaties Delivered Before St. Cyprian Lodge. No. 13, June 24, 1853, by Martin R. Delany. 40 pages.

My Bondage and My Freedom, by Frederick Douglass, 1855, 464 pages.

The Anti-Slavery Movement, by Frederick Douglass, 1855.

The Claims of the Negro Ethnologically Considered, An Address Before the Literary Societies of Western Reserve College (at commencement, July 12, 1854), by Frederick Douglass, 1854. 37 pages.

The Colonization Scheme Considered, in its Rejection by the Colored People—in its tendency to uphold Caste—in its unfitness for Christianizing and Civilizing of the Aborigines of Africa—and for putting a stop to the African Slave Trade, by Samuel E. Cornish and Theodore S. Wright, Newark, 1840. 26 pages.

Tables

Table I

Proportion of Free Blacks and Slaves of Mixed Racial Ancestry, 1860*

	Free Blacks	Slaves
United States	36.2%	---
North	30.9	---
South	40.8	10.4%
Upper South	35.0	13.4
Lower South	75.8	8.5
Delaware	14.6	4.6
D.C.	40.4	4.9
Kentucky	38.1	19.2
Maryland	19.1	10.2
Missouri	46.9	19.1
North Carolina	71.6	6.9
Tennessee	58.7	13.6
Virginia	40.5	14.3
Alabama	78.0	7.9
Arkansas	60.4	12.6
Florida	69.0	8.5
Georgia	57.2	8.0
Louisiana	81.3	9.8
Mississippi	77.7	8.4
South Carolina	72.0	5.3
Texas	76.9	13.7

*Source: U.S. Bureau of the Census, *Negro Population of the United States, 1790–1915* (Washington, D.C., 1918), p. 220.

Table 2

Percentage of Blacks in U.S. Population in 1790*

New England	
Maine	0.6%
New Hampshire	0.6
Vermont	0.3
Massachusetts	1.4
Rhode Island	6.3
Connecticut	2.3
Middle States	
New York	7.6
New Jersey	7.7
Pennsylvania	2.4
Upper South	
Delaware	21.6
Maryland	34.7
Virginia	40.9
North Carolina	36.8
Kentucky	17.0
Tennessee	10.6
Lower South	
South Carolina	43.7
Georgia	35.9

*Source: U.S. Bureau of the Census, *Negro Population of the United States, 1790-1915* (Washington, D.C., 1918), p. 51.

Table 3

Proportion of the Total Populations of Free Blacks, Whites and Slaves Residing in Urban Areas*, 1860

	Free Blacks	Whites	Slaves
United States	47.3%	32.9%	---
North	61.4	40.6	---
South	35.2	14.8	5.0%
Upper South	32.3	16.7	6.2
Lower South	53.2	11.4	4.3

*All places, incorporated and unincorporated, greater than 10,000 in population.

Table 4

Proportion* of Urban Population Residing in Large Cities, †1860

	Free Blacks	Whites	Slaves
United States	62.5%	52.2%	---
North	55.7	48.5	---
South	72.7	68.7	46.8%
Upper South	69.2	69.4	41.8
Lower South	85.5	66.7	51.4

*All places, incorporated and unincorporated, greater than 10,000 in population.

†*Source* (both tables): *Population of the United States in 1860* (Washington, D.C., 1864).

*Percentages represent the portion of each group's entire population who reside in urban areas, not a percentage of the entire urban area.

Table 5

Free Black Population, 1755-1810*

	Pre-1790	1790	1800	1810
United States		59,466	108,395	186,446
North		27,109	47,154	78,181
South		32,357	61,241	108,265
Upper South		30,158	56,855	94,085
Lower South		2,199	4,386	14,180
Delaware		3,899	8,268	13,136
D.C.			783	2,549
Kentucky		114	741	1,713
Maryland	1,817[a]	8,043	19,587	33,927
Missouri				607
North Carolina		4,975	7,043	10,266
Tennessee		361	309	1,317
Virginia	1,800[b]	12,766	20,124	30,570
Georgia		398	1,019	1,801
Louisiana	165[c]	(1,303)[d]	(1,768)[e]	7,585
Mississippi			182	240
South Carolina		1,801	3,185	4,554

[a]1755   [b]1782   [c]1769   [d]1785   [e]1803

*Between 1790 and 1810, the Federal census enumerated free blacks as "all other Free persons," (1790) and "all other Free Persons, except Indians not taxed" (1800, 1810).

Source: *Population of the United States in 1860* (Washington, D.C., 1864), pp. 600-01.

Table 6

Proportion of Free Blacks, Whites, and Slave Females, 1860

	Free Black	White	Slave
United States	52.0%	48.6%	---
North	51.4	48.7	---
South	52.6	48.5	49.9%
Upper South	52.3	48.9	49.7
Lower South	54.5	47.9	49.9
Urban South[a]	56.9	48.4	52.2
Larger Southern Cities[b]	58.5	49.1	53.5
Rural South	50.3	48.5	49.7

[a]Places greater than 2,500 in population.
[b]Places greater than 10,000 in population.

Source: *Population of the United States in 1860* (Washington, D.C., 1864).

Table 6A
Slave Population, 1755–1860

	1790	1800	1820	1840	1860
United States	697,897	893,041	1,538,125	2,487,455	3,953,760
North	40,370	35,946	19,108	1,129	64
South	657,527	857,095	1,519,017	2,486,326	3,953,696
Upper South	521,169	648,051	965,514	1,215,497	1,530,229
Lower South	136,358	209,044	553,503	1,270,829	2,423,467

Sources: Condensed statistics of *Gentlemen's Magazine and Historical Chronicle*, XXIV (1764), p. 261; Lawrence Kinnaird, ed., "Spain in the Mississippi Valley, 1765–1794," in *Annual Report of the American Historical Association for the Year 1945*, 4 vols. (Washington, D.C., 1946), II, pt. 1, p. 196; "Appendix" to *An Account of Louisiana*, being an Abstract of Documents in the Offices of the Department of State and the Treasury (Philadelphia, 1803), pp. 84–7; *Annals of Congress*, 8th Cong. 2nd. Sess., pp. 1574–6; *Population of the United States in 1860* (Washington, D.C., 1864), pp. 598–605.

Table 7

Positions Advocated by Leading Spokesmen and Editors, 1827–1840

Individual Growth: Improvement within the context of the American system (moral suasion-integrationist)	Universal Freemen Betterment: Development of political power via separate social institutions	Resettlement Development of separate communities in territories not having slaves	Emigration/Colonization A) Colonization to Liberia B) Emigration to Haiti, Caribbean, W. Africa
1. Maria Stewart 2. Frederick Douglass 3. William Wells Brown 4. Samuel Cornish (*Rights of All*, 1829–37; *Colored American*, 1837–42) 5. William Nell 6. James N.C. Pennington 7. David Ruggles (*The Mirror of Liberty*, 1837–?)	1. "Augustine" (Lewis Woodson) 2. "Sidney" 3. David Walker 4. Daniel Payne 5. Charles Ray (*Colored American*, 1838) 6. Henry Highland Garnet 7. Samuel Ringgold Ward (*National Watchman*)	*Canada* 1. Wilberforce settlement (1829–36), the Reverend Nathanial Paul Israel Lewis *United States* 1. Nashoba settlement, Tenn. (1825–30), Francis Wright 2. Augustus Wattles settlement, "Carthagena" (Mercer County, Ohio, 1835)	1. Lott Cary; Baptist missionary to Liberia, 1821–28 2. John Brown Russwurm (*Freedom's Journal*, 1827–29) 3. The Reverend Daniel Coker (emigrated, 1820, via ACS) 4. Samuel Wilson, businessman (emigrated, via ACS)

3. Robert Rose, settlement at Silver Lake, Penn. (1836–38)

5. The Reverend Thomas Paul (emigrated to Haiti as missionary)
6. Richard Allen (advocated Haitian emigration prior to 1825, rejected it by 1827)

8. James McCune Smith
9. William Whipper
10. Robert Purvis
11. Charles Lenox Remond
12. James Forten
13. Van Rensselaer (*Ram's Horn*, 1846–48)
14. Phillip A. Bell (*Weekly Advocate*, 1837; *Colored American*, 1838)
15. William H. Day (*The Aliened American*)

Table 7A

Positions Advocated by Leading Spokesmen and Editors, 1840–1861

Individual Growth: Improvement within the context of the American system (moral suasion-integrationist)	Universal Freemen Betterment: Development of political power via separate social institutions	Resettlement: Development of separate communities in territories not having slaves	Emigration/Colonization A) Colonization to Liberia B) Emigration to Haiti, Caribbean, W. Africa
1. Samuel Cornish (anti-emigration and colonization, but sympathetic to resettlement within the terr. in the U.S. Editor of *The Colored American*, 1837–42) 2. William Nell 3. James C. Pennington 4. Charles Lenox Remond 5. James Forten 6. Maria Stewart 7. Robert Purvis 8. David Ruggles (*The Mirror of Liberty*, 1837–?; *Genius of*	1. "Augustine" (Lewis Woodson) 2. "Sidney" 3. David Walker 4. Daniel Payne 5. Bishop Richard Allen	*Canada:* 1. Elgin Community (1849–73), Samuel Ringgold Ward (*The Aliened American*; emigrated 1851) 2. Refugee Home Society (1850–65) 3. Mary Shadd (*Provincial Freemen*, 1853–57) 4. Henry Bibb (*Voice of the Fugitive*, 1851–53) 5. Charles Ray (*The Colored American*, 1838) 6. Samuel R. Ward (*Na-*	1. William Wells Brown (emigrationist in 1859) 2. *William Whipper (The Northern Star*, emigrationist in 1856) 3. Henry Highland Garnet (*National Watchman*, emigrationist in 1849) 4. The Reverend Lott Cary, missionary-colonizer, 1821–28, Liberia 5. The Reverend Daniel Coker, missionary-colonizer, 1820 6. The Reverend Thomas Paul, emigrationist

Freedom, 1845–47)
9. Phillip A. Bell (*Pacific Appeal*, 1857–?)
10. James McCune Smith
11. Frederick Douglass (resigned to possibility of emigration *if* conditions remained the same)

tional Watchman; Impartial Citizen; Provincial Freemen, in Canada)
7. William H. Day (*The Aliened American*, pro-emigrationist in 1856)

7. The Reverend Alexander Crummell, emigrated to Liberia, 1853–73
8. Martin R. Delany (*The Mystery*, 1846; *The North Star*); favored emigration yet joined Union Army during Civil War as a major
9. James T. Holly (emigrated to Haiti, 1861)
10. John Brown Russwurm (*Freedom's Journal*, 1827–29; *Liberia Herald*); emigrated 1829

Table 8

The Illiteracy of Colored Adults in 1870 (These figures are representative only for those blacks who were contacted or were aware of the census. Ex: Ohio's black population at census was 63,000. Only 30,000 were contacted for census.)

States and Territories	Colored Persons of 21 years of age and upward			Colored males of 21 years of age and upward			Colored females of 21 years of age and upward		
	Enumerated No.	Returned as unable to write No.	%	Enumerated No.	Returned as unable to write No.	%	Enumerated No.	Returned as unable to write No.	%
Maine	1,151	128	11.1	629	69	11.0	522	59	11.3
New Hampshire	341	70	20.5	182	38	20.9	159	32	20.1
Vermont	491	87	17.7	284	47	16.5	207	40	19.2
Massachusetts	8,440	1,876	22.2	4,126	826	20.0	4,314	1,050	24.2
Rhode Island	3,149	728	23.1	1,440	296	20.6	1,709	432	25.3
Connecticut	5,747	1,353	23.5	2,756	634	23.0	2,991	719	24.0
New York	30,668	8,875	29.0	14,737	3,952	26.8	15,931	4,923	30.9
New Jersey	16,134	6,393	39.0	7,879	2,882	36.6	8,255	3,511	42.5
Pennsylvania	35,664	13,232	37.1	17,093	5,760	33.7	18,571	7,472	40.2
Ohio	30,391	15,621	51.4	15,649	7,535	48.1	14,742	8,806	54.9
Michigan	7,858	3,233	41.1	4,226	1,532	36.2	3,632	1,701	46.8
Indiana	11,661	6,440	55.2	6,161	3,212	52.1	5,500	3,228	58.7

Wisconsin	1,666	463	27.8	897	244	27.2	769	219	28.5
Illinois	14,349	8,061	56.2	7,706	3,974	51.6	6,643	4,087	61.5
Minnesota	756	334	44.2	495	154	39.0	361	180	49.9
Iowa	2,792	1,310	46.9	1,556	635	40.8	1,236	675	54.6
Nebraska	479	157	32.8	298	96	32.2	181	61	33.7
Kansas	8,091	5,920	73.2	4,191	2,900	69.2	3,900	3,020	77.4
Northern Division	179,828	74,281	41.3	90,205	34,786	38.6	89,623	39,495	44.1

Source: Bureau of Education, *Circulars of Information* (1884), Nos. 1–7.

Table 9

Table 9

*Navy Ration for Each Day of the Week**

	BREAD	BEEF	PORK	FLOUR	RICE	DRIED FRUIT	PICKLES	SUGAR	TEA/CHOICE	COFFEE	BUTTER	CHEESE	BEANS	MOLASSES	VINEGAR	WATER
Sun.	14	1		½		¼		2	½	1						1
Mon.	14		1					2	½	1			½			1
Tues.	14	1			½			2	½	1	2	2				1
Wed.	14		1				¼	2	½	1				½		1
Thurs.	14	1		½		¼		2	½	1						1
Fri.	14	1	1		½			2	½	1	2	2		½		1
Sat.	14						¼	2	½	1			½		½	1
	98	4	3	1	1	½	½	14	3½	7	4	4	1	1	½	7

*Every emigrant should be provided with a mattress two feet wide, and holding a gallon tin can (for water), a tin cup, a tin plate, a knife and fork, a few pounds of soap, and towels, with such extra utensils as may be deemed necessary to hold the daily rations.

Source: *The Weekly Anglo-African*, April 6, 1861, p. 4.

Bibliography

Books

Abby, Edward S. *Journal of a Residence and Tour in the United States of America.* 3 Volumes. London: J. Murray, 1835.
Aptheker, Herbert. *American Negro Slave Revolts.* New York: Columbia University Press, 1943.
Bassett, John. *Slavery in the State of North Carolina.* Johnson Press (repr.), 1899.
Bell, Howard. *Minutes of the Proceedings of the National Negro Convention, 1830–1864.* New York: Arno, 1969.
―――. *A Survey of the Negro Convention Movement.* New York: Arno, 1970.
Berelson, Bernard and Morris Janowitz, eds. *Reader in Public Opinion and Communication.* Glencoe: Free Press, 1950.
Berlin, Ira. *Slaves Without Masters: The Free Negro in the Ante-Bellum South.* New York: Vintage, 1976.
Bisseret, Noelle. *Education, Class, Language and Ideology.* London: Routledge and Kegan Paul, 1979.
Brown, Isaac Van Arsdale. *Biography of the Reverend Robert Finley.* New York: Arno, 1969.
Brown, William Wells. *The Blackman: His Antecedents, His Genius and His Achievements.* New York: Arno, 1969 (repr.).
Coffin, Joshua. *An Account of Some of the Principal Slave Insurrections.* New York: American Anti-Slavery Society, 1860.
Coker, Daniel. *Journal of Daniel Coker.* Baltimore: Edward J. Coale, 1820.
Cox, Oliver. *Caste, Class and Race.* New York: Modern Reader, 1948.
Cromwell, John W. *The Negro in American History: Men and Women Eminent in the Evolution of the American of African Descent.* New York: Basic Afro-American Reprint Library, 1969.
Dann, Martin. *The Black Press, 1827–1890: The Quest for National Identity.* New York: Capricorn, 1972.
Davis, David B. *The Problem of Slavery in Western Culture.* Ithaca: Cornell University Press, 1976.
Delany, Martin Robinson. *The Condition, Elevation, Emigration and Destiny of the Colored People of the United States.* New York: Arno/N.Y. Times, 1969 (repr.).
Dexter, Lewis A. and David M. White, eds. *People, Society, and Mass Communication.* New York: The Free Press, 1964.
Douglass, Frederick. "The Present and Future of the Colored Race in

America." In *Negro Social and Political Thought*, ed. by Howard Brotz. New York: Basic Books, Inc., 1966, pp. 267-77.
Douglass, William. *Annals of the First African Church in the United States of America, now styled the African Episcopal Church of St. Thomas, Philadelphia.* Philadelphia: King and Baird Printers, 1862.
DuBois, W.E.B. *Souls of Black Folk.* New York: New American Library, 1969.
Durkheim, Emile. *The Elementary Form of Religious Life: A Study in Religious Sociology.* London: Allen and Unwin, 1915.
Fanon, Frantz. *Towards the African Revolution.* New York: Grove, 1965.
Foner, Eric. *Free Soil, Free Labor, Free Men: The Ideology of the Republican Party Before the Civil War.* New York: Oxford University Press, 1970.
Franklin, John Hope. *The Free Negro in North Carolina, 1790-1860.* New York: Norton, 1943.
_____. *The Negro Family in the United States.* New York: The Dryden Press, 1951.
Frazier, Franklin. *The Negro Church in America.* New York: Schocker, 1963.
Garnet, Henry Highland. "The Past and Present Condition and Destiny of the Colored Race." In *Negro Social and Political Thought*, ed. by Howard Brotz. New York: Basic Books, 1966.
George, Carol. *Segregated Sabbaths: Richard Allen and the Emergence of Independent Black Churches, 1760-1840.* New York: Oxford University Press, 1973.
Giddens, Anthony. *New Rules of Sociology Research: A Positive Critique of Interpretive Sociologies.* New York: Basic Books, Inc., 1976.
Goffman, Erving. *Frame Analysis: An Essay on the Organization of Experience.* New York: Harper and Row, 1974.
_____. *Gender Advertisements.* New York, Harper and Row, 1976.
Gottlieb, Avi and William Ickes. "Attributional Strategies of Social Influence." In *New Directions of Attribution Research.* New York: Halstead Press/Wiley, pp. 261-96, 1976.
Graff, Harvey. *The Literacy Myth: Literacy and Social Structures in the 19th Century.* New York: Academic Press, 1979.
Jones, Edward E., David F. Kanouse, Harold H. Kelly, Richard E. Nisbett, Stuart Valins and Bernard Weiner, eds. *Attribution: Perceiving the Cause of Behavior.* New Jersey: General Learning Press, 1971.
King, Grace. *New Orleans, the Place and the People.* New York: Macmillan Company, 1915.
Mannheim, Karl. *Ideology and Utopia.* New York: Harvest/HBJ Books, 1936.
Marx, Karl. *The Communist Manifesto.* New York: Schaerr and Frantz, 1883.
Memmi, Albert. *The Colonizer and the Colonized.* Boston: Beacon Press, 1968.
Meyers, Marvin. *The Jacksonian Persuasion: Politics and Belief.* Stanford: Stanford University Press, 1957.
Miller, Floyd. *The Search for Black Nationality: Black Emigration and Colonization, 1787-1863.* Chicago: University of Illinois Press, 1975.
Nichols, Marie H., ed. *Rhetoric and Criticism.* Baton Rouge: Louisiana State University Press, 1967.
Phillips, Urich B. *American Negro Slavery: A Study of the Supply, Employment and Control of Negro Labor as Determined by the Plantation Regime.* New York: Appleton and Company, 1928.
Porter, Dorothy, ed. *Negro Protest Pamphlets.* New York: Arno/N.Y. Times, 1969.
Quarles, Benjamin. *Black Abolitionist.* New York: Oxford University Press, 1969.
_____. *Frederick Douglass.* New York: Oxford University Press, 1976.

———. *The Negro in the American Revolution*. Durham: North Carolina University Press, 1961.
Robinson, Donald. *Slavery in the Structure of American Politics, 1765-1820*. New York: Norton Press, 1979.
Ruechkert, William H., ed. *Critical Responses to Kenneth Burke*. Minneapolis: University of Minnesota Press, 1969.
Sennett, Richard. *Authority*. New York: Random House, 1981.
———. *The Fall of Public Man*. New York: Alfred A. Knopf, 1977.
Smith, William E. *The Francis Preston Blair Family in Politics*. DaCapo Press, 1933.
Staudenraus, P.J. *The African Colonization Movement*. New York: Columbia University Press, 1961.
Sterkx, H.E. *The Free Negro in Ante-Bellum Louisiana*. New Jersey: Fairleigh Dickinson University Press, 1972.
Stokes, Issac Newton. *Iconography of Manhattan Island, 1498-1909*. New York: R.H. Dodd, 1918.
Stucky, Sterling. *The Ideological Origins of Black Nationalism*. Boston: The Beacon Press, 1972.
Sweet, Leonard I. *Black Images of America, 1784-1870*. New York: Norton and Company, 1976.
Tajfel, Henri. "The Roots of Prejudice: Cognitive Aspects." In *Psychology and Race*. Edited by Peter Watson. Chicago: Aldine Publishing Company, 1973.
William, George. *History of the Negro People in America, 1619-1880*. New York: Arno Press, 1968.
Woodson, Carter. *The Education of the Negro Prior to 1861*. New York: Arno Press, 1968.
———. *Free Negro Heads of Families in the United States, 1830*. Washington, D.C.: Association for the Study of Negro Life and History, 1925.
———. *The Mind of the Negro as Reflected in Letters Written During the Crisis of 1800-1860*. Greenwood Press, 1926.
———. *Negro Orators and Their Orations*. Russell Press, 1925.

Periodicals

Bitzer, Lloyd. "The Rhetorical Situation." *Philosophy and Rhetoric*, 1:1 (1968): 1-14.
Brown, Delindus R. "Free Blacks' Rhetorical Impact on African Colonization: The Emergence of Rhetorical Evidence." *Journal of Black Studies*, 9:3 (March 1979): 251-265.
Cathcart, Robert S. "New Approaches to the Study of Movements: Defining Movements Rhetorically." *Western Speech*, 36:2 (Spring 1972): 82-88.
Cole, Michael and Silvia Schribner. "The Psychology of Literacy." *New York Times Book Review* (December 13, 1981): 1.
David, Dodge. "The Free Negroes in North Carolina." *Atlantic Monthly*, 57 (January 1886): 20-30.
Dowling, John. "Sketches of New York Baptists." *Baptist Monthly Record*, 4 (1849): 297.
Festinger, L. "A Theory of Social Comparison Process." *Human Relations*, 7:2 (1954): 117-140.
Fisher, M.W. "Lott Cary: The Colonizing Missionary." *Journal of Negro History*, 7:4 (October 1922): 380-418.

Franklin, Vincent P. "Education for Colonization: Attempts to Educate Free Blacks in the United States for Emigration to Africa, 1823-1833." *Journal of Negro Education*, 43:1 (Winter 1974): 91-103.
Gitlin, Todd. "News as Ideology and Contested Area: Toward A Theory of Hegemony Crisis and Opposition." *Socialist Review*, 9:48 (November-December 1979): 11-54.
Gonos, George. "Situation Versus Frame: The Interactionist and the Structuralist Analysis of Everyday Life." *American Sociological Review*, 42 (December 1977): 854-867.
Harvey, John and Gary Wells. "Do People Use Consensus Information in Making Causal Attribution." *Journal of Personality and Social Psychology*, 35 (May 1977): 279-293.
Hudson, Gossie Harold. "John Chavis, 1763-1838: A Social-Psychological Study." *Journal of Negro History*, 64:2 (Spring 1979): 142-156.
Kelly, Harold M. "Attribution Theory in Social Psychology." *Nebraska Symposium on Motivation*, 15 (1967): 192-238.
Moses, Wilson J. "Civilizing Missionary: A Study of Alexander Crummell." *The Journal of Negro History*, 60:2 (April, 1975): 229-251.
Porter, Dorothy B. "The Organized Education Activities of Negro Literary Societies, 1828-1846." *Journal of Negro Education*, 5:4 (October 1936): 555-576.
Storms, Michael D. "Videotape and Attribution Process: Reversing Actor's and Observer's Points of View." *Journal of Personality and Social Psychology*, 27:2 (August 1973): 165-175.
Toplin, Robert B. "The Spector of Crisis: Slaveholders' Reaction to Abolitionism in the United States and Brazil." *Civil War History*, 18: 1 (June 1972): 129-138.
Wells, Gary and John Harvey, "Do People Use Consensus Information in Making Causal Attribution. *Journal of Personality and Social Psychology*, 35 (May 1977): 279-293.

Newspapers and Journals

African Repository and Colonial Journal. Vol. 4, 11 (Washington, D.C.), 1825-1827.
The Anglo-African Magazine, Vol. 1, Nos. 4 and 10 (New York), 1859.
Baton Rouge Daily Gazette and Comet (Baton Rouge, Louisiana), 28 January 1859.
The Colored American (New York), 11 March 1837-10 July 1841.
Douglass' Monthly (Rochester, N.Y.), May 1861.
Frederick Douglass' Paper (Rochester, N.Y.), 1851-1855.
Freedom's Journal (New York), 2 November 1827.
Genius of Universal Emancipation (Ohio), Vol. 4, 1824.
The Liberator (Boston), 11 August 1832.
Maryland Colonization Journal (Baltimore), 1841.
National Enquirer and Constitutional Advocate of Universal Liberty (Philadelphia), 21 September 1837.
National Era (New York), 3 May 1849.
New York Daily Tribune (New York), 9 July-10 July 1851.
New York Times (New York), 3 March 1853.
New Orleans Semi-Weekly Creole (New Orleans), 5 November 1854.
The North Star (Rochester, New York), 16 February, 23 March, 13 April 1849.

Opelousas Patriot (Louisiana), 19 February 1859.
The Pacific Appeal (San Francisco, Calif.), 23 August 1862.
The Provincial Freemen (Toronto), 25 March 1854; 31 January 1857.
Rights of All (New York), 12 June, 7 August, 14 August 1829.
Voice of the Fugitive (Sandwich, Canada West), 1851.
The Weekly Advocate (New York), 14 January 1837.
The Weekly Anglo-African 1859-1861.

Pamphlets

Address of the Board of Managers of the Haitian Emigration Society of Colored People to Emigrants Intending to Sail to the Island of Hayti in the Brig. De Witt Clinton. New York: Mahlon Day, 1824. pp. 3-8.
Address to Parents and Guardians of Children Belonging to the New York African Free School by the Trustees. New York: 1818.
Benezet, Anthony. *A Serious Address to the Rulers of America on the Inconsistency of their Conduct Respecting Slavery.* Trenton, N.J., 1783. Reprinted by J. Phillips.
Cornish, Samuel E. and Theodore S. Wright. *The Colonization Scheme Considered: Its Rejection by the Colored People.* Newark: Aaron Guest, 1840.
Constitution of the American Society of Free Persons of Color and the Proceedings of the Convention, 20 Sept.-24 Sept., Philadelphia, 1830.
Debates of the Iowa Constitutional Convention, 1857.
Journal of Proceedings of Bethel Church, 1822-1831.
Manheim, Ernest. *A Paper Presented at the Annual Meeting of the American Sociological Association*, 1958.
Menzel, Herbert. "Communication Through Institutions and Social Structures." Presented at *Speech Association of America*, 1967.
_____. "Quasi-Mass Communication and the Active Audience." Presented at *Conference on Communication in Community Health*, 17 April 1969.
Payne, Daniel. *The Semi-Centenary and Retrospective of the African Methodist Episcopal Church in the United States of America.* Freeport, NY: Books for Libraries Press, 1972 (repr. of an 1866 pamphlet).
Sketches of the Higher Class of Colored Society in Philadelphia. Philadelphia: Merrihew and Thompson, 1841.
Seventh Annual Report of the Baptist Board of Foreign Missions in the Latter Day Luminary. Vol. 2 (May 1821).
Wymms, James. *The Blackman: His Antecedents, His Genius and His Achievements.* New York, 1883.

Pamphlets of National Freemen Conventions

Minutes of the Fifth Annual Convention for the Improvement of the Free People of Colour, ... 1835. Philadelphia: William P. Gibbons.
Minutes of the National Convention of Colored Citizens, ... 1843. Buffalo, NY: Piercy and Reed.
Proceedings of the National Convention of Colored People, ... 1847. Troy, NY: J.C. Kneeland and Company.
Report of the Proceedings of the Colored National Convention, ... 1848. Cleveland, OH: John Dick.

Proceedings of the Colored National Convention, ... *1853.* Rochester, NY: Office of *Frederick Douglass' Paper.*

Proceedings of the Colored National Convention, ... *1855.* Salem, NJ: *National Standard* Office.

Documents and Letters

Census of the United States:

1811. *Third Census of the United States, 1810.* Washington, D.C., N.P.
1832 *Fifth Census of the United States, 1830.* Washington, D.C.: Puff Green.
1853 *Seventh Census of the United States, 1850.* Washington, D.C.: Robert Armstrong.
1864 *Black Population by Free-Slave Status and Change in Slave Population by Region: 1790 to 1860.* United States Department of Commerce. Washington, D.C.

Clark, Walter, ed. *The State Records of North Carolina, 1777–1790.* 10 Volumes, 1895. AMS Press (reprint).
Garrison, William Lloyd. "Garrison to His Wife (October 20, 1847)." Letter in collection of Boston Public Library.
Hazard's Register, Vol. 5, p. 26, 1830.
Laws of Louisiana, 1816–1817. New Orleans, Louisiana, 1817.
Petitions, Slavery and the Negro. Delaware State Archives, 1832.
Report by the United States Commission on Education, 1870.
Smith, Gerrit. *Gerrit Smith Miller Collection of Gerrit Smith.* Syracuse University Library.
United States Bureau of Education, Circular of Information. Washington, D.C., 1884. Nos. 1–7.

Index

abolitionists 102, 104, 108, 110
African Aid Society (England) 153
African American press: as a non-monolithic institution 155; as a director of political thought 157; influence on emigration 158–160; as a catalyst 170
African Baptist Church 31
African Civilization Society of New York 153
African Education Society of the United States 32
The African Free School (New York City) 56, 57
African Methodist Church 30
African Methodist Episcopal Church (AME) 24, 26, 36, 69; membership 39; separate but equal status 44
African Methodist Episcopal Zion Church 24
African Mission School of Hartford 25
African nationalism: 152, 175; "Negro" nationality 138; "Colored" nationality 188
African Protestant Church 31
African School (Parsippany, New Jersey) 31
African Union Society 27; views on free blacks 28
The Alien American 2
Allen, Bishop Richard 3, 28, 29, 31–32, 37, 44, 69, 72; on emigration 26; attacks Haitian emigration 42; Free African Society 52
AME *see* African Methodist Episcopal Church
The American (preamble) 172
American Anti-Slavery Society 70

American Colonization Society 4, 30, 35–36, 38, 67, 70, 73, 89–90, 93, 95, 104, 128, 163, 172, 175; for the interest of whites 40
American Missionary Assoc. 91, 153
American Moral Society 34
Anglo-American Magazine 98; opposing views 40
Anthony, J.P. 151–152
Ashmun, Jehudi 32, 128, 178
assimilation 45, 53, 55 174; "passable" 49–50; "passing" 59; appeals 118
"Augustine" *see* Woodson, Lewis

Baptist Board of Foreign Missions 38
The Baptist Monthly Record 30
Bell, Phillip 84, 118, 173, 181, 186
Berry, Rev. S.V. 145
Bibb, Henry 89, 156, 175; and Canadian emigration 114
black nationalism *see* African nationalism
black press *see* African American press
Blair, Francis P. 102, 166, 178
British American Institute 91
Brown, George: "Letter from Liberia" 126
Brown, John, Jr. 136
Brown, John, Sr. 150
Brown, William W. 51
Butler, Benjamin 85, 88

Cameron, Simon 160
Canada 80, 90, 91–92, 120, 161, 175
Cary, Lott 24–25, 38, 178

231

Chambliss, Rolin 2
Charlotte Corday (ship) 29
Chase, Senator Salmon P. 167
Chatham Planet 150
Chavis, John ("stump" preacher) 43, 46, 118
Christian education: on social elevation 33
Christian morality 35; American socialization 43, 47, 60, 118, 152; civilization and Christianity 154
Cincinnati Haytien Union 29
Clarkson, Thomas 102, 106, 107
Clay, Henry 34, 93-94, 107-108, 122, 128, 132, 163, 166-167, 169, 193; colonization scheme 123-124; advocacy for colonization 164-165
Coker, the Reverend Daniel: emigration to Liberia 31
colonization 4, 26; anti-colonization 38
The Colored American 2, 34, 45, 50, 56, 58, 61, 65-66, 79-80, 173, 180-181; on social etiquette 21; racial definition 33; West Indian laborers 81, 82, 85, 110, 113, 115, 117, 125-126, 132, 159, 161, 163, 170; preamble 172
"The Colored Baltimorean" (pseudonym) 83, 102
"colored" nationality 188
"The Colored Presbyterian Minister" 146, 151
Concordia (ship) 29
Congregational Church 24
Connecticut Legislature 7
Cooper, David 10
Cornish, Reverend Samuel 7, 42-43, 56, 66-68, 73, 80-82, 84-89, 118, 121, 125, 127, 156, 159, 173, 178, 180-181, 185-187 social etiquette 21; on missionaries 25; abilities of free blacks 26, 33, 34; rejects emigration 38; on racial labeling 112; editorial rights 115
Crummel, Alexander 72, 96-97, 132

Delany, Martin: on separation 35, 60-61, 68, 82, 89, 91-92, 95, 98-99, 116, 119, 121, 136-137, 142, 145, 147-148, 150, 152, 156, 158, 163, 166-167, 170, 177, 187, 193
The Demosthenian Institute 55
Dessaline, Jean Jacques 148
De Witt Clinton (ship) 29
Dodge, David: description of North Carolina free blacks 19
Douglass, Frederick 70-71, 82, 84-85, 92-97, 105, 118, 119, 121, 141, 160, 163, 164-166, 170-171, 173-174, 177, 181, 183, 185-188; colonization 131; Clay's colonization scheme 167-169; selective emigration 184
Douglass' Monthly viii, 93, 150, 171, 174-175, 188
Dred Scott decision (1857) 61
Dresser, Amos 53
Dubois, W.E.B.: on two-ness 40; 59
Durnford, Andrew (free black planter) 19, 46-47

Edgeworth Literary Association 55
Ellison, Ralph 49
Emerson, Ralph Waldo 27
emigration 60, 97, 152; definition 4

Felinghuyser, Theodore 85, 88
Festinger, L.: on consensus formation 118
Fillmore, Millard 116
Finley, the Reverend Robert 28, 35-36
Forten, James 26, 28-29, 63, 69, 86, 170; attacks Henry Clay 83-84
Frederick Douglass' Paper viii, 2, 65, 93, 97, 110, 129, 131, 174-175, 182
Free African Society (Philadelphia) 52
free blacks (freemen) 9-12, 22-24, 36-37, 45, 47-52, 54, 56, 60, 61, 63, 69, 83, 86, 94, 96, 100, 110, 112, 118-120, 167-168, 171, 177-178, 182, 187; population figures 13-15; racial purification 16; socio-economic conditions 17; on education 57-58
Freedom's Journal vii, xii, 2, 38, 65-66, 73-75, 132, 173; emigrants' departing 126-127
Freeman, M.H. 54

freemen *see* free blacks
Fugitive Slave acts (1850) 61, 63, 85, 186

Garnet, Henry H.: 68, 96, 136-137, 142, 145-146, 148, 151, 160, 163; on emigration 78-79; defends position 135; assails Delany 150
Garrison, William Lloyd 65, 85, 93, 174; convention of 1830 22
George, Carol 30
The Globe 193
Gloucester, Reverend James 135, 146
Goffman, Erving: on consensus 161
Goffman, Irving vii
Goheen, Dr. 125
Gurley, the Reverend Ralph 104, 128

Haiti 26, 82, 134-140, 148, 185; emigrants 41-42; criteria for emigrants 143; nationalism 145; economics 152
Hamilton, Thomas 132, 135, 170
Haytien Emigration Society of Coloured People 29
Haytien Emigration Society of Philadelphia 29
Hepburn, John 149
The Herald 58-59
Hinton, Frederick A. 34
Holcomb, J. 79, 80
Holly, James Theodore 99, 101, 119, 133, 136-138, 143, 145; on emigration 40-42, 82, 89-91; "Thoughts on Hayti" 98; "vindication..." 98; defends emigration 147-150, 152-154, 156, 163, 166-167, 177, 193
Hopkins, Samuel 27
Hugo, Victor 106

individual growth 60, 75-76

James, C.L.R. 158
Jay, John 56
Jay, William 33
Jefferson, Thomas 32, 103
Jones, Absalom 52

Kelly, Harold 66
Kennedy, John H. 102, 104-105
Kosciuszko Fund 32

Latrobe, John H.B.: on abolition 106
Lawrence, George 135, 141, 163, 170, 171
"Letter from Liberia" 126
Lexington Observer and Reporter 122, 163
The Liberator 65
Liberia 30-34, 42-43, 65, 74, 161, 175, 177-178, 185; Maryland colony 80, 82, 87, 90, 97, 110, 121, 122-132; settlers 159
Liberia Herald 74, 125
Locke, John 179
Lovejoy, Owen 104
Louisiana (state) 14; St. Landry Parish 15; complexion hierarchy 16, 18
Lowell, James Russell 27

Madison, James 103
Mannheim, Karl 6
Marx, Karl 129
Maryland Colonization Society 31, 105
Massachusetts Anti-Slavery Society 174
Methodist Episcopal Church 39
Methodist Protestant Church (whites only) 37
Minerva Literary Association 55
Morel, Junius C. 34
Moten, Rashey B. 2
mulattoes 9, 12, 39
Myrdal, Gunner 48
The Mystery 68, 94

National Convention (1835) 33, 70, 162; (1838) 34; (1843) 160; (1847) 94; (1848) 95, 116, 117, 160
The National Watchman 94
Nebraska Bill (1854) 183
"Negro" nationality 138, 152, 175
New Jersey 57
New Jersey Colonization Society 31
Newman, William P. 149
New York (state) 57
The New York Tribune 57, 129
Nicaragua 82
Niger Valley Exploration Party 137
Nigeria 134
Nisbett, Richard 155
North Carolina, Act of 1787 10, 19
The North Star 2, 35, 70, 78, 93-95,

Index

97, 108, 110, 116–117, 122, 163–165, 173–175
The Northern Star 69

Ohio 57; black laws 167; state convention (1849) 171
Ohio Abolition Society 53
Orville, Dr. 57

The Pacific Appeal 85
Paul, Nathaniel 27
Payne, the Reverend Daniel 39, 69
Pennington, Dr. 142
Pennsylvania 57
The Pennsylvania Inquirer 65
The Pennsylvania Society for Promoting the Abolition of Slavery 10, 66
The Philadelphia Library Company of Colored Persons 55
The Philamathean Society 56
Phillips, Wendell 148
The Phoenix Society 56
The Pine and Palm 173
Porter, Dorothy 119
The Protestant Episcopal Church 24
The Provincial Freeman 91–92
Purvis, Robert 34

The Ram's Horn 94, 170
Ray, the Reverend Charles B 173
Read, J.B. 19
Redpath, James 136–137, 139, 142, 145, 147–148, 150–151
Refugee Home Society 91
religious separatism 26
Remond, Lenox 51
resettlement: in Canada 60, 77–78; definition of 76,
The Rights of All 2, 25, 42, 68, 125, 173
Ruggles, David 84, 118, 181, 186
The Rush Library Company and Debating Society of Pennsylvania 55
Russwurm, John 38, 73–74, 85, 96, 132, 193

St. Phillips Church (New York City) 36–37
Sennett, Richard 50
Shadd, Mary Ann 91, 100, 119, 121, 156

"Sidney" (pseudonym) 58, 61
Sketches of the Higher Class of Colored Society 51
Smith, Gerrit 93, 96, 110
Smith, Dr. James McCune 57, 93, 135, 137, 142, 145, 146–147, 163, 180; on emigration 133–134
Smith, Robert 14
The Society for Improving the Conditions of the African Race 10
The Society for the Relief of Free Negroes Unlawfully Held in Bondage 10
South Carolina 176
Starkey, J.R. 16
Stowe, Harriet 95, 97

Tappan, Arthur 56
Tappan, Lewis 110
Trumbull, Lyman 103

universal betterment 60, 76
University of Glasgow (Scotland) 57, 133; city of 175

Valens, Stuart 155
Van Rensselaer, Thomas 170
Virginia House of Delegates 57
The Voice of the Fugitive 65, 89–92; Canadian emigration 114, 159, 173

Wagoner, H.O. 171
Walker, David 14, 30
Ward, Samuel R. 91, 96
Webster, Daniel 166
The Weekly Advocate (preamble) 173
The Weekly Anglo African 58–59, 113, 121, 132, 135, 137, 140–145, 150–151, 170–171, 173, 177, 187; Liberia 130; H.H. Garnet 163
Wesley Methodist Church 39
Whipper, William 34, 69–70, 85
William, the Reverend Peter 29, 36
Woodson, Carter 9
Woodson, Lewis (pseudonym: "Augustine") 15, 50, 52, 60, 80, 102, 170; black church 34–35; ideological confusion 45
Wright, Theodore 85–88, 127, 178